THE PHILOSOPHY
OF
CHRYSIPPUS

THE PHILOSOPHY
OF
CHRYSIPPUS

BY

JOSIAH B. GOULD

STATE UNIVERSITY OF NEW YORK PRESS
ALBANY

Published by State University of New York Press
Thurlow Terrace, Albany, New York 12201

International Standard Book Number 0-87395-064-X
Library of Congress Catalog Card Number 78-112606

PRINTED IN THE NETHERLANDS

CONTENTS

ACKNOWLEDGEMENTS

I should like to acknowledge with gratitude the help given me in the preparation of this book by the Philosophy Department of the Johns Hopkins University, the Samuel Fels Foundation, and the Rockefeller Institute (now Rockefeller University). I am also grateful to the editor of *Phronesis* for his permission to use my article, "Chrysippus: on the Criteria for the Truth of a Conditional Proposition" (*Phronesis*, Vol. XII, 1967). Above all I wish to acknowledge the guidance and encouragement provided me by an eminent scholar and a good man, Professor Ludwig Edelstein. It is to his memory that I dedicate this book.

CHAPTER ONE

INTRODUCTION

In this book I attempt to formulate a well-evidenced statement of the philosophical doctrines belonging to the Stoic philosopher, Chrysippus. Only fragments of his writings are extant, and in dealing with these remains of his philosophy I have not deviated from the following principle: unless the author of a cited fragment states explicitly in the body of the fragment that a given doctrine belongs to Chrysippus, that it is to be found in one of his books, or that the words themselves are taken verbatim from Chrysippus, it may not be admitted as evidence for any assertion about Chrysippus' philosophical position. This is not to say that I have precluded the use of fragments purporting to convey general Stoic doctrine. I shall, however, make use of such fragments only to elucidate doctrines explicitly ascribed to Chrysippus in other fragments and not to make inferences about the philosophy of Chrysippus on the strength of the suspect assumption that what is Stoic is of necessity Chrysippean.

It can be argued that such a procedure ought to be followed generally when dealing with philosophers whose works are no longer extant, but of whose works there exist in the writings of others numerous quotations and summaries.[1] And this method of proceeding seems especially apposite with respect to Chrysippus, for in the discussions of the past several decades [2] another method has been employed so that, at present, it is hard to say precisely and specifically what Chrysippus taught.

The methodological principle, which I am here rejecting, was given authoritative support and emphasis in Arnim's monumental

---

[1] *Cf.* Ludwig Edelstein, "The Philosophical System of Posidonius", *American Journal of Philology* (Vol. LVIII, July 1936), pp. 286-325. Here such a method is used in an investigation of Posidonius' philosophical system and on pp. 286-288 are explained some of the problems that have arisen from a failure to attend exclusively to the explicitly attested Posidonian fragments.

[2] Hans von Arnim, "Chrysippos," *Paulys Realencyclopädie der Classischen Altertumwissenschaft* (Stuttgart: Alfred Druckenmüller, 1899), cols. 2502-2509. Émile Bréhier, *Chrysippe* (Paris: Felix Alcan, 1910). Max Pohlenz, *Die Stoa*, 2. Auflage, 2 Vols. (Göttingen: Vandenhoeck and Ruprecht, 1959).

work,[1] published at the beginning of the century, in which for the first time all or nearly all [2] the fragments of the ancient Stoa were made accessible; for in the determination of what material was pertinent Arnim employed one standard for all the philosophers [3] except Chrysippus and another for Chrysippus. With respect to the first group Arnim admitted material to his collection only if it was relevant by explicit testimony, only, that is, if the name of the philosopher appeared in the passage under scrutiny. With regard to Chrysippus Arnim, in addition to passages relevant by explicit testimony, admitted also passages which convey the doctrines of the Roman Stoa or the Stoa as it existed in the age of the emperors.

Arnim's reason for employing this criterion with respect to Chrysippus lay in his belief that the doctrines of the Roman Stoa were derived *in toto* from Chrysippus.[4] This premise permitted him the inference that the fragments from the Roman Stoa which bear upon Stoic doctrine are *ipso facto* mineable for Chrysippean doctrine. Arnim, then, in two volumes of his work, includes enough fragments to exhibit as fully as possible "that form of the doctrine which existed in the age of the emperors," [5] even though this procedure involved the inclusion of many fragments which are not in an obvious way pertinent to Chrysippus, for his name does not appear in them. Arnim's supposition, to be sure, is more moderate than that of Stein, who had maintained that *every* doctrine introduced with the expression, "the Stoics", could be regarded as a declaration of Chrysippus' view, unless it had been shown to be the doctrine

---

[1] *Stoicorum Veterum Fragmenta*, Vol. I, 1905; Vol. II, 1903; Vol. III, 1903; Vol. IV (Index), 1914, Leipzig. The fragments are henceforth cited by number and volume; for example, II 386 is fragment 386 in Vol. II.

[2] Max Pohlenz, in his enthusiastic review of the second volume of Arnim's work (*Berliner Philologische Wochenschrift*, XXIII (August 1, 1903), pp. 962-971), mentions several fragments (*infra*, note 2, p. 131) overlooked by Arnim. I miss the definition of philosophy attributed to Chrysippus by Isidore of Pelusium (*Patrologia Graeca*, V, 78, p. 1637, Migne) and cited by Bréhier (*op. cit.*, p. 29, note 1).

[3] Zeno of Citeum, Aristo, Apollophanes, Herillus, Dionysius of Heracles, Persaeus, Cleanthes, Sphaerus, Zeno of Tarsus, Diogenes of Babylonia, Antipater of Tarsus, Apollodorus of Seleucia, Archedemus of Tarsus, Boethus of Sidon, Basilides, Eudromus, and Crinis.

[4] *Stoicorum Veterum Fragmenta*, Vol. 1, p. III.

[5] *Ibid.*, p. V. An important modern study which presupposes the correctness of this view is Otto Rieth, *Grundbegriffe der Stoischen Ethik* (Berlin: Weidmannsche Buchhandlung, 1933). See p. 20 of Rieth's study for his view of Arnim's work.

of another Stoic thinker.[1] Stein's view was rightly not accepted, but Arnim's more qualified view has met with general approval; for example, Pohlenz clearly sides with Arnim when he (Pohlenz) writes that, in the Age of the Empire, "Chrysippus indisputably prevailed as the real authority and protector of orthodoxy." [2]

It might, of course, be true that the doctrines of Chrysippus and the Roman Stoa are identical, though even Pohlenz, undermining his own thesis, suggests the contrary, for he himself in the course of his book, makes clear "how many new and different trends appear in the philosophy of the Roman Stoics." [3] In any event the problem of Chrysippus' relation to the Roman Stoa can never be satisfactorily resolved until we possess a statement, as comprehensive as the explicit evidence allows, of Chrysippus' philosophical doctrines.

Émile Bréhier's study [4] is the only one since the publication of Arnim's work which claimed to provide such a reconstruction. Bréhier, too, holds that Chrysippus was assigned a "place prépondérante" by the Roman Stoa,[5] but he does not systematically introduce material from that period for assertions about Chrysippus. Even so, his success in providing the desired reconstruction is, as I shall now try to make plain, ostensible only.

The first section of Bréhier's book, entitled *Chrysippe* in 1910, deals with Chrysippus' life and works. It is the only part of his book in which Chrysippus alone is considered. The remaining three sections, apparently concerned with the philosophical doctrines of Chrysippus, contain, in fact, expositions of philosophical doctrines belonging to "the Stoics" with only occasional references to Chrysippus. Bréhier himself evidently became aware that he had given his book an inexact title, for the ninth edition, which appeared in 1951, bore the more telling title, *Chrysippe et L'Ancien Stoicisme*.

Of course a book about Chrysippus and Stoicism is better than

---

[1] Ludwig Stein, *Die Psychologie der Stoa* (Berlin: S. Calvary, 1886), p. 173.

[2] Pohlenz, *Die Stoa*, I, 292. And in his review of Volume II of Arnim's work (*op. cit.*, p. 963), Pohlenz wrote, "Vorläufig begrüsse ich es immer mit Freuden, dass Chrysipp in den Mittelpunkt des Ganzen gestellt ist und offenbar als der Vertreter der orthodoxen Stoa erscheinen soll."

[3] Ludwig Edelstein, review of *Die Stoa* by Max Pohlenz, *American Journal of Philology*, (LXXII, October, 1951), p. 429.

[4] Émile Bréhier, *op. cit.*

[5] *Ibid.*, p. 3.

no book at all about one of the ancient Stoics. But Bréhier's inclusion in his book about Chrysippus of an excessive amount of material having to do with the Stoics, Stoicism, and Stoic doctrine blurred his account of Chrysippus. The substantiated assertions which one can make about the Stoics generally are far more in number than those which one can make about the philosophy of Chrysippus. This circumstance, I believe, lured Bréhier into saying a great many more things about the Stoics and Stoic doctrine than about Chrysippean doctrine. The end result is that one who reads Bréhier's book acquires a rather comprehensive view of Stoic doctrine, but neither the distinctive features of Chrysippus' thought nor his contributions to Stoic philosophy are brought into sharp focus.[1]

Bréhier's study is replete with comments upon "the Stoics" and "Stoic doctrine". [2] To say it once more, if it could be known with certainty that at least Chrysippus is denoted by "the Stoics" in every assertion containing that expression, then a well-evidenced book indeed might be written about Chrysippus' philosophical position. But, in advance of an independent investigation of the explicitly Chrysippean testimony, it cannot be assumed that a doxographer or biographer who refers to the Stoics is at the same time referring, either wittingly or unwittingly, to Chrysippus. Bréhier's book cannot satisfy the requirements which one who wishes to get at the philosophy of Chrysippus based upon a rigorous exclusion of all evidence not explicitly Chrysippean must impose on oneself.

---

[1] Bréhier himself had in the Introduction to his book contrasted the diversity and original features of the various Stoic thinkers with the traditional and arrested contours of Epicurean thought. But as one moves through Bréhier's book, with its innumerable "les Stoïciens" and its occasional "Chrysippe", one cannot help but get the impression that the uniformity of Stoic thought is in degree not less than that of Epicurean philosophy. Consequently Bréhier himself unwittingly betrays one of the valuable insights which characterize his work. Bréhier's chapter on the writings of Chrysippus, a chapter in which he attempts to make intelligible some of the titles in Diogenes Laertius' incomplete list of Chrysippus' writings, is concerned exclusively with Chrysippus and is one of the most illuminating parts of his book.

[2] Bréhier, op. cit., pp. 59-276, passim. For example, in the first chapter of Book II, there are 39 occurrences of the expressions "les Stoïciens" and "la doctrine stoicienne", while "Chrysippe" appears only 29 times. And these statistics, which may seem picayunish, are genuinely indicative of the real subject of Bréhier's book.

The foregoing remarks have, I trust, made it clear that the work I have undertaken is justified on methodological grounds as well as by the present state of investigations into the philosophy of Chrysippus. It should contribute to the establishment of an articulate criterion by which what is and what is not Chrysippean can be distinguished not only in the doctrines of the Roman Stoics, but in all the doxographical material about the Stoics in general. But, as was stated at the outset, the primary aim of the book is to give a well-substantiated picture of Chrysippus' philosophy.

A further consideration would be a careful examination of the authors of just those fragments which purport to be about Chrysippus. Why were they citing Chrysippus or some one of his books? Were they trying to understand, undermine, or propagate his doctrines?

Cicero is interested in Chrysippus and our philosopher appears several times in the ἀπόγραφα of the Roman, and Cicero seems in general to report fairly.[1] Diocles Magnes mentions Chrysippus more infrequently, but when he does so, his report is a reliable one. Sextus Empiricus gives us some of our most detailed accounts of Chrysippus' logical doctrines, and they seem correct.

Galen and Plutarch, perhaps, constitute our richest sources, but unhappily each is hostile towards Chrysippus. Galen's reports are biased because he uses Posidonius, whose acid criticisms of Chrysippus are attested.[2] Plutarch makes no secret of his antagonism towards the Stoics. One of his books, De Stoicorum Repugnantiis, is written explicitly to set forth, from Plutarch's point of view, the contradictions infecting Stoic principles and the discrepancies between the lives of some of the Stoics and the doctrines which they professed. Such a writer might be disposed to snatch at straws, for example, to take what is an apparent contradiction for a real contradiction. To cite a case in point, it is no contradiction, as Plutarch would have us believe,[3] to affirm that the parts of philosophy are ordered in two ways—in one way with respect to their logical relation to one another and in a second way with respect to the manner in which they ought to be introduced to the student.

---

[1] One passage constitutes an exception; I discuss it in detail, infra, pp. 77-79.

[2] Ludwig Edelstein, "The Philosophical System of Posidonius," pp. 306, 323.

[3] II 30; II 37; II 50.

But Plutarch can make it appear to be a contradiction by ignoring [1] the respects in which the two arrangements of the philosophical disciplines differ. It becomes the task of the interpreter to scrutinize carefully the sometimes not-so-artful devices of such hostile writers.

These are indeed important issues and deserve close scrutiny. In this book they receive cursory attention only, for to investigate fully the motives and principles according to which later writers may have used Chrysippean material would have led me too far away from my task—not a mean one—to reconstruct the thought of Chrysippus from the fragmentary remains of his writings and summaries of his doctrines to be found in other writers. Before the statue can be rounded and smoothed the stone has to be hewn. This fundamental step, it is hoped, is accomplished in the following formulation of Chrysippus' philosophical doctrines, based on the kind of evidence that has been described.

---

[1] He himself has preserved for us the knowledge of these different "respects". But since they resolved the contradiction which he wished to attribute to Chrysippus, he ignored them. *Cf.* Max Pohlenz, "Plutarchs Schriften gegen die Stoiker." *Hermes*, Vol. 74 (1939), pp. 1-33.

CHAPTER TWO

CHRYSIPPUS—LIFE AND REPUTATION IN ANTIQUITY, AND MODERN ASSESSMENTS

1. LIFE AND REPUTATION IN ANTIQUITY

It would, of course, be an advantage if we possessed some direct reports about Chrysippus' career by his contemporaries such that we might construct a solidly detailed biography. As the case stands we have to rely on fragments reporting the barest particulars and on a few colorful anecdotes. Chrysippus, born in Soli, a town in Cilicia to which his father had emigrated from Tarsus,[1] died in the 143rd Olympiad (208-204 B.C.) at the age of seventy-three (II 1). He led a busy life of lecturing and writing and isolated himself somewhat from social life. When someone reproached him because he would not, with the crowd, attend the lectures of Aristo, he said, "If I had followed the crowd, I should not have studied philosophy" (II 1). He did not dedicate any of his books to the kings and he refused to go to Ptolemy's court when that king wrote to Cleanthes requesting that he himself come or that he send someone from his school (II 1). In spite of his scholarly preoccupations he tended his family duties, for when his sister was indisposed, or when she died, he sent for her sons and helped them (II 1). He was remembered in Athens by one of these nephews with a statue placed in the Ceramicus.[2] His lectures attracted students, and he was a man confident of his abilities. When an anxious father asked Chrysippus with whom his son ought to study, Chrysippus replied, "Me. For if I suspected that there were someone better than myself, I should myself be studying philosophy with him." (II 6)

He studied with Cleanthes for a long period of time and his attitude towards his teacher, it appears, was ambivalent. On one hand, he himself inveighed against Cleanthes and said more than once that he was not content in his association with him (II 1). On the other, he is reported to have protected him from the young wiseacres who sought to disarm him with sophisms (II 19); and

---

[1] (II 1); (II 1); (II 24).
[2] (II 1); (II 3); (II 3).

this exhibits a kind of respect for his old teacher. It also reveals a certain competency in reasoning power; and his self-confidence regarding this capacity is manifest in his practice of saying to Cleanthes that all he wanted was to be told what the theories were, for he himself would find the proofs for them (II 1).

He was a methodical and industrious writer, setting for himself the completion of a specific number of lines everyday.[1] He wrote more than 705 books (II 1). Little is attested about the quality of his work and what we do have is unfavorable;[2] we cannot control these reports on the basis of the few quotations preserved in the fragments.

Though the paucity of direct accounts about Chrysippus is to be lamented, we are fortunate in possessing a number of fragments which tell us something of his reputation in antiquity. There are first the conventional, but by no means insignificant, reports of men outside the Stoic school who were unanimous in viewing Chrysippus as an extraordinarily able philosopher. Diogenes Laertius in his account of Chrysippus retails the ascription, "outstanding philosopher" (II 1), and he says in the same passage that Chrysippus "was exceedingly acute in every branch of philosophy." Origen by implication places him in the class of "genuine philosophers" (II 23). Cicero says he was believed to be the "sharpest-witted among men and as not having failed to satisfy the demands of philosophy" (II 26). Chrysippus, it is evident, was viewed as a man of imposing stature in philosophy. Though the comprehensiveness of his interests is attested[3] his reputation, it seems, rested in large measure on his unfathomable competence as a dialectician. Dionysius says that no one knew the dialectic arts better than Chrysippus did (II 28). And Diogenes shows in his account that Dionysius' judgment was shared by many men. For, as he says, Chrysippus "was so greatly renowned in the field of dialectic that most people believed, if that branch of philosophy were favored by the gods, it would be no other than Chrysippean dialectic" (II 1).

An especially good characterization of Chrysippus is preserved,

---

[1] 500 of them (II 1).

[2] We are told (II 1; II 27) that his books were padded with repetitions, frequent corrections, and many quotations of authorities; and that they were difficult (II 19). Dionysius of Halicarnassus said that no one worthy of mention composed his sentences in a worse order than Chrysippus (II 28).

[3] "Among Stoic doctrines what is there that has been omitted by Chrysippus?" (II 34).

by a lucky stroke of chance, in an account concerning Carneades' relation to Chrysippus. It is evident that Chrysippus was looked upon as the philosopher who had defended the open-flanked Stoa against the attacks of the Academic sceptics. He always immersed himself in his adversary's position, presumably on the plausible theory that the better you understand your enemy, the more likely you are to withstand his attacks and launch effective countermoves (II 1). Carneades, who studied all of the early Stoics and particularly the books of Chrysippus and who became famous because he spoke out against them, said, "Without Chrysippus where should I have been?" [1] In fact he was charged by others with having spoken nothing original but with having borrowed his weapons from Chrysippus, who had set forth so thoroughly the arguments for positions contrary to his own (II 32). Again Carneades is reported (II 32) to have exclaimed when arguing against Chrysippean doctrines, with a slight change in a Homeric phrase (*Iliad* vi. 407), "Unlucky one, your strength will destroy you."

That Chrysippus was believed to have revived the Stoa after the crushing blows dealt it by Arcesilaus and other Academics appears to be the purport of the ancient saying, "If there had been no Chrysippus, there would be no Stoa" (II 6). In antiquity, then, even outside the school, Chrysippus was regarded as an eminently capable philosopher, as an extraordinarily skilful dialectician, and as one who came to the defense of the Stoa in a crucial moment, namely, when it was about to encounter its death blow from a rival school in Athens, the Academy, which had then become the stronghold of scepticism.

If we ask ourselves, "How was Chrysippus viewed by later generations *within* the school?" and seek an answer based on the extant testimony, the results point to an influence which, in time, was far-reaching indeed. Among the fragments of Panaetius,[2] the next philosopher of stature in the tradition after Chrysippus and the thinker who "was destined to introduce Stoicism to Roman society", [3] we do not find even one sentence in which Panaetius makes a judgment about Chrysippus. We are able, however, from

---

[1] Diogenes Laertius iv. 62.

[2] *Panaetii Rhodii Fragmenta* collegit iterumque edidit Modestus Van Straaten, Leiden: E. J. Brill, 1952 (reprinted with supplement, 1962).

[3] E. Vernon Arnold, *Roman Stoicism* (New York: The Humanities Press, 1958, first published 1911), p. 98.

the Posidonian fragments [1] to glean something of Panaetius' successor's attitude towards our philosopher. Unfortunately we have no direct assessment by Posidonius of Chrysippus as a philosopher. He was antagonistic towards Chrysippus' moral philosophy,[2] and perhaps it is safe to infer from the bitter attack he launched against Chrysippus [3] for deviating from Plato and Aristotle [4] that, in Posidonius' eyes, Chrysippus' influence in the school was sufficiently prevalent to make mandatory a detailed criticism of those of his doctrines thought to be erroneous and heretical. Arnim [5] sees the "reaction against Chrysippus' authority" in the middle of the second century B.C. as a fact from which we can infer that Chrysippus' books down to that date had been regarded as "the source for an essence of Stoic wisdom." I believe this goes too far. Aside from the fact that Chrysippus is not mentioned in any of the fragments—admittedly few in number—of his immediate successors in the Stoa,[6] it seems unlikely that his works, as influential as they may have become, would have immediately eclipsed the works of Zeno and Cleanthes. Bearing in mind that our judgment is based upon fragmentary remains of the literature of the period, we may conclude that Chrysippus' influence was forceful within the Stoa during the two centuries following his death, even though he was believed by Posidonius to have defected from some of the Stoic ethical principles.

This conclusion, based as it is upon oblique testimony, is more directly attested when we turn to the writers of the Roman Stoa through whose extant writings the modern world has become familiar with Stoicism. I have in mind, of course, Seneca, Epictetus, and Marcus Aurelius.

In the whole body of Seneca's works there are fifteen allusions to Chrysippus.[7] If one reads through in turn the passages in which

---

[1] Ludwig Edelstein, *The Fragments of Posidonius* with a commentary (unpublished).

[2] *Ibid.*, p. 54.

[3] *Supra*, p. 5.

[4] And, *ipso facto*, for defecting from Zeno and Cleanthes who, according to Posidonius, shared the views of Plato and Aristotle with regard to the soul. Edelstein, *Commentary*, pp. 53, 54.

[5] Arnim, "Chrysippos", *Realencyclopädie*, cols. 2505, 2506.

[6] Zeno of Tarsus, Diogenes of Babylonia, Antipater of Tarsus, Apollodorus, Archedemus, Boethus, Basilides, Eudromus, and Crinis. Fragments can be found in the third volume of *Stoicorum Veterum Fragmenta*.

[7] *On Leisure* vi. 4, 5; viii. 1 (III 695); *On Benefits* i. 3, 8; i. 4, 1 (both in

they occur, one cannot fail to discern that, in Seneca's mind, Chrysippus is *one* of the pillars of the Porch. Seneca usually mentions him in the same breath with other esteemed philosophers—in large measure, Stoic philosophers—for example, Zeno;[1] Zeno and Cleanthes;[2] Zeno and Socrates;[3] Cleanthes;[4] Plato, Zeno, and Posidonius;[5] Zeno, Cleanthes, Panaetius, and Posidonius.[6] And in each of these passages it is obvious that Seneca is pointing out great men to his readers; representative is this sentence from *On Benefits*:[7] "I shall not remind you of Socrates, of Chrysippus, of Zeno, and the others, truly great men—in fact, too great, because envy sets no bounds to our praise of the ancients." While it is not at all apparent that Chrysippus, in Seneca's estimation, is in any way a *unique* authority in the Stoic tradition, one who has cast a shadow on any of the other prominent figures in the school—he alludes to Cleanthes thirteen times and to Zeno, twenty-two—it is at the same time manifest that Chrysippus is viewed as one among the solidly preeminent spokesmen for and exemplars of Stoic principles.

Even in those passages [8] in which Seneca is critical of the manner in which Chrysippus treats a subject in one of his books, he calls him "a great man" (*magnus vir*) and speaks of his "famous acumen" which is "so keen and pierces to the very core of the truth."

In the remaining passages [9] Seneca introduces distinctions, analogies, definitions, and precepts belonging to Chrysippus, and the mere fact that he chooses Chrysippus as one of his authorities in itself testifies to the respect Chrysippus continued to enjoy in the school some 265 years after his death.

Before turning to Epictetus I pause for a glance at his teacher, a contemporary of Seneca's, and a Stoic whose influence was so

---

III 726); vii. 8, 2; ii. 17, 3 (III 725); ii. 25, 3 (III 726); iii 22 (III 351); *ep.* cviii. 38, 39; *ep.* xxii. 11; *ep.* xxxiii. 4; *On the Firmness of the Wise Man* xvii., (II 11); *On Tranquillity of the Soul* i. 10 (III 695); *ep.* ix. 14 (III 674); *ep.* cxiii. 23 (II 836).

[1] *Ep.* xxii. 11.
[2] *On Leisure* vi. 4, 5; *On Tranquillity of the Soul* i. 10.
[3] *On Benefits* vii. 8, 2.
[4] *Ep.* cxiii. 23.
[5] *Ep.* xcviii. 38, 39.
[6] *Ep.* xxxiii. 4.
[7] vii. 8, 2. Loeb Library trans. (John W. Basore).
[8] *On Benefits* i. 3, 8; i. 4, 1.
[9] *On Benefits* ii. 17, 3; ii. 25, 3; iii. 22, 1; *On the Firmness of the Wise Man* xvii. 1; *On Leisure* viii. 1; *ep.* ix. 14.

great that, according to one modern scholar, "we may almost regard him as a third founder of the philosophy." [1] The philosopher is Musonius. In the fragments of his works [2] are to be found three mentions of Zeno, two of Cleanthes, and none of Chrysippus. This circumstance, too, lends some weight to the hypothesis, better evidenced in Epictetus, that however strong Chrysippus' influence may have become in the first century A.D., it did not completely overshadow that of his predecessors.

Epictetus in all of his writings refers to Chrysippus about fourteen times.[3] It becomes plain to the reader of these passages that Chrysippus' books are now being read as texts in the school. This is presupposed in Epictetus' admonitions that to be serene is not merely to have read many treatises of Chrysippus,[4] that virtue is not to be equated with a knowledge of Chrysippus,[5] that to be a philosopher it does not suffice to read a few introductions and some books of Chrysippus,[6] and that one undervalues his moral purpose if he constantly worries about whether men will think he has read Chrysippus or not.[7] Even this comment on the obscurity of Chrysippus' style makes it patent not only that people in the Roman Stoa were reading Chrysippus but that those who comprehended him were pluming their feathers: "When a person gives himself airs because he can understand and interpret the books of Chrysippus, say to yourself, 'If Chrysippus had not written obscurely, this man would have nothing about which to give himself airs'." [8]

It is equally clear, however, that Chrysippus is not the sole tutor of the first century Stoa. Epictetus mentions along with Chrysippus' works the treatises of Antipater and Archedemus in three different passages [9] and a treatise on ethics by Diogenes.[10] He refers twelve times to Zeno and ten times to Cleanthes. And in his characteristically homilitic vein he says in one place, "And what do I lose? says

---

[1] Arnold, *op. cit.*, p. 117.

[2] G. Musonii Rufi, *Reliquiae*, ed. O. Hense (Leipzig: B. G. Teubner, 1905).

[3] *Discourses* i. 4, 5; i. 4, 28-32 (III 144); i. 10, 10; i. 17, 11-16 (II 51); ii. 6, 9 (III 191); ii. 16, 34; ii. 17, 34 (II 280); ii. 17, 39-40; ii. 19, 13-14; ii. 23, 44; iii. 2, 13-14; iv. 9, 6; *Encheiridion*, 49.

[4] *Discourses* i. 4, 5.

[5] *Ibid.*

[6] *Discourses* ii. 16, 34; *cf.* ii. 17, 39-40.

[7] *Discourses* iii. 21, 6-7.

[8] *Encheiridion*, 49.

[9] *Discourses* ii. 17, 39-40; iii. 2, 13-14; iii. 21, 67.

[10] *Discourses* ii. 19, 13-14.

somebody.—Man, you used to be modest, and are no longer so; have you lost nothing? Instead of Chrysippus and Zeno you now read Aristeides and Evenus; have you lost nothing?" [1] Finally, at the conclusion of an argument in which he has tried to show that logic is not a barren discipline, he invokes as authorities for his view not only Chrysippus, but also Zeno, Cleanthes, Antisthenes, and Socrates.[2]

It is evident that Epictetus, like Seneca, esteems Chrysippus as one of the great men of the Stoa. But he goes further than Seneca in that he takes Chrysippus to be the preeminent teacher of the Stoa. It is Chrysippus who is the interpreter of nature.[3] And it is from Chrysippus that one may learn how the universe is administered, what place the rational animal has in it, the nature of one's self and the nature of one's good and evil.[4] That his writings were earnestly studied and commented upon in the first and second centuries A.D. is further evidenced by the contemporary criticisms of the school. Writers who wished to attack the school—critics such as Plutarch, Galen, and Alexander of Aphrodisias—aimed their polemic first and foremost at Chrysippus.[5]

Marcus Aurelius alludes to Chrysippus in two passages, one of which is significant.[6] Aurelius, it is apparent, wished in this passage to introduce some noteworthy names in philosophy. His whole point is: renowned though men be, they cannot withstand the obscurity in which time engulfs them. And what names came to his mind for this purpose? Those of Chrysippus, Socrates, and Epictetus—and in that order.

If our reading of the evidence is correct, Chrysippus' influence in the school persisted until the third century A.D., when Stoicism itself begins to lose ground and to be absorbed piecemeal into Neoplatonic and Christian thought. It is true that some of Chrysippus' doctrines were attacked by Posidonius, but, as one scholar has observed,[7] it was "characteristic of the Stoic movement that from

---

[1] *Discourses* iv. 9, 6—Loeb. trans.

[2] *Discourses* i. 17, 11-16 (II 91).

[3] *Encheiridion*, 49.

[4] *Discourses* i. 10, 10.

[5] Arnim, "Chrysippos", *Realencyclopädie*, col. 2506.

[6] *Meditations* vii. 19; vi. 42. In the second he identifies a play by describing it as "the one Chrysippus mentions."

[7] Edelstein, *Commentary*, p. 54. Edelstein cites Numenius, who attests that Antipater wrote a whole book on the differences between Cleanthes and Chrysippus.

its beginning dissension existed among the various scholarchs." The esteem with which Chrysippus is regarded by later generations of Stoics is shared with Zeno, Cleanthes, and even Socrates. Not until one reaches the first entury A.D. does one get the impression that Chrysippus' books are being read *more than* those of other Stoics, indeed that they are being used as texts and provided with introductions.

2. MODERN ASSESSMENTS OF CHRYSIPPUS' POSITION IN THE STOA

Modern interpretations of Chrysippus' position *vis-à-vis* the Stoic school, some of which reflect the ancient evaluations, fall roughly into four categories: (i) Chrysippus systematizes and strengthens Stoic doctrine; (ii) Chrysippus is more or less original: his relation to his predecessors, Zeno and Cleanthes; (iii) Chrysippus argues more acutely than his predecessors and was responsible for the importance logic assumed in the Stoa; (iv) Chrysippus' works remained for centuries the recognized standard of orthodoxy. No one of these categories excludes the other; in theory one's interpretation might embrace all four views.

As for the first category, I have used Arnold's phraseology [1] in its formulation because, so articulated, it is sufficiently general to embrace all the differences in the modern views. Arnold, to whom I have just referred, and Pearson fundamentally agree. The former maintains that Chrysippus "devoted his whole energies" [2] to systematizing and strengthening Stoic doctrine; Pearson, that he did nothing beyond consolidating and defending Stoic doctrine. The only difference in their views lies in the fact that Arnold's is a general verdict made *en passant* while Pearson attempts to show in detail that the "true essence" of Stoicism was contributed by Zeno and Cleanthes, holding that Chrysippus' task then became that of preserving what his predecessors had originated. [3] Petersen, Arnim, Bréhier, and Pohlenz agree with Arnold and Pearson insofar as they, too, claim that Chrysippus, by means of his uncommon dialectical skill, defended the Stoa against its adversaries in one of the dark hours of its history, [4] but in their opinion this is not the

---

[1] Arnold, *op. cit.*, p. 91.

[2] *Ibid.*

[3] A. C. Pearson, *The Fragments of Zeno and Cleanthes.* (London: C. J. Clay & Sons, 1891), p. 48.

[4] "...harum [definitionum] fundamenta reconditius perscrutatus sit et, si qua laberentur, omni qua posset diligentia restituerit, eaque firmiora

only way in which Chrysippus strengthened the Stoa. The additional ways in which he, in their view, added vigor to the Porch will come to the fore as we examine their stance with respect to the remaining categories.

With regard to the second category, Chrysippus' originality or his relation to Zeno and Cleanthes, the scholars are not in agreement. None of them thinks that Chrysippus is wholly original or that he defected from his predecessors on every point in favor of some other philosopher, though some of them do take the view which occupies the other end of the continuum—namely, the view that Chrysippus only adopts the opinions of Zeno and Cleanthes. We have already seen this to be true of Pearson.[1] Bréhier, too, is of the opinion that Chrysippus was not given to the invention of new doctrines and was more of an apologist than a philosopher.[2] Like Pearson, he feels that Chrysippus did not create but consolidated Stoic doctrines.[3] But, more than Pearson, Bréhier emphasizes the new power with which Chrysippus furnished the Stoa by means of his clear awareness of traditional concepts and those resulting from rational reflection, opposed concepts which, in Bréhier's view, it was the Stoa's self-imposed task to unify and harmonize.[4] Petersen holds that Chrysippus' originality lies in his elaboration of a doctrine of categories which contributed to a strengthening of the Porch.[5]

---

redderet necesse est; quod quidem factum esse eo probatur, quod cum in omnibus philosophiae partibus, quarum fragmenta tantum supersunt, restant vestigia, in quibus vincula ista atque firmamenta systematis agnoscantur...." Christian Petersen, *Philosophiae Chrysippi Fundamenta* (Altons and Hamburg, 1827), p. 21.

"Es [his detailed study of Academic philosophy] befähigte ihn, den stoischen Dogmatismus, der zu Kleanthes Zeiten von Arkesilaos in die Enge getrieben worden war, durch sorgfältige, begriffliche und logische Durchbildung gegen die skeptischen Grunde zu verschanzen...." Arnim, "Chrysippos", *Realencyclopädie*, col. 2503.

"...il a fondé une seconde fois le stoicisme, en le defendant contre les dissidents comme Ariston, et contre les adversaires." Bréhier, *op. cit.*, p. 3.

"Und mit dieser Dialektik hat er in schwerer Zeit sieghaft den Kampf gegen die Akademiker wie gegen die Häretiker seiner Schule geführt." Pohlenz, *op. cit.*, I, 29.

[1] *Supra*, note 3, p. 14.
[2] Bréhier, *op. cit.*, p. 59.
[3] *Ibid.*   [4] Bréhier, *op. cit.*, p. 3.
[5] Petersen, *op. cit.*, pp. 21, 22. For a discussion of this subject, *infra*, pp. 103-107. Petersen's work, dedicated to a discussion of the categories in Stoic doctrine, is vitiated insofar as Chrysippus is concerned by Petersen's contention that "those things which are attributed to the Stoics generally are to be referred to Chrysippus." *op. cit.*, p. 22.

Baguet thinks that it was only in natural philosophy that Chrysippus tended to adopt the views of Zeno and Cleanthes.[1] This is similar to, though not identical with, Arnim's belief that Chrysippus, in natural philosophy and ethics, in part follows Zeno; in part, Cleanthes; and, in part, seeks a middle position between the two.[2] Pohlenz, more than any of the other interpreters, finds in Chrysippus an original philosopher who "under the pressure of hostile objections as well as through the consistency of his own thought saw himself in many ways constrained to diverge from Zeno and Cleanthes, and he has in many areas laid wholly new ground for Stoic doctrine."[3]

That Chrysippus argues more acutely than his predecessors in the Stoa and that he was responsible for the importance logic assumed in the school is Baguet's view and, indeed, the main thesis of his book. Baguet would, in the absence of Aristotle, be willing to confer on Chrysippus the authorship of logic.[4] Chrysippus "treats with more exactitude" and works "more subtly and more carefully" than Zeno and Cleanthes, and what they left unproved he "interprets at length, demonstrates, and defends with brilliance."[5] All of our interpreters, each in his own way, agree with Baguet concerning the prominent position given to logic within the Stoic system by Chrysippus.[6]

The view that Chrysippus' works remained for centuries the recognized standard of orthodoxy, our fourth category, is perhaps most forthrightly held by Arnim. He maintains that, although the

---

[1] F. N. G. Baguet, *De Chrysippo* (Annales Accademiae Lovaniensis, 1822), p. 75.

[2] Arnim, "Chrysippos", *Realencyclopädie*, cols. 2508, 2509.

[3] Pohlenz, *op. cit.*, I, 29.

[4] Baguet, *op. cit.*, p. 59.

[5] *Ibid.*, pp. 63, 75.

[6] "Etenim cum non logicen tantum prioribus fusius et subtilius exponeret, sed definitiones maxime et emendaret et melius fundaret. . . ." Petersen, *op. cit.*, p. 20.

"Die Neuerungen des Ch. in der Lehre liegen besonders auf dem Gebiete der Logik." Arnim, "Chrysippos", *Realencyclopädie*, col. 2506.

". . .it is clear that Zeno's logical treatises had been cast into the shade by the more elaborate performances of Chrysippus." Pearson, *op. cit.*, p. 28.

"La dialectique stoicienne est, comme l'on sait, une invention de Chrysippe. . . ." Bréhier, *op. cit.*, p. 60.

"Zenon schätzte allerdings die Dialektik gering ein, und auch Kleanthes lag sie wenig. Dafür war Chrysipp der geborene Dialektiker, dessen Sätze bald auch weit über den Kreis seiner Schule hinaus 'soviel galten wie die Sprüche Apollos.' Zielbewusst hat er die Schullehre auf eine ganz neue Grundlage gestellt." Pohlenz, *op. cit.*, I, 49-50.

attacks of Carneades and the defection of Panaetius and his followers from "Chrysippean orthodoxy" constituted a temporary threat,
the form the Stoic doctrine assumed for later generations was
Chrysippean.[1] Though Bréhier admits that the rejuvenated Stoa of
Panaetius and Posidonius abandons on many points the doctrines
of Chrysippus, he thinks that Chrysippus established some of the
traits which became definitive for the Stoa, especially a kind of
rationalism which gives a richer significance to physical, moral,
and religious concepts; [2] and he agrees that Chrysippus was assigned
a predominating position by the Roman Stoa.[3] Pohlenz' view with
respect to the position occupied by Chrysippus in Stoic philosophy
is curious in that he both is and is not in agreement with Arnim
and Bréhier. As has already been indicated [4] Pohlenz underwrites
the Arnim assessment when he makes assertions like the following:
"The later period knows the Stoic doctrine only in the form which
Chrysippus has given it." [5] But Pohlenz, as was also observed
earlier,[6] subverts his own thesis (and that of Arnim) by describing
innovations introduced into Stoic philosophy by Musonius, Seneca,
Epictetus, and Marcus Aurelius, all members of the Roman Stoa.

Some criticism of holders of the fourth view who employ it
methodologically to unveil Chrysippus' thought has already been
voiced. But it is, of course, now too early to judge these assessments
in and of themselves. This task I postpone, for obvious reasons, to
the concluding chapter.

---

[1] Arnim, "Chrysippos", *Realencyclopädie*, col. 2506. In this article Arnim
holds that "the knowledge of Stoic philosophy, which in the first and second
centuries A.D. was common property of the educated, is related in essentials
to the Chrysippean form of the doctrine. As has already been pointed out
(*supra*, p. 2) Arnim, several years later, putting his position even more strongly
said the Roman Stoa was *wholly dependent* on Chrysippus.

[2] Bréhier, *op. cit.*, p. 276.

[3] *Ibid.*, p. 3.

[4] *Supra*, p. 3.

[5] *Pohlenz, op. cit.*, I, 30, 32.

[6] *Supra*, p. 3.

THIRD CENTURY INTELLECTUAL CURRENTS

Just as the philosophy of any thinker is more readily apprehended when the intellectual milieu in which it arose is understood, so Chrysippus' philosophical views become more intelligible to one who has some comprehension of what might be called "philosophy's condition" at the end of the fourth and during the third century. Some of the ground that we cover will be familiar to the reader, but this makes even more necessary a review of the period because so much has changed and is being debated in the assessments of post-Aristotelian philosophy in Greece that the interpreter cannot afford to take for granted the picture the standard histories give.[1]

1. Two traditional characterizations of Hellenistic philosophy

In the traditional representations of early Hellenistic philosophy two characterizations of it are outstanding: (i) it is *Lebensphilosophie* or philosophy concerned with the conduct and goals of life; (ii) it exhibits an abandonment of fourth century idealism. Serious misunderstandings ensue unless each of these descriptions is carefully qualified.

The charge that hellenistic philosophy is a *Lebensphilosophie* has taken several forms. We hear of "the predominantly practical direction"[2] which philosophy now takes. The Greek philosophical schools after Aristotle, we are told, were "elaborated rather to meet a practical need than to satisfy speculative curiosity."[3] Philosophy,

---

[1] The works of recent years have considerably altered the views prevalent forty years ago, and this makes it all the more necessary for me to discuss early Hellenistic philosophy, because the literature on the subject, especially the English literature (which was published at the beginning of the century and some of which is appearing in new editions) and even portions of the most recent German treatise on the Stoa, does not reflect the modified assessment of philosophical activity in the third century B.C.

[2] Eduard Zeller, *Die Philosophie der Griechen* (5th edit., Vol. III, Pt. 1, Darmstadt: Wissenschaftliche Buchgesellschaft, 1963), p. 12.

[3] Edwyn Bevan, *Stoics and Sceptics* (Cambridge: W. Heffer and Sons, Ltd., 1959 (first published 1913)), p. 31. For Bevan's views about the *practical* bent of the Stoa in particular, see pp. 39-41.

in the hellenistic age, becomes "extremely practical and realistic" and a similarity in the systems of Epicurus and Zeno is that both give "expression to the desire for means to practical ends." [1] Stoicism and Epicureanism, in contrast to philosophies before them, become "character philosophies." [2] Or, as it is also frequently put, this is an age which chiefly needs "not theoretical knowledge", but moral strengthening.[3] What this dichotomy between the practical and theoretical means in terms of the three branches of philosophy is not merely that moral philosophy now becomes of vital concern to a great many individuals—this is true—but that epistemology and cosmology are no longer cultivated in a disinterested spirit, but are merely formulated as auxiliaries to ethical conclusions.[4] As it has been most recently expressed, "The demand for a coherent world view remained; however it was only to form the basis for a way of life which assured to the individual tranquillity and happiness independently of every external circumstance as well as of the community." [5] Another reason for which, we are sometimes told,[6] post-Aristotelian schools attended to the construction of a consistent world view was the continuing influence of Attic philosophy even on foreigners. One scholar even "regrets" that the Stoics felt

---

[1] R. D. Hicks, *Stoic and Epicurean* (New York: Charles Scribner's Sons, 1910), Preface.

[2] Paul Barth. *Die Stoa* (Stuttgart: Fr. Frommanns (E. Hauff), 1903): "Duhring...hat Recht, wenn er die Stoiker, wie die Epikureer im Gegensatze zu ihren Vorgängern "Charakter-philosophen nennt." p. 32. *Cf.* W. Windelband's, "Even such comprehensive systems as the Stoic and the Neoplatonic work only with the conceptions of Greek philosophy, in order to gain a theoretical basis for their practical ideal." p. 157. *A History of Philosophy* (second edit. revised. trans. by James H. Tufts. New York: The Macmillan Company, 1901).

[3] Zeller, *op. cit.*, p. 12.

[4] Of all those who have perpetuated the idea of this dichotomy, perhaps Bevan has stated most clearly what it means in the following sentence: "It was not that Zeno addressed himself to the Universe with a pure disinterested curiosity to know the truth of things for the sake of knowing, but he wanted to make sure of such things about it as should justify a certain emotional and volitional attitude in men." *Op. cit.*, p. 40. *Cf.* Zeller: "Die wissenschaftliche Erkenntniss ist den Stoikern...nicht Selbstzweck, sondern nur ein Mittel zur Erzeugung des richtigen sittlichen Verhaltens: alle philosophische Forschung steht mittelbar oder unmittelbar im Dienste der Tugend." *Op. cit.*, p. 355.

[5] Pohlenz, *op. cit.*, I, 19.

[6] "...und so weit hatte die attische Philosophie doch auch auf die Fernstehenden gewirkt, dass sie das Bedürfnis nach einer geschlossenen Anschauung von der Welt weckte." *Ibid.*

compelled to accompany their utterances about conduct with meta-physical statements.[1] In summary, the overwhelming impression one gets from the traditional histories is that Greek philosophy after Aristotle suffers a collapse from within. Having erected the fiction that the world after Alexander plunges into a state of decay, modern scholars then go on to point out that philosophy, now become religion,[2] ministers to the moral needs of the people,[3] and, if it continues to formulate Weltanschauungen at all, it does so either to provide a basis for its moral dicta or because it succumbs to the not-yet-expired momentum towards metaphysics embedded in Attic philosophy.

Now there is no denying that post-Aristotelian philosophy put a greater emphasis on ethics and particularly on the problem of defining adequately the nature of happiness. But the traditional interpretations go too far in leading one to believe that philosophers either gave themselves over wholly to ethics or that their reflections on epistemological issues and problems in natural philosophy were entirely subordinate to and functions of their solutions in the realm of moral philosophy. It cannot be my purpose here to deal with all the issues involved. But at least three considerations have to be introduced which show that the traditional interpretation must be modified to a certain extent and that one has to look at this period from a vantage point different from the traditional.

The first point is that the third century in Greece was not, as the nineteenth century thought, [4] a period of decay and corruption. Greece was prosperous down to the time of Sulla.[5] Its wealth is evidenced in "the enormous expansion of trade, the growth of clubs,

---

[1] Reported by Bevan (op. cit., p. 30) of Heinrich Gomperz in his Die Lebensauffassung der griechischen Philosophen.

[2] Zeller, op. cit., p. 12.

[3] "...die stoische Philosophie wollte eine Lebenskunst sein...." Pohlenz, op. cit., I, 32. "Die Stoa will dem einzelnen Menschen den rechten Weg für sein Leben zeigen." Ibid., I, 34. "Für die meisten Menschen [in the third century B.C.] gab es nur eine Führerin, die Philosophie...wurde jetzt ihr Ziel, das Individuum an sich selbst zu stellen und ihm Frieden und Glück-seligkeit auch unter den widrigsten äusseren Umständen zu sichern." Ibid., I, 19.

[4] Zeller, op. cit., pp. 10-12. "The Hellenistic period has often been treated as one of decline, even of decay; but probably few would now care to argue this was true of the third century." Sir William Tarn, Hellenistic Civilisation, 3rd edit. (London: Edward Arnold & Co., 1952), p. 4.

[5] Tarn, op. cit., p. 120. Though as contrasted with the fourth century, the gap which separated rich and poor grew wider in the third century.

of new festivals, of luxury in women's dress, of better-planned cities, improved private houses, and more elaborate furniture." [1] Attractive tasks in political, economic, and cultural spheres beckoned to the individual.[2] One of the recent interpreters conveys well the enthusiasm and excitement of the age: "Men had a clear consciousness that they were experiencing a radical change of times and were at the beginning of a new epoch. They rejoiced at the signs of progress which they had everywhere before their eyes, and were astounded by the magnificence and splendor which unfolded themselves in an unheard-of measure." [3] Now since Zeller [4] linked the practical character of the post-Aristotelian philosophies with the material decadence of the period, a realization that the period was not at all bereft of money, energy, and enthusiasm ought to render *prima facie* plausible the suggestion that the philosophies promulgated in the third century, like their predecessors, could well be full-fledged philosophies—with emphasis on ethics to be sure—but with genuinely disinterested views concerning the nature of knowledge and the nature of the world.

The second point to be considered is that also in the philosophies of Plato and Aristotle much attention is given to "practical" topics. They, too, sought to answer questions about man's final end and his conduct. Indeed, if we exclude the *Timaeus* (and not even all of that), the *Critias*, the *Euthydemus*, and the *Parmenides*, which Platonic dialogue is *not* concerned with problems most of which are right at the core of man's existence? And Aristotle devotes one of his longest works, not to mention his investigations of the soul and man in society, to defining man's final end, happiness, and to stating the way in which it might be attained.

My third point is the obverse of the second. Just as Plato and Aristotle, deeply concerned as they were with practical issues, ascended to cosmological problems, so did hellenistic philosophy, in fact, continue to explore these theoretical questions—questions about the nature of the cosmos—which had vexed the hellenic philosophers.[5] Of course, as has already been pointed out, there was a new surge of interest in ethical questions and, if people turned

---

[1] *Ibid.*, p. 111. *Cf.* also p. 113: "...the days when the Hellenistic world was called 'poverty stricken' are, or should be, long past."

[2] Pohlenz, *op. cit.*, I, 16.

[3] *Ibid.*

[4] *Supra*, note 4, p. 20.

[5] This does not apply to the Academy after it turns sceptical.

away from Platonic and Aristotelian solutions, it was because those solutions either entailed involvement with ideal and therefore un-real entities or implied an anachronistic attachment to the city state—an institution virtually defunct. But there was not, as if by way of compensation, any diminution of interest in questions about the nature of the cosmos. On the contrary, as one should almost expect, there is now more incentive than ever to know the nature of the cosmos. Is it not one's natural habitat? Epicurus may think the cosmos is studded with innumerable worlds; Aristotle, that there is only one. Plato may be a dualist, the Stoa, monistic. Nonetheless all four are voices in the tradition of cosmology and metaphysics. The Epicureans and Stoics certainly claimed to possess fully developed systems which took account of problems in episte-mology and natural philosophy as well as in ethics. If they rejected the idealism of Plato and Aristotle, they nonetheless studied the writings of these philosophers intensively.

And this brings me to the second traditional characterization of hellenistic philosophy—that it represents an abandonment of Platonic and Aristotelian idealism, a charge which also requires qualification, I believe. For when historians of ancient philosophy speak of either the motives or the precedents for the materialism that ensued, their accounts have been seriously misleading. Zeller, for example, says that when we turn away from the Platonic or Aristotelian philosophy to the Stoic there appears to us nothing more "astonishing" than the outspoken materialism of the latter.[1] To the question, how have the Stoics arrived at this materialism, Zeller replies that its distinctive motive is to be found "in the practical character of Stoic philosophy." [2] Praechter and others hold that, given Plato's and Aristotle's idealism, hellenistic philosophy, in its materialistic physics, had to go back to the pre-Socratics for precedents and models.[3] One is thus led to believe that, if it had not been for the Stoics and Epicureans, the tradition of Platonic and Aristotelian idealism would have continued to flourish un-challenged and that the two major hellenistic schools represent a

---

[1] Zeller, *op. cit.*, p. 119.

[2] *Ibid.*, p. 127.

[3] Karl Praechter, *Die Philosophie des Altertums*, 12th edit. (Berlin: E. S. Mittler & Sohn, 1926), p. 419, 450-451. Hicks (*op. cit.*) speaks of Heraclitus as Zeno's precursor (p. 10) and of the "retrograde tendency" in the Stoa's cosmic pantheism (p. 20). Zeno, according to Arnold (*op. cit.*), "broke down the barrier which Socrates had set up against the Ionic philosophers." p. 70.

radical break in the most recent philosophical tradition. To accept such a view would be to be misled.

One of the most important and too-frequently ignored facts about philosophy in Athens in the fourth century is that Platonic and Aristotelian idealism had been rejected before the century drew to a close. Plato and Aristotle later penetrated Christian theology and in the modern period they have been read and reread so much—on occasion with some degree of partisanship—that it is difficult for us to realize that, even though men continued to study Plato and Aristotle, within the same century in which these men died their philosophies were impugned and found wanting.[1] Once we understand this we shall hardly find it "astonishing" to discover materialistic doctrines emerging in the following century. Nor shall we find any reason for believing that hellenistic philosophers sought to revive the then moribund pre-Socratic systems for lack of a non-idealistic tradition in late fourth century philosophy. I do not mean to suggest that they might not have taken an interest in the reinterpreting of some of the old pre-Socratic philosophies, but the interest in the pre-Socratics came *after* their commitments to materialism and not the other way about.[2]

For fourth century philosophy the emergence of idealism had been decisive. Plato claimed to resolve the metaphysical problem of the pre-Socratics—what is the ultimate constitution of matter or what is the nature of things—with his theory of ideas. The eternal, immutable, incorporeal Ideas constitute what is real in comparison with which the transient, mutable, and corporeal phenomena are only shadows. The Ideas, or at least one of them, are the source which gives to all existing things their being. They constitute not only objective ideals for ethics but objects of knowledge for science. If it is true that the Presocratic achievement was the discovery of nature,[3] it is also true that "for Plato it is not nature alone that reigns over the world. Nature, the catchword of Presocratic philosophy, the symbol of its materialism, is of

---

[1] For an analysis of the demise of philosophical idealism in the fourth century, from which I have profited, see Ludwig Edelstein, *The Meaning of Stoicism* (Cambridge, Massachusetts: Harvard University Press, 1966), pp. 19-22.

[2] Zeller, an exception, saw this. *Op. cit.*, p. 126-127.

[3] F. M. Cornford, *Before and After Socrates* (Cambridge: The University Press, 1960 (1st published, 1932)), pp. 7, 8.

secondary importance in the Platonic scheme."[1] Plato's was one of those post-Socratic reassertions of the spiritual whose existence the pre-Socratics had denied.[2]

But in Aristotle nature already assumes a more important role in the idealists' understanding of the world. There is a more intimate relationship between forms and things. Forms reside in things and things have dispositions to realize the forms inchoate in them. Teleology is immanent in nature, and in no other way can becoming and perishing be understood. Thus idealism had obviously been toned down in Aristotelian metaphysics. Visible phenomena are no longer explained in terms of a receptacle in which the Ideas imperfectly reproduce themselves. The phenomena, having positive qualities of their own, no longer serve as a mere foil to heighten the immutability and eternality of the Ideas. The status of the Ideas is severely limited.

Moreover, both philosophies, that of Plato and that of Aristotle, often taken to be the undisputed masters of the philosophical scene, were defeated in the fourth century on epistemological grounds. The Cynics, with whom Zeno studied, deny the existence of the universal. Plato's immediate successor, Speusippus, sought to resolve the epistemological problem by resorting to a sense perception which apprehends the common element in things. One generation later the Academy is in the hands of the sceptics.

Within the Lyceum the naturalizing tendency is continued.[3] But while Aristotle's cautious empiricism had merely tended towards an increasing acknowledgment of the power of facts, Theophrastus and Strato, the two succeeding leaders of the Peripatos, put a growing emphasis upon the practice of observation. Theophrastus opposes Aristotle's doctrine of motion with the criticism that movement is "proper both to nature in general and the celestial system in particular" and hence does not require a special explanation.[4] He also is doubtful of Aristotle's teleological

---

[1] Edelstein, *The Meaning of Stoicism*, p. 20.

[2] "Science [pre-Socratic] drew the conclusion, not that the spiritual world had been misconceived, but that there was no such thing: nothing was real except tangible body composed of atoms. The result was a doctrine that philosophers call materialism...." Cornford, *op. cit.*, p. 27.

[3] Werner Jaeger, *Diokles von Karystos* (Berlin: Walter De Gruyter & Co., 1938), p. 228.

[4] "Surely, then, if the life in animals does not need explanation or is to be explained only in this way, may it not be the case that in the heavens too, and in the heavenly bodies, movement does not need explanation or is

principle and recommends that it be used with discrete restraint: "With regard to the view that all things are for the sake of an end and nothing is in vain, the assignation of ends is in general not easy, as it is usually stated to be...we must set certain limits to purposiveness and to the effort after the best, and not assert it to exist in all cases without qualification." [1] Finally, he attacks the doctrine of the four elements and, on the basis of his observations of the qualities of fire, he challenges its being called a primordial element when it obviously is a compound, requiring, as it does, another material for its own nutriment.[2]

In Strato the tendency towards observation culminates [3] and philosophy turns into scientism. Wehrli, the most recent commentator on the text, speaks of Strato's "positivistic science" [4] and observes, "The sharp decline in the number of students in the Lyceum was probably in general provoked by the common neglect of educational activity, of instruction in rhetoric and ethics; the school consequently lost its wide circle of students who had come for a general education and it became more exclusively than earlier the place for scientific research." [5] Even this kind of research seems to have expired after Strato in the Lyceum itself, though treatises in the special sciences—botany, physics, anatomy, physiology, mathematics, astronomy, geography, mechanics, music, and grammar—continue for the next 200 years to issue from the Lyceum's "offshoot"—the Museum of Alexandria.[6]

If the Peripatos after Aristotle is critical of some of its founder's major doctrines, the Academy goes much further in the abandon-

---

to be explained in a special way?' Theophrastus *Metaphysics* 10ª 16-29, (Ross trans.).

[1] *Ibid.*, 10ª 22-**24**; 11ª 1-3.

[2] Theophrastus περὶ πυρός. Cap. I. *Theophrasti Eresii opera Quae Supersunt omnia.* 3rd vol. Fragmenta. Friderick Wimmer. Leipzig: Teubner, 1862.

[3] Benjamin Farrington, *Greek Science* (Baltimore: Penguin Books, 1949), p. 171.

[4] Fritz Wehrli, *Die Schule des Aristoteles. Texte und Kommentar.* Heft V. *Straton von Lampsakos* (Basel: Benno Schwabe & Co., 1950), p. 46.

[5] Wehrli, *Ibid. Cf.* Pierre Duhem, *Le Système du Monde*, Vol. I, p. 243.

[6] Farrington, *op. cit.*, p. 157. *Cf.* K. O. Brink, "Peripatos", *Realencyclopädie*: "Der Schwerpunkt seiner [Strato's] Tätigkeit liegt auf der physikalischen Einzelforschung. Es will wenig besagen, wenn von ihm Logik, Rhetorik, Ethik, Politik daneben weiter gelehrt werden (auch kulturhistorische Titel begegnen): eigene Bedeutung kann ihnen nicht mehr zukommen. Zu seiner Zeit hatte die alexandrinische Forschung bereits eingesetzt. Die von Demetrios und Theophrast angesponnenen Verbindungen zu den Ptolemäern und dem Museion führte er fort." Col. 931.

ment of the Platonic philosophy. After Xenocrates speculative investigations languished and the Academy tends to limit itself to moral philosophy. Soon after the beginning of the third century simple neglect of theoretical knowledge turns into the positive conviction that such knowledge is impossible.[1]

Thus Arcesilaus directed his attack against both rational knowledge and empirical knowledge, and since he was persuaded that every possibility of rational knowledge had been overthrown,[2] the empiricists—that is, the Stoics and Epicureans—constituted his primary target. He criticized in particular the Stoic kataleptic presentation, one of the definitions [3] of which was that it was a presentation which is incapable of becoming false. Arcesilaus maintained that no such presentation existed.[4] And since apprehension is based on the kataleptic presentation, it results that all things are non-apprehensible and even the Stoic sage must withhold judgment.[5]

Finally, Arcesilaus recommended as a rule of conduct for those who suspend judgment about everything the criterion of "the reasonable." [6] A right act, he maintains, is one which has a reasonable justification.[7] To be wise is to be able to produce such a justification for one's actions, and to be wise is to be happy.[8]

But the sceptic element predominated. Even Diogenes Laertius says of Arcesilaus that with him "begins the Middle Academy; he was the first to suspend his judgment owing to the contradictions of opposing arguments. He was also the first to argue on both sides of a question, and the first to meddle with the system handed down by Plato and, by means of question and answer, to make it more closely resemble eristic." [9] Diogenes' statement is worth keeping in mind for the interpreter of Chrysippus since the latter studied with Arcesilaus at the Academy.

---

[1] Zeller, op. cit., p. 496.

[2] Ibid., 508-509.

[3] Sextus Empiricus, adv. math. vii. 151. Infra, pp. 58-60.

[4] Ibid., vii. 154.

[5] Ibid., vii. 155.

[6] Sextus Empiricus, adv. math. vii. 158.

[7] εὔλογος ἀπολογία Ibid. This, interestingly enough, has at least a verbal affinity with Toulmin's doctrine: "All that two people need (and all that they have) to contradict one another about in the case of ethical predicates are the reasons for doing this rather than that or the other." p. 28, Stephen Toulmin, Reason in Ethics (Cambridge: The University Press, 1960).

[8] Sextus Empiricus, adv. math. vii. 158.

[9] Diogenes Laertius iv. 28 Loeb trans. (R. D. Hicks).

It should now be clear that the Epicureans and Stoics were not the only ones responsible for the collapse of philosophical idealism, but that they continued a tradition of rejection that had already begun within the Lyceum and Academy themselves in the latter part of the fourth century. In view of the fact that the Lyceum turned to a cultivation of the special sciences and the Academy turned sceptical, it ought also to be evident that if philosophy in the traditional sense was cultivated anywhere in Athens in the third century, it can only have been in the Garden and in the Porch.

2. EPICUREANISM

To speak of Epicurus' school first, as recent investigations have shown,[1] it is indeed true that he was much more of a philosopher than had been thought. He established his school in Athens about 306 B.C. Epicurus claimed to know what the goal of life is and how it is to be attained.[2] He also formulated a closely-knit epistemology and natural philosophy.[3]

He maintained that pleasure was the final end of life.[4] Feeling, and specifically the feelings of pleasure and pain, is the criterion by which men judge of things to be sought and of things to be avoided.[5] It is because the experience of needing pleasure signifies the presence of pain that one can, according to Epicurus, call pleasure "the alpha and omega of a blessed life." [6] Epicurus means by pleasure "the absence of pain in the body and of trouble in the soul." [7] He believed that anyone who observed sufficiently the behavior of young animals could only conclude that they pursue

---

[1] Cyril Bailey, *The Greek Atomists and Epicurus* (Oxford: The Clarendon Press, 1928). Norman W. DeWitt, *Epicurus and His Philosophy* (Minneapolis: University of Minnesota Press, 1954). Benjamin Farrington, *The Faith of Epicurus* (London: Weidenfeld and Nicolson, 1967).

[2] "And to say that the season for studying philosophy has not yet come, or that it is past and gone, is like saying that the season for happiness is not yet or that it is now no more." D. L. x. 122. Letter to Menoeceus. (Hicks trans.).

[3] In addition to the books cited by Bailey and DeWitt, see also Zeller (*op. cit.*) and Epicurus' letters: Letter to Herodotus, Diogenes Laertius x. 35-83; Letter to Pythocles, D.L. x. 84-116; Letter to Menoeceus, D. L. x. 122-135.

[4] D.L. x. 128, 129. Letter to Menoeceus.

[5] *Ibid.* x. 129.

[6] "When we are pained because of the absence of pleasure, then, and then only, do we feel the need of pleasure. *Wherefore* we call pleasure the alpha and omega of a blessed life." *Ibid.* x. 128 (Hicks trans., italicising my own).

[7] *Ibid.* x. 131.

pleasure as the chief good and avoid pain as the chief evil. And as long as they remain unperverted they will seek pleasure and avoid pain in accordance with or as prompted by nature.[1]

Since "trouble in the soul" is caused by fear, Epicurus can define the final end of life as freedom from pain and fear,[2] or stated positively, health of body and tranquillity of mind.[3] Presumably health of body comes under the jurisdiction of the gymnastic trainer and the doctor. But for peace of mind a knowledge of the nature of things is required, and it was Epicurus' intention to provide such knowledge.[4] Since fear, and specifically fear of the gods and fear of death, is the main obstacle to attaining an unperturbed mind, this fear has to be extirpated, and it can be if men understand the nature of the gods and the nature of death.

The gods themselves live a blessed and hence unperturbed life.[5] The gods are simply not concerned about the destinies of any terrestrial creatures; to impute such concern to them would be to attribute to them something which does not cohere with the bliss which they enjoy. If a supervision of revolutions of bodies in the sky, solstices, and celestial risings and settings cannot be assigned to the gods on the ground that "troubles and anxieties and feelings of anger and partiality do not accord with bliss", [6] then *a fortiori* it must be concluded that a concern either to punish or to reward

---

[1] "Hence Epicurus refuses to admit any necessity for argument or discussion to *prove* that pleasure is desirable and pain to be avoided. These facts, he thinks, are perceived by the senses, as that fire is hot, snow white, honey sweet, none of which things needs be proved by elaborate argument. It is enough merely to draw attention to them." Cicero *de finibus* i. 9, 30, Loeb trans. (H. Rackham).

[2] "For the end of all our actions is to be free from pain and fear..." Letter to Menoeceus. D.L. x. 128.   [3] *Ibid.*

[4] "In the first place, remember that, like everything else, knowledge of celestial phenomena, whether taken along with other things or in isolation, has no other end in view than peace of mind and firm conviction." D.L. x. 85. Why this has to be interpreted to mean "one may regard the phenomena in any way one likes provided a tranquil state of mind ensues," I fail to understand. The following do not sound like the words of one who is not eager to know exactly how things are: "Further, we must hold that to arrive at accurate knowledge of the cause of things of most moment is the business of natural science, and that happiness depends on this (viz. on the knowledge of celestial and atmospheric phenomena), and upon knowing what the heavenly bodies really are, and any kindred facts contributing to exact knowledge in this respect." *Letter to Herodotus*. D.L. x. 78, Loeb trans. (R. D. Hicks).

[5] *Letter to Menoeceus*. D.L. x. 123.

[6] *Letter to Herodotus*. D.L. x. 76, 77, Loeb trans. (R. D. Hicks).

terrestrial creatures is alien to the unperturbed mind. How fear of
the gods destroyed one's peace of mind is vividly expressed in a
passage from Cicero's *Academica* in which the interlocutor is observing how Strato's concept of God (he makes God immune from
any very extensive exertion) frees him from fear: "Assuredly he
frees the deity from a great task, and also me from alarm! For who
holding the view that a god pays heed to him can avoid shivering
with dread of the divine power all day and all night long, and if
any disaster happens to him (and to whom does it not?) being
thoroughly frightened lest it be a judgment upon him?" [1] The
gods, according to Epicurus, were even more exempt from terrestrial
concerns than Strato thought, so no mortal need fear that they
dog his footsteps.

The fear of death, Epicurus taught, was equally groundless and
this he sought to show with his well-known doctrine that where
death is we are not and where we are death is not.[2] Body and
soul, like everything else, are composed of small, indivisible,
impenetrable particles, that is, atoms of matter in the void. Death
marks the dispersal of these atoms, and since the dispersion of the
soul atoms spells the end of sentience,[3] death cannot be evil, "for
good and evil imply sentience." [4] And if something cannot be
painful when it is present, it is groundless to be pained by the
thought of its occurrence.[5]

One further doctrine of Epicurus, which forms an important
intellectual current against which Chrysippus swam, was his view
on causation.[6] The causes of the motions of particles of matter are
weight and impact,[7] but impact is not a primitive cause. The
impact, itself, comes about through a spontaneous swerve [8] in the

---

[1] ii. 38, 121. Loeb trans.   [2] *Letter to Menoeceus*. D.L. x. 125.

[3] "...so long as the soul is in the body, it never loses sentience through
the removal of some other part...But the rest of the frame, whether the
whole of it survives or only a part, no longer has sensation, when once
those atoms have departed, which, however, few in number, are required
to constitute the nature of the soul." *Letter to Herodotus*, D.L. x. 65. (Loeb
trans.).

[4] *Letter to Menoeceus*. D.L. x. 124.

[5] *Ibid.*, x. 125.

[6] The topic must have been discussed in the *Physics*, but all of it that is
extant is found only in the Big Epitome, represented by Lucretius' poem.
DeWitt, *op. cit.*, pp. 5, 169.

[7] Lucrt. ii. 84, 85.

[8] "...incerto tempore ferme
incertisque locis spatio..."   *Ibid.*, ii. 218, 219

downward course of the atoms.[1] This swerve is an important cause in Epicurus' view, for it accounts for two otherwise unexplained phenomena. One is the existence of complex bodies. If there were no swerve, there would be no impact, and hence "the motions by means of which nature generates things would not vary."[2] That is, unless there was a spontaneous swerve in the atoms, natural objects would not exist. The second phenomenon which would be left unexplained if there were no uncaused swerve in the atoms is free will. The passage must be quoted, for it states so well an issue with respect to which the Epicureans and Stoics clash head-on: "Again, if all movement is always interconnected, the new arising from the old in a determinate order—if the atoms never swerve so as to originate some new movement that will snap the bonds of fate, the everlasting sequence of cause and effect—what is the source of the free will possessed by living things throughout the earth?"[3] Epicurus believed that volition was a cause of movement; or, to put it more accurately, that its source,[4] the slight swerve, is a cause. As we shall see, any such uncaused movement is anathema for Chrysippus.[5]

It is profitable to keep this résumé of Epicurean doctrines in mind since, in all probability, the Epicurean School was founded before the Stoa,[6] and not just Chrysippus, but the early Stoa generally, could not afford to ignore its existence. We now turn to

---

[1] "Quod nisi declinare solerent . .

. . . .

nec foret offensus natus nec plaga creata
principiis. . . . ."   *Ibid.*, ii. 221-224.

[2] *Ibid.*, ii. 241, 242.

[3] *Ibid.*, ii. 250-256 (R. E. Latham's trans.).

[4] *Ibid.*, ii. 286. "...*unde* haec est nobis innata potestas" (Italics, my own). De Witt's account appears confused on this point. He says, "Motion is initiated in the mind, situated deep in the breast, and is communicated to all the parts of the body. In this case, therefore, the swerve of the atom is no longer a cause, as it was described at the outset, but the result of another cause, namely, volition." *Op cit.*, 169, 170. Lucretius says plainly in lines 289-294 (Book ii) that the spontaneous swerve of the atom makes possible (*id facit*) the mind's freedom from necessity.

[5] Cicero, wittingly or unwittingly, expresses the Stoic view in his criticism of Epicurus' doctrine of the swerve: "The swerving is itself an arbitrary fiction, for Epicurus says the atoms swerve without a cause,—yet this is the capital offence in a natural philosopher, to speak of something taking place uncaused." i. 6, 19. *de finibus*, Loeb trans. (H. Rackham).

[6] *Cf.* Pohlenz, *op. cit.*, I, 20-21. Also Edelstein's review of Pohlenz. *Die Stoa*, p. 426.

the school which most attracted Chrysippus and to whose leadership he fell heir.

3. The Stoa of Zeno and Cleanthes

Zeno came to Athens in 312/311 at the age of twenty-two.[1] He studied at the Academy, with the Megarian logicians, and with Crates the Cynic. He probably began taking pupils soon after 300 B.C.[2] The Athenians had great respect for Zeno's character and, though he never accepted their offer of citizenship, the Assembly passed a decree shortly before his death awarding him a golden crown and, at the time of his death, a public funeral in the Ceramicus.[3]

Zeno divided philosophy into three parts—logic, physics, and ethics. He did not give much attention to formal logic, but considered the most important problem in logic to be that of the standard of knowledge. He held the senses to be infallible, but the impressions they convey may be in error, and an impression is not to be trusted unless it is "in itself perspicuous." [4] If the strength of tension in the impression is sufficiently strong when it strikes the sense organ, the impression must be coming from an external object and, in such case, the mind grasps it and assents to it. Such an impression Zeno called kataleptic presentation.[5]

---

[1] For a summary of Stoic doctrines attributable to Zeno and Cleanthes the reader may be referred to Pearson, *op. cit.* In this sadly neglected work Pearson, by the way, employs the same methodological principle with respect to Zeno and Cleanthes which I here use in regard to Chrysippus.

[2] Pearson, *op. cit.*, p. 4. Pohlenz (*op. cit.*, I, 23) thinks Epicurus "has certainly contributed to the ripening of Zeno's decision to establish a philosophical school." Zeno's students, at first called Zenoians, later adopted the name of Stoics because Zeno gave his lectures at the Stoa Poikile. Pearson, *op. cit.*, p. 4.

[3] Pearson, *op. cit.*, pp. 4, 5. "Whereas Zeno of Citium, son of Mnaseas, has for many years been devoted to philosophy in the city and has continued to be a man of worth in all other respects, exhorting to virtue and temperance those of the youth who come to him to be taught, directing them to what is best, affording to all in his own conduct a pattern for imitation in perfect consistency with his teaching, it has seemed good to the people—and may it turn out well—to bestow praise upon Zeno of Citium, the son of Mnaseas, and to crown him with a golden crown according to the law, for his goodness and temperance, and to build him a tomb in the Ceramicus at the public cost." D.L. vii. 10, 11, (Hicks trans.).

[4] *Ibid.*, p. 8.

[5] *Ibid.* Diogenes Laertius (vii. 54) reports that "certain of the older Stoics taught that "right reason" (ὀρθὸς λόγος) is the standard of truth. Pearson, following Stein, regards "the doctrine of ὀρθὸς λόγος as a concession

In physics Zeno begins from the proposition that nothing exists but body. This is derived from the view, enunciated by Plato in the *Sophist* (247ᵈ8-ᵉ4), that things which have real existence are those which can affect other things or can be affected by other things, and the principle that body alone is capable of acting and being acted upon. There is an active principle and a passive principle which work together to produce the material world. The active principle is God and the passive is matter. More specifically God is the fiery ether which penetrates the universe in the way that honey passes through a honeycomb. His essence is one, but is differentiated in the variety of existing things. He may be called nature, forethought, or fate. Matter is formless, indeterminate, and finite in extent. The action of God upon matter results in the creation of the world. This action consists in a metamorphosis of the creative fire, which, passing through an intermediate watery stage, becomes the four elements—fire, air, water, and earth. And everything is composed from them.

The world is, by no means, eternal. A time will come when it will burn and will be absorbed into the primordial fire. Indeed, there are some visible signs of its destructibility. Is not every substance with which man is acquainted mortal? Did not all living creatures, including the human species, have a beginning in time? After the conflagration the world will, as the embryo is created from the seed, be formed anew. "For the purpose is unvarying no less than never-ending; a new Heracles will free a young world from its plagues, and a new Socrates will plead his cause against the same accusers." [1] The cosmos and the individual suffer the same fate. They are also alike in that the cosmos is a living unity, sentient, rational, and wise.

The universe is a sphere at whose circumference there is a revolving sheath of aether in which are embedded the celestial bodies, sun, moon, and stars—divine beings which are products of the creative fire. Outside the universe there is unlimited void; within it there is none. The universe does not dissolve into this void because its parts are attracted to the center where the earth is situated.

---

to rationalism. Right reason becomes, in this view, a subsidiary and secondary criterion, so that the results of thought must be confirmed by experience." *Ibid.*, p. 9. *Cf. Infra*, note 1, p. 45.

[1] *Ibid.*, p. 11.

To go from cosmology to anthropology, the soul is conceived by Zeno as a warm breath or as a sentient exhalation. "For the soul is fed by exhalation from the blood, just as the heavenly bodies are by particles from the lower elements." [1] The soul is corporeal and grows with the body.[2] Its growth is influenced by external impressions and reason is perfectly developed at the age of puberty. The soul is one in essence but has several faculties extending out from the ruling faculty, situated in the heart. It permeates the whole body and death is its separation therefrom. However the soul is not eternal, though it does endure for a time after its departure from the body.

Zeno was of course a monotheist, but he could easily accommodate the polytheism of the popular religion, regarding it "as implying a recognition of the ubiquity of the divine presence." [3] God's manifestation in aether, air, and water is represented by Zeus, Hera, and Poseidon respectively. Divination is a legitimate activity, in Zeno's view, because there is forethought in the divine government of the world.

The final end of life, according to Zeno, is to live in accordance with virtue. The first impulses of man are directed, not towards virtue, but towards self-preservation. "These natural impulses require the guidance of reason, and in their proper subordination to it is to be found the condition of happiness, which may be described as the unruffled flow of life." [4] Virtue is sufficient for happiness, and only what is morally evil can diminish the satisfaction of the virtuous. All things other than virtue and vice are therefore morally indifferent. But within the class of indifferent things a gradation exists—passing from negative value through the absolutely indifferent to positive value. Things which possess positive value are in accordance with nature, and things which possess negative values are not. These value properties are not permanent traits of the things having them; what has one degree of value in one set of circumstances may not have it in another.

---

[1] *Ibid.*, pp. 12, 13.
[2] A view expressed in the verse
"For nature, crescent, does not grow alone
In thews and bulk, but as this temple waxes,
The inward service of the mind and soul
Grows wide withal." *Hamlet* i.3.
[3] Pearson, *op. cit.*, p. 13.
[4] *Ibid.*, p. 14.

The same does not hold for things that are *good*. To this classification of objects there is an analogous classification of actions. Virtue is one permanent condition of the ruling faculty of the soul, and it is identical with wisdom which manifests itself in such diverse circumstances as justice, courage, and temperance.

Zeno, unlike Plato and Aristotle, declares all emotions to be bad. These emotions, of which pleasure, grief, fear, and desire, are the chief representatives, result from "an irrational and unnatural movement in the soul, or an excess of impulse." [1] Zeno dwells more upon their effects on the soul than upon their causes.

According to him, the wise man is motivated only by virtue; the fool, only by vice. "Friendship, freedom, piety, riches, beauty, the arts of kingship and generalship, even success in culinary operations belong to the wise man alone: He is never mistaken, never regrets what he has done, feels no compassion, and is absolutely free from every form of emotion." [2] It is possible to progress from a state of folly to a state of wisdom. This progress is marked by a purgation of the soul, under the influence of reason, from its emotions. Suicide belongs to the class of indifferent things, and if circumstances point to that exit, the wise man will take it.

With respect to social ethics Zeno of course rejects the aristocratic ideal state delineated by Plato. His state "comprises the whole of mankind living together like a herd of cattle", [3] and its presiding deity is Eros, god of friendship and concord. In Zeno's state there will be no coinage, a community of wives, and a thoroughly revised educational system.

We must now briefly outline the contributions of Cleanthes, Chrysippus' immediate predecessor, who led the Stoa from 264 to the time of his death in 232.[4]

Deeply-rooted conviction and religious fervor are the hallmarks of Cleanthes' character and they led him to emphasize the theological branch of philosophy [5] and also issued in his poetical expressions

---

[1] *Ibid.*, p. 16.

[2] *Ibid.*

[3] *Ibid.*, p. 17. *Cf.* André-Jean Voelke, *Les rapports avec autrui dans la philosophie grecque d'Aristote à Panétius* (Paris: Librairie Philosophique J. Vrin, 1961), pp. 123-128.

[4] For Cleanthes, see Pearson, *op. cit.*; Hans von Arnim, "Kleanthes", *Realencyclopädie*, cols. 558-574; Nicola Festa, *I frammenti degli Stoici antichi* (Vol. II, Bari: Guiseppe Laterza e Figli, 1935), pp. 75-176.

[5] Arnim, "Kleanthes", col. 567.

of praise for the divine. Cleanthes did not possess a combative nature, and even while he was nominally heading the Stoa, Chrysippus, his student, was the prime defender of the Porch against the assaults of the Epicureans on its ethics and those of the Academics on its logical theories.

Cleanthes held that there were six major divisions of philosophy: dialectic, rhetoric, physics, theology, ethics, and politics.

He rests epistemology on an even stronger empirical basis than Zeno had. The latter had described a presentation simply as "an impression on the soul." This was interpreted by Cleanthes to mean "an actual material concavity impressed by the object." [1]

Cleanthes calls the divine permeating essence, which Zeno had called aether, "pneuma." As has been observed [2] Cleanthes is the author of the doctrine that "the world is God." Agreeing with Zeno that God, working through the four elements, creates the world and noting the constant mutation of these elements, Cleanthes looked for the cause. Inferring the nature of the cosmos from the nature of the individual, he concluded that this ceaseless movement in the cosmos was caused by the "tension" between its parts; for it is this tension which causes movement in the human frame. "Thus the phenomenal world is created and again destroyed by the successive phases in the ever varying tension of the fiery breath, which is at once identified with God and with the universe." [3]

Cleanthes, having noted that everything requires warmth for its existence and having thereafter inferred that the essence of things is constituted by warmth, taught that the ruling part of the cosmos is located in the sun.[4] As a matter of fact, the sun *is* the ruling part of the world. At the time of the conflagration, everything will become like the sun, which is the fiery breath in its purest form. The sun moves in an oblique course through the zodiac and, since it strikes the world with its rays, it is called a plectrum.

Cleanthes contributes two proofs for the doctrine that the soul is corporeal—one based on "the mental resemblance between parents and children" and the other on "the sympathy of the soul with the body." [5]

---

[1] Pearson, *op. cit.*, p. 38.
[2] *Ibid.*, p. 41.
[3] *Ibid.*, p. 42. *Cf.* Arnim, "Kleanthes", cols. 565-566. Festa, *op. cit.*, p. 123
[4] Festa, *op. cit.*, p. 118.
[5] Pearson, *op. cit.*, p. 42. *Cf.* Arnim, "Kleanthes", col. 566.

In theology Cleanthes refuses to make the divine agency responsible for evil. He gives five distinct reasons for the existence
of God.[1] Zeus is the one eternal god, for the others will be destroyed
at the time of the conflagration. Like Zeno, Cleanthes believed that
popular religion was a manifestation of the truth, but that its real
meaning required interpretation.

In ethics Cleanthes seems for the most part to have accepted the
principles established by Zeno. We have already seen him employ
a principle which he regards of the utmost importance, namely,
that there is a parallelism between the macrocosm that is the world
and the microcosm that is the individual. "The more, therefore, that
man brings himself into harmony with the spirit which breathes
throughout the universe, the more does he fulfil the role to which
he is destined."[2] Cleanthes' doctrine of tension is applied to two
topics in Zeno's ethics—the nature of virtue and the emotions. The
air current in every body is always in some state of tension. When
it is strong enough to do what is fitting this tension is called
strength and power, and as manifested in different circumstances,
this power is one of the four virtues—self-control, courage, justice,
or temperance.[3] The weakness of soul, which explains the occurrence
of emotions comes about when the tension is relaxed. "Thus the
essence of virtue and emotion, which Zeno had left unexplained on
the physical side, is traced to a single science, and this source is the
same power which is the origin of all movement and life."[4] Cleanthes
engaged in controversy with the Epicureans in his *On Pleasure* where
he maintains that pleasure is without value and absolutely contrary
to nature. He also wrote a number of treatises in the area of applied
morals, and here we find involved the general principle that it is
not the nature of the deed but the disposition of the agent which

---

[1] "(1) the ascending series of organisms from plants to man, which shows
that there must be some being who is best of all, and this cannot be man
with all his imperfections and frailties, (2) the foreknowledge of coming
events, (3) the fruitfulness of the earth and other natural blessings, (4)
the occurrence of portents outside the ordinary course of nature, and (5)
the regular movements of the heavenly bodies." Pearson, *op. cit.*, p. 43.

[2] *Ibid.*, p. 44.

[3] "It will be observed that ἐγκράτεια here occupies the position which
by Chrysippus and his followers is assigned to φρόνησις. Thus Cleanthes
fortifies his main position that strength of tension is the necessary starting-
point of virtue by a tacit appeal to the authority of Socrates, who had pointed
to ἐγκράτεια as κρηπὶς ἀρετῆς." Pearson, *op. cit.*, p. 45.

[4] *Ibid.*, p. 45.

constitutes virtuous conduct or, put another way, the same action "may be either vicious or virtuous, according to the motive which prompts its performance." [1]

This has been a sketch of that third century school of philosophy [2] which most appealed to Chrysippus and which he was to defend, reshape, and develop. Before we see how he did this, since I surely cannot speak of intellectual currents in the third century without saying something of the scientific movement, I conclude this chapter with some observations on the relation of the special sciences to philosophy.

4. THE SPECIAL SCIENCES

It is well-known that some of the special sciences—mathematics, medicine and biology, physics, astronomy, grammar and philology —developed apace in the third and second centuries B.C. [3] Moreover it is held in some quarters that theoretical interest in knowledge for its own sake, during this period, "developed essentially in the individual sciences." [4] Furnished with such reports the modern reader may get the impression that the philosophical schools in the Hellenistic period were utterly detached from the sciences and that, while individuals at a considerable remove from the philosophical schools made progress in one science or another, the philosophers themselves were completely and exclusively involved with problems relating to man's inner life and human conduct. Such an impression would be grossly unhistorical. The relation between philosophy and the sciences was an especially intimate one and the features of this compenetration of one by the other can perhaps be suggested by the following remarks. [5]

---

[1] *Ibid.*, p. 47.

[2] In the chapters which follow on Chrysippus' logic, natural philosophy, and moral philosophy, I deal in more detail with some of the Zenonian and Cleanthian doctrines described in this section rather generally.

[3] Marshall Clagett, *Greek Science in Antiquity* (2nd edit. New York: Collier Books, 1963 (f.p. 1955), pp. 54-126. Benjamin Farrington, *Greek Science* (Baltimore: Penguin Books, 1953), pp. 155-242. George Sarton, *Ancient Science and Modern Civilization* (New York: Harper & Brothers, 1959 (f.p. 1954), pp. 3-36. *Les Stoiciens* (Textes traduits par Émile Bréhier édites sous la direction de Pierre-Maxime Schuhl. Paris: Éditions Gallimard, 1962), p. LXIV.

[4] W. Windelband, *A History of Philosophy* (2nd edit. trans. by James H. Tufts. New York: MacMillan Co., 1901), p. 156.

[5] Edelstein has done invaluable service in the task of giving us a picture of the relation between philosophy and science in antiquity. See his "Recent

In the first place there are a number of germinal ideas advanced by pre-Socratic philosophers and philosophers of the fourth century which were to reappear in and affect the development of science in subsequent centuries. Marshall Clagett [1] has given a clear formulation of some of these ideas: the indestructibility of the material substratum, the consequences and accompaniments of change of phase in the material substratum; the notion that physical forces stimulate change and movement; the infinitude of space and the infinitude of worlds like our own in that space; the evolutionary development of living things; the healing power of nature. Another of these ideas, discussed by Edelstein,[2] and one which says something about the philosophical motivation for scientific research is that to make a discovery in the realm of nature, say, in biology or astronomy, is both to realize the divine element in oneself and to unveil that element in nature. It is to employ reason, that feature or function in man which makes him akin to the gods.[3] The scientist in the third century B.C., by his association with one of the philoso-

---

Interpretations of Ancient Science", *Journal of the History of Ideas*, Vol. XIII (October, 1952), pp. 573-604; "Motives and Incentives of Science in Antiquity (paper read at International Conference on the History of Science, Oxford, July, 1961); "The Development of Greek Anatomy" (unpublished paper read in a seminar course on the history of philosophy). For an instance of negative influence, which exhibits compenetration all the same, see Pierre Duhem, *Le Système du Monde* (Paris: Librairie Scientifique A. Hermann et Fils, 1913), Vol. I, pp. 424-426.

[1] *Op. cit.*, pp. 51-53.

[2] Edelstein, "Motives and Incentives...", p. 6 For the presence of this motif in Isaac Newton's work, see Max Jammer, *Concepts of Space* (New York: Harper & Brothers, 1960 (f. p. 1954), p. 26.

[3] "But such a life would be too high for man; for it is not in so far as he is man that he will live so, but in so far as something divine is present in him; and by so much as this is superior to our composite nature is its activity superior to that which is the exercise of the other kind of virtue. If reason is divine, then, in comparison with man, the life according to it is divine in comparison with human life. But we must not follow those who advise us, being men, to think of human things, and being mortal, of mortal things, but must, so far as we can, make ourselves immortal, and strain every nerve to live in accordance with the best thing in us; for even if it be small in bulk, much more does it in power and worth surpass everything. This would seem, too, to be each man himself, since it is the authoritative and better part of him. It would be strange, then, if he were to choose not the life of his self but that of something else. And what we said before will apply now; that which is proper to each thing is by nature best and most pleasant for each thing; for man, therefore, the life according to reason is best and pleasantest, since reason more than anything else *is* man." Aristotle *Ethica Nicomachea* 1177[b] 27-1178[a] 8 (trans. by W. D. Ross).

phical schools, gains "a ruling principle for the treatment of separate questions which interested him." [1] One such ruling principle, though it is probably more general than those which the author just cited had in mind, is the researcher's notion that his discoveries were tantamount to revelations of the divine at work in nature. As Edelstein has put it, "Whenever the Greek or Roman confronts phenomena that reflect eternal laws, he hears in the eternal the voice of the divine; "eternal" and "divine" are interchangeable expressions." [2] The penetration of science by philosophy, then, is evidenced by this motive, peculiarly philosophical, which provides the scientist a stimulus for his investigations.

Secondly, the method of experiment, which, in spite of recent assertions to the contrary,[3] was practiced in antiquity,[4] was not the special monopoly of scientists—of an Erasistratus or a Galen. Just because a philosopher suggests only one experiment for a certain physical hypothesis, as Chrysippus does, for example, in support of his theory of mixture,[5] one cannot allege that he is unscientific, on the ground that only the scientists of the day are carrying on systematic experimentation. For, as has been pointed out,[6] though the two attitudes—that of repeated, systematic experimentation and that of occasional experimental proof of a speculative theory—existed side by side, they cannot be assigned to the scientist and philosopher respectively. ". . . if some of the ancients clearly saw the advantage of repeated, systematic experimentation, others lacked this insight. No less an anatomist than Galen was unwilling to investigate all phenomena, wherever this did not seem to serve his purpose." [7] That the method of experiment cuts across the not-so-distinct division between science and philosophy in antiquity is further evidence of their compenetration.

Thirdly, philosophers, if they do not possess expert knowledge

----

[1] Windelband, op. cit., p. 156. It is perhaps significant that it is Windelband himself, who elsewhere accentuates the development of the special sciences (supra, note 4, p. 37), admits this.

[2] Edelstein, "Motives and Incentives. . .", p. 6.

[3] S. Sambursky, The Physical World of the Greeks, (Trans. by Merton Dagut, London: Routledge and Kegan Paul, 1956), pp. 2, 95.

[4] Edelstein, "Recent Interpretations. . .", pp. 574, 575. Benjamin Farrington, "Strato and the Experimental Method of Research", op. cit., pp. 169-185.

[5] II (471, 473).

[6] Edelstein, "Recent Interpretations. . .", p. 577.

[7] Ibid.

in some area of investigation, borrow such knowledge from some
one of the individual scientists. An instance of this relying on the
expert is attested with respect to Chrysippus. Our philosopher,
as we shall see,[1] maintained that the soul's ruling function had its
locus in the heart, and in order to give his theory scientific support,
he appealed to the physician, Praxagoras, who held that the nerves
have their origin in the heart.[2] And Steckerl rightly infers that
Chrysippus' use of Praxagoras' opinion in his argument "shows
that Praxagoras was considered to be an outstanding authority on
medical questions during the third century." [3]

Fourthly, it is well to remind ourselves that the methods of
analysis and synthesis, which were to play such a significant role
in the development of Euclidean geometry in the third century,[4]
were methods upon which much attention had been lavished by
the philosophers, Plato and Aristotle. For example, Plato's description of the use of hypothesis in the *Meno* ($87^{b}2$-$^{c}10$) is a near description of the method of analysis, and his account in the *Republic*
(511 B-C) of the descent of the dialectician through Ideas matches
the description of the method of synthesis given by Pappus of

---

[1] *Infra* p. 133.

[2] III 897. *Cf.* Fritz Steckerl, *The Fragments of Praxagoras of Cos and His
School* (Leiden: E. J. Brill, 1958), pp. 49-53.

[3] Steckerl, *op. cit.*, p. 4. From the fact that Chrysippus appealed to
Praxagoras, whose theory was fifty years old when Chrysippus became
leader of the Stoa, instead of to the more recent and different theories of
Herophilus and Erasistratus, Solmsen concludes that Chrysippus' "feeling
for scientific progress may not have been very vivid." p. 195. "Greek
Philosophy and the Discovery of the Nerves", *Museum Helveticum* (Vol. 18,
Fasc. 4), pp. 169-197. Also Friedrich Solmsen, *Cleanthes or Posidonius?
The Basis of Stoic Physics* (Amsterdam, 1961), p. 24. But it is questionable
that there existed at all in the third century B.C. such a phenomenon as
"the feeling for scientific progress." Edelstein, who has discussed the
lack of agreement among scientists in the Hellenistic centuries, says that in
this age, "there remained a great variety of doctrines, and adherence to any
one of them was optional, as it were....and these divergencies did not
imply a distinction between science and non-science; they merely characterized
rival systems of thought which continued to exist side by side." pp. 601,
602, "Recent Trends in the Interpretation of Ancient Science." Even
though the special sciences are coming into being in the third century, they
are nevertheless still very much in what Thomas Kuhn would call "the
pre-paradigm period" of their development (for Kuhn's analysis of the
development of sciences in terms of the adoption and abandonment of
paradigms, see his *The Structure of Scientific Revolutions* (Chicago: The
University of Chicago Press, 1962)).

[4] Clagett, *op. cit.*, pp. 71-73.

Alexandria.[1] And Aristotle uses one form of analysis, the *reductio ad absurdum* argument, time and time again in his disproof of invalid syllogisms.[2] The interest in demonstrative proofs, as will be made evident in the following chapter, was not a monopoly of the mathematicians in the third century either; an interest in sound argument was also exhibited in the philosophical schools.

Finally, and perhaps most significantly, certain problems discussed in the philosophical schools, had considerable bearing on the manner in which specifically scientific investigations were conducted.[3] Consider, for example, the problem of causation debated heatedly in the Stoa and the Garden. The manner of work of a scientist, it seems, would be materially affected by his commitment to (or his denial of) the principle that everything that occurs has a cause; that if that cause is not evident, this means, not that it does not exist, but that it works in a concealed manner, and that further investigation might divulge it. This was precisely the theory of causation advanced by the Stoa (II 973).

A more dramatic and more specific manifestation of this dynamic relation between discussions of philosophical problems in the schools and the character of specific scientific investigations is seen in the development of Greek anatomy.[4] In the fifth and fourth centuries B.C. it was the practice of physicians to dissect dead and living animals and then to base their claims about the human body on

---

[1] Pappus of Alexandria: "*Analysis*, then, takes that which is sought as if it were admitted and passes from it through its successive consequences to something which is admitted as the result of synthesis: for in analysis we assume that which is sought as if it were (already) done and we inquire what it is from which this results, and again what is the antecedent cause of the latter, and so on, until by so retracing our steps to the class of first principles, and such a method we call analysis as being solution backwards.

But in *synthesis*, reversing the process, we take as already done that which was last arrived at in the analysis and, by arranging in their natural order as consequences what were before antecedents, and successively connecting them one with another, we arrive finally at the construction of what was sought; and this we call synthesis." *The Thirteen Books of Euclid's Elements* (2nd edit. trans. with introduction and commentary by T. L. Heath. New York: Dover Publications, Inc., 1956) Vol. I, p. 138.

[2] *Prior Analytics* i. 3-6 *passim*.

[3] And this is probably what Windelband had in mind when he said that the scientist got from the philosophical schools "a ruling principle for the treatment of separate questions and subjects which interested him." *op. cit.*, p. 156.

[4] Edelstein, "The Development of Greek Anatomy", *Supra* note 5, p. 37.

inferences from the animal body.[1] Dissection and vivisection is practiced on human bodies soon after the beginning of the third century. Given that the Greeks had such a fear of dead bodies and regard the burial of every corpse as a duty, how could dissection of the human body ever arise as a practice? It was a general belief in the sixth and fifth centuries that the human body after death is still sentient. This belief becomes radically changed by the Platonic philosophy which maintains that the person is his soul, not his body, so that after death the corpse is not to be identified with the person that was.[2] Plato believes that

> the soul is wholly superior to the body, and that in actual life what makes each of us to be what he is is nothing else than the soul, while the body is a semblance which attends on each of us, it being well said that the bodily corpses are images of the dead, but that which is the real self of each of us, and which we term the immortal soul, departs to the presence of other gods.[3]

Aristotle propounds a similar view of the soul and the Hellenistic physicians who first performed dissections on the human body are disciples of these philosophers. The view that the soul is the person or that where the soul is not, the person is not, is present in the whole of Hellenistic philosophy. Expressed by Epicurus in the words, "The wise man will not think about burial", [4] it appears in its most extreme form in the Stoic view that the wise man will make no objections to the practice of eating the cadavers of one's parents (III 747, 748).

Even if the discussions by philosophers of the nature of the soul made it possible to perform dissections, why should physicians suddenly find this practice, certainly not any more agreeable because of the new attitude, necessary? This question, too, is answered by reference to discussions in the philosophical schools, and specifically discussions regarding the propriety of the analogical method.

In the fifth and fourth centuries B.C. the method of explanation

---

[1] *Ibid.*, p. 237.
[2] *Phaedo* (115c-e).
[3] *Laws* 959a-b. (trans. Bury).
[4] Epicurus, fr. 578, in Usener *Epicurea* (Leipzig, 1887); quoted by Edelstein, p. 243.

by analogy is accepted because of "the belief that there exists an
all-embracing uniformity in nature." [1] Since everything, so it was
believed, is ultimately one thing, one could compare men and
animals, animals and plants, and, indeed, human behavior and the
behavior of celestial bodies. Belief in analogy, however, begins to
wear thin in the fourth century. Aristotle begins to criticize statements based on analogy.[2] "And he makes no inferences from the organs of animals to those of human beings, except in comparing
their functions. Analogies become an uncertain basis for study." [3]
Theophrastus was even more critical of the analogical method [4] and
Erasistratus, one of the first and greatest anatomists of antiquity,
was his pupil. Do we not have here a clear-cut case of a special
scientist getting his "ruling principle" from a philosophical school?

In summary, it is well to bear in mind when we observe individual
sciences beginning to form and even to flourish in the third century
B.C. that these special sciences and philosophy do not develop
wholly independently of one another. The sciences partake of
philosophy's motivation, they share with it a method, and they
often derive from philosophy their governing principles; and
philosophers sometimes rely on the theories of individual scientists.

This sketch of some of the intellectual currents present in
Chrysippus' century provides a background which will perhaps
facilitate our interpretation of the fragments of Chrysippus'
philosophy. It should be clear, for example, that Chrysippus lives
in an era that is recoiling away from Platonic-Aristotelian idealism.
And we cannot be surprised when we come upon fragments which
point to nominalism in logic and materialism in metaphysics. We
now know that this is a period in which the boundaries of the
individual's habitat are greatly expanded, and therefore if we find
fragments which permit us to get a glimpse of discussions about the
nature of the cosmos, we shall welcome them as if expected. It is
an age in which men are desperately eager to discover what happi-

---

[1] Edelstein, "Development..." p. 245.
[2] "It is equally absurd to suppose that anything has been explained by
calling the sea 'the sweat of the earth', like Empedocles. Metaphors are
poetical and so that expression of his may satisfy the requirements of a
poem, but as a scientific theory it is unsatisfactory." *Meteorologica* 357ª 24-28.
Oxford trans. of Aristotle's Works.
[3] Edelstein, "Development..." p. 246.
[4] Benjamin Farrington, *op. cit.*, pp. 164-166.

ness is, and Epicurus has told them that happiness is pleasure. Epicurus is taken seriously by a great number of persons and, if Chrysippus wishes to propose a contrary thesis about happiness, he, too, must take Epicurus seriously. Chrysippus is surely familiar with the doctrines of Zeno and Cleanthes, and he knows skepticism from the inside. He has to defend the Stoa in the wake of the Skeptical Middle Academy's attack on it. This fact will perhaps throw light on some of the logical fragments. This is a century, as has been seen, not only of reaction against philosophical idealism, but also one of development in the special sciences. In the light of our discussion of the intimate relation between these sciences and philosophy, it would be folly to suppose that Chrysippus, the head of one of the major philosophical schools at Athens, was not aware of these developments. Though we shall not permit our background picture to draw us into a violation of the methodological principle enunciated in the first chapter, we shall refer to it when it appears that a given fragment will thereby say more to us.

CHAPTER FOUR

LOGIC

Chrysippus defined philosophy as "the cultivation of rightness of reason." [1] What he can have meant by this expression will emerge only after we have some understanding of his view of reason and the way in which he regarded the branches of philosophy. Like Zeno, [2] Chrysippus believed that there were three subjects of investigation (θεωρήματα), as he called them, belonging to the philosopher (II 42). The three divisions of philosophy are logic, physics, and ethics (II 37). Chrysippus, like Aristotle, as will be seen presently, believed that the student ought to learn logic before studying the other parts of philosophy; but unlike the Peripatetic, who not only regarded logic as a propaedeutic subject but also excluded it altogether from his classification of the sciences,[3] Chrysippus makes logic a division of philosophy coordinate with the other divisions of it. And my presentation of Chrysippus' logic provides a clue, I believe, as to why Chrysippus found so congenial the tripartite division of philosophy, [4] which makes logic a member in good standing in the circle of philosophical disciplines.

---

[1] Isidore of Pelusium attributes (*Patrologia Greca*, V, 78, p. 1637, Migne) this definition (ἐπιτήδευσις λόγου ὀρθότητος) to Chrysippus. It does not appear as such in Arnim's collection, but B. Keil ("Chrysippeum", *Hermes*, 1905, p. 155) found this definition of philosophy in Herculaneum Papyrus 1020, which appears in *SVF* II as fragment 131. The definition appears at line 28, p. 41. *Cf.* Bréhier, *Chrysippe et L'Ancien Stoicisme*, p. 29, note 1. Sextus Empiricus reports a similar Stoic definition of philosophy: "cultivation of wisdom" (ἐπιτήδευσις σοφίας); wisdom is "the knowledge of things divine and human." (*SVF* II 36)

[2] *Supra*, p. 31.

[3] Aristotle, *Meta.* 1005[b] 3, 1026[a] 18 and W. D. Ross, *Aristotle*, 5th edit. (New York: Barnes & Noble, 1949), p. 20.

[4] Epicurus, too, divided philosophy into three parts: canonic, physics and ethics. Canonic, or the study of the criterion of truth, was usually combined with physics, *D.L.* x.30. Cicero, following Antiochus, attributes this threefold division of philosophy to Plato's disciples, Speusippus, Aristotle and Xenocrates, and to Polemo and Theophrastus. *de finibus* iv. 2, 3-8. The division certainly does *not* belong to Aristotle. *Cf.* Sextus Empiricus, *adv. math.* vii. 16. For an argument by which "the Stoics" sought to prove that logic is not merely an instrument of, but a branch of philosophy, see the remarks of Ammonius in his commentary on Aristotle's *Prior Analytics* (p. 8, 20 Wallies) in *SVF* II 49.

As for the order in which the branches of philosophy ought to be studied, logic-ethics-physics was the arrangement recommended by Chrysippus.[1] Diogenes Laertius (II 43) says that Chrysippus put physics second and ethics third, but Plutarch's report merits more credence, because he confirms it with a quotation from one of Chrysippus' books. It is worthy of note, however, that, while Chrysippus recommends the logic-ethics-physics order as the order of study or learning, he explicitly affirms that natural philosophy has but one aim, and that is to help students of it to distinguish between good things and bad things (III 68). This would indicate that natural philosophy is logically prior to ethics. Incidentally, while we can certainly infer from this report that the primary concern of Chrysippus, as of the century, was with ethics, it would be logically unsound to conclude from this assertion alone that Chrysippus was not interested in logic and physics at all or that, while interested, he allowed his ethical doctrines to distort his conclusions in these spheres. To assume the first alternative would in addition be an error in fact. To assume the second in advance would be to make less fruitful an otherwise sympathetic approach to the Chrysippean fragments. It appears to me that Chrysippus was intensely interested in legitimate modes of inference and the nature of the cosmos, but the fragments might seem to be less eloquent on this point to one who approached them with the attitude that because Chrysippus was a moralist, he could not have been a logician or a cosmologist.

Our exposition of Chrysippus' doctrines will follow the logic-natural philosophy-ethics order.[2]

---

[1] *SVF* II 42. Chrysippus' view was familiar to Hume through Plutarch. "The method I [Demea is speaking] follow in their education is founded on the saying of an ancient, 'That students of philosophy ought first to learn logics, then ethics, next physics, last of all the nature of the gods.'" *Dialogues Concerning Natural Religion* (ed. with an introduction by Henry D. Aiken. New York: Hafner Publishing Co., 1948), p. 5. Demea's remark sounds like a verbatim translation of Chrysippus' statement in *SVF* II 42.

[2] Plutarch, whose avowed purpose in writing the *De Stoicorum Repugnantiis* is to set forth Chrysippus' allegedly contradictory doctrines (II 1125), mistakenly observes that Chrysippus' practice does not agree with his recommendations. For, Plutarch reports, while recommending that natural philosophy, and more specifically, theology, be studied last, Chrysippus prefaced everything he wrote with words about God, Fate, and Providence (x II 30). But surely, for one who maintains that students should study natural philosophy last in order, and who asserts that the truths of natural philosophy undergird those of ethics, there is nothing irregular about placing

It is somewhat ironic that, in order to reconstruct for ourselves Chrysippus' views on logic, we have only seventy-six fragments, one of them (II 13-17) containing a list which indicates that he wrote 262 books on logic. These 262 books constitute a little less than half of his literary work; and if we assume [1] that the other 443 books written by him dealt with natural philosophy and ethics exclusively, then the mentioned irony comes statistically to this: while we possess more than 400 Chrysippean fragments having to do with either ethics or natural philosophy, we have only seventy-six such fragments having to do with logic, the branch of philosophy to which Chrysippus devoted more than a third of his many books.[2]

A rather large group of books dealt with the various forms of propositions and here one finds among others the titles *On Negative Propositions, On the Subject-What are False Propositions*, and *On Imperatives*. These titles appear to denote subjects that have occupied a central place in discussions by contemporary philosophers.[3] In a group which considers logic in relation to words and sentences there appear the titles, *Sentences Opposed to Ordinary Usage, On Ambiguity in a Conditional Proposition, An Introduction to The Study of Ambiguity*. Included in a set of titles dealing with arguments and moods there are *Introduction to the Liar Argument, On the Analysis of Syllogisms*, and *Reply to Those Who Think that a Proposition Can be Both False and True*.

It would be an advantage both to the historian of philosophy and to the logician if something of the contents of these works could

---

the truths of natural philosophy at the beginning of his lectures and books. Plutarch confuses Chrysippus' recommended order of learning philosophy with Chrysippus' view about the logical order (and this is probably the tradition from which Diogenes Laertius got his report referred to in the text above) of the divisions of philosophy. Plutarch himself furnishes us evidence for concluding that, for Chrysippus, while natural philosophy and its most important subdivision, theology, are *posterior* to logic and ethics in the order of study, at least natural philosophy is logically prior to ethics (*supra*, p. 5).

[1] An unlikely assumption. In the seventy-six extant logical fragments seventeen of Chrysippus' books are named; only six of them are to be found in Laertius' catalogue.

[2] In *SVF* II 1 Chrysippus is reported to have written more than 705 books.

[3] A. J. Ayer, "Negation", *Journal of Philosophy*, Vol. XLIX (Dec. 18, 1952), pp. 797-815. Bertrand Russell, *The Problems of Philosophy* (New York: Oxford Univ. Press, 1959; first published, 1912), Chapter XII "Truth and Falsehood", pp. 119-130. R. M. Hare, *The Language of Morals* (Oxford: The Clarendon Press, 1952), Chapter 2: "Imperatives and Logic", pp. 17-31.

be established.[1] Although it is indeed regrettable that we do not
have any of Chrysippus' logical treatises, the titles of which are
so tantalizing, we are nevertheless able on the basis of the fragments
we possess to make out some of his views on logic.

I. THEORY OF KNOWLEDGE

We have no fragment stating into what branches Chrysippus
divided logic. The evidence indicates, however, that what we today
call theory of knowledge was a topic of importance for the Stoa
generally and that for Chrysippus in particular it was a subject to
be taken up by students of logic. And it comes from a good source;
it is moreover a rather extensive and detailed account.

According to Sextus Empiricus the main types of philosophy are
three: there are first those who claim they have discovered the truth
(these are the dogmatists); secondly are those who maintain that
the truth cannot be apprehended (the sceptics); then there are
those who continue to look for the truth (the academics). As
examples of dogmatic philosophers Sextus mentions Aristotle,
Epicurus, and the Stoics.[2] Since the Stoics are philosophers who
claim to have discovered the truth, they must have held that things
can be known. One might think that, had they been unopposed in
their view that things are knowable, they may through, say,
indolence, never have reflected upon the epistemological foundations
of their doctrines. But they were not unopposed in their claims. On
the contrary, the early Stoa was constantly dogged by the New
Academy whose devotees believed that things cannot be known.[3]

---

[1] In another place I intend to make an analysis of these titles, comparing
the terms in them with uses of them by Aristotle, the Stoics generally,
and Galen, with a view to determining something about the subjects dealt
with in Chrysippus' logical books. In this way it will perhaps be possible,
as Mette has put it, "to trace back to Chrysippus himself a number of the
concepts of Stoic logic." H. J. Mette, Review of *Die Stoa* by Max Pohlenz.
Gnomon (Band 23/1951, pp. 27-39), p. 31.

[2] *P.H.* i. 1-4. Diogenes Laertius, in the Prologue to his *Lives and Opinions
of Eminent Philosophers*, points out similarly that a possible classification
of philosophers is that which divides them into dogmatists and sceptics.
Dogmatists are all those philosophers who make assertions about things
on the ground that they can be known. Sceptics are all those philosophers
who withhold assertions about things on the ground that they cannot be
known.

[3] Eduard Zeller, *Die Philosophie der Griechen in ihrer geschichtlichen
Entwicklung.* (Dritter Teil; erste Abteilung, 6, unveränderte Auflage.
Darmstadt: Wissenschaftliche Buchgesellschaft, 1963), pp. 507-508.

The Stoa, then, even if not drawn to a consideration of epistemology by any other motive or circumstance, would certainly have been compelled to attend to it by philosophers like Arcesilaus and Carneades, who maintained that the things the Stoa claimed to know are among those things which cannot be known at all. But, aside from these attacks by the Academy, it is hardly credible that the Stoa, even if disposed towards intellectual sloth, in the wake of Plato's and Aristotle's concern with epistemology and the doubts raised by Pyrrho about the possibility of knowledge, could have refrained from dealing with the problem of knowledge.[1] So much for the Stoa in general. What about Chrysippus?

Again there is evidence in Sextus Empiricus supplemented by that in Epictetus that Chrysippus reflected upon the problem of knowledge, and that, for him, this problem came within the purview of logic. Sextus gears his treatise, *Against the Logicians*, to "the investigation of the criterion", as he puts it,[2] and to the replies which different schools of philosophy have given to the question: Does a criterion of what is exist and, if so, what is its nature?[3] When the Stoic school comes up for consideration, Sextus introduces and discusses Chrysippus' view.[4] That the topic is embraced by logic is shown in an illuminating passage from Arrian's accounts of Epictetus' discourses.[5] There the point made is that the reason for which Chrysippus placed logic in the forefront is the same as that for which one examines the measure before he measures the grain. Just as the modius and balance are standards by which one measures other things, logic is that with which one distinguishes and examines things other than logic. Or rather, through studying logic, one comes to "understand" thoroughly the standard[6] of other

---

[1] Plato, *Theaetetus*. Aristotle, *Posterior Analytics* 99ᵇ15-100ᵇ16; *de anima* 425ᵇ23-430ᵇ7. For Pyrrho, see *D.L.* ix. 61-108; also V. Brochard, *Les Sceptiques Grecs*. Nouvelle édition conforme à la deuxième (Paris: Librairie Philosophique J. Vrin, 1959), pp. 51-76; and Mary Mills Patrick, *The Greek Sceptics* (New York: Columbia Univ. Press, 1929), pp. 31-56.

[2] *Against the Logicians* i. 27 (*adv. math.* vii. 27)—ἡ περὶ τοῦ κριτηρίου ζήτησις.

[3] *Ibid.*, i. 29, 46-48.

[4] *SVF* II 56. For a detailed discussion of this criterion, *infra*, pp. 52-56.

[5] *SVF* II 51 (typographical error in Arnim lists this as 54). Arnim extracted so little from the text here that the fragment as constituted by him is hardly intelligible.

[6] Epictetus uses the same term (κριτήριον) which Sextus (*supra*, note 2) was to use. Diocles Magnes (II 52) states clearly that and why the Stoa generally assigned to the doctrine of the criterion a place of priority: "The

things or the standard through which other things are apprehended (Epictetus i. 17, 8). Logic provides a standard by applying which one can decide whether or not a given body or object really exists. Chrysippus' theory of knowledge, then, is incorporated in his logic. Like dialectic and rhetoric, theory of knowledge is a division of logic.

This placement of theory of knowledge squarely within the confines of logic is noteworthy for two reasons. In the first place, it appears to denote a move by Chrysippus, and the early Stoa generally, towards a more rigorous systematization of philosophy. Aristotle had discussed the process whereby the mind attains knowledge in his logic (*Post. An.* 99^{b}20-100^{b}17), in his psychology (*de anima* 425^{b}11-432^{a}12), and in his metaphysics (*Meta.* 980^{b}25-981^{a}13); Plato had introduced the same subject into a number of dialogues. Secondly, the fact that theory of knowledge became a division of logic is a clue, in my opinion, as to the reason why logic itself came to occupy a position in philosophy coordinate with philosophy's other major divisions. Epistemology makes of the branch of philosophy to which it belongs something far more important than a mere preparatory study.

Having established something as to the relation of epistemology and logic for Chrysippus, let us now see what can be made of his theory of knowledge, itself, insofar as the fragments afford a glimpse of it. Let us be clear about the question, an answer to which I try to elicit from the Chrysippean fragments. What I here try to determine is whether or not there is for Chrysippus some standard by which one may judge that a thing or things really exist; and if there is, what its nature is. Chrysippus' answer to the first part of the question is, as suggested by the remarks made above, in the affirmative. To show further that this is so and to extract an answer to the second part of the question necessitates a brief glance at Chrysippus' doctrine of the soul.

One of the cardinal features of the soul in Chrysippus' view is its unity. He explicitly rejects the Platonic tripartite soul and substitutes a soul having functions and states or conditions. [1] The soul

---

Stoics prefer to give a position of priority to the doctrine of presentation and sense perception inasmuch as the *criterion* by which the truth of things is known is generically a presentation and inasmuch as the doctrine of assent, apprehension, and thought, while prior to other topics, is not acquired without presentation" (emphasis my own). My remarks in the text above show clearly that Diocles is here reporting the view of Chrysippus.

[1] These functions will be discussed shortly with reference to sense percep-

and body, both of which are corporeal, interpenetrate one another completely (II 471, 473, 634). The soul is said to have eight "parts", but it appears that seven of them, the five senses, the reproductive organs, and the voice, are functions of the eighth "part", the ruling element. The ruling element of the soul is situated in the heart (II 880, 885, 910). Reporting Chrysippus' view of the way in which the soul functions in knowledge getting, Chalcidius says in one of the richest fragments we possess (II 879):

> The whole soul extends its senses, which are functions of it, like branches, from that ruling part, as from a tree; and these senses are to be reporters of those things which they perceive, while the ruling part itself, like a king, passes judgment upon those things which the senses will have reported. Moreover these things which are sensed, namely, bodies, are composites, and thus each sense perceives some one ingredient in the composition; this one, color; another, sound; and while that one discerns the flavor of fluids, this one discerns the aromas of substances, and that one by touch distinguishes roughness and smoothness. And all this is concerned with what is present; however, no sense remembers what is past or apprehends what is future. Rather it is the peculiar function of inner deliberation and reflection to observe the affection of each sense and to infer what this object is from those data which the senses report, and to apprehend what is present, and moreover to remember what is no longer present, and to foresee what will happen.[1]

In this fragment we discover that the soul, in order to acquire knowledge of the external world, functions in a variety of ways: (i) each of the senses reports[2] some of the qualities of the object impinging upon it; (ii) from the data reported by the senses, the ruling function of the soul infers, after deliberation and reflection,

---

tion; the soul's condition, insofar as that topic relates to epistemology, will be discussed below in relation to Chrysippus' doctrines of presentation.

[1] Compare this with Heraclitus' soul/spider analogy (Diels, *Die Fragmente der Vorsokratiker*, 22B67ª. Chrysippus also (*SVF* II 879) uses the spider model. See also Solmsen's "Greek Philosophy and the Discovery of the Nerves", *Museum Helveticum* (Vol. 18, Fasc. 3, pp. 150-167), p. 157, note 46.

[2] In *SVF* II 867, where he talks about seeing, Chrysippus says that through the air extended outwards as through a stick the object seen is *reported* (or *announced*): τὸ βλεπόμενον ἀγγέλλεσθαι. Plato, too, had spoken of sensation as "reporting" (παραγγέλλειν) something to the soul (*Rep.* 524ª3).

what the object before it is; it apprehends objects which are present; (iii) this ruling function of the soul also remembers objects no longer present and concerning which, consequently, there are no longer reports from the senses; (iv) finally it is a function of the soul to foresee things which will happen. Using the evidence that other fragments provide, I shall consider each of these points in detail.

In what way do the senses, functions of the soul, constitute messengers from the external world?[1] What happens when one of the senses is affected by an external object? The object impinges upon the sense organs, either immediately or mediately,[2] and engenders movements in them which, Chrysippus maintains, are passed along to the ruling part of the soul.[3] From another fragment (II 866) we learn that, in Chrysippus' view, a pneumatic current (the substance of the soul is pneuma, a body composed of fire and air (II 841, 879)) extends from the ruling part of the soul to the pupil of the eye and on occasion out beyond the pupil into the surrounding air. Pneumatic currents, which function as extensions of the soul, go out to each of the sense organs (II 826), and presumably it is they which transmit the movements, engendered in the sense organs by external objects, to the ruling part of the soul.

---

[1] Pohlenz employs a bridge figure to express the phenomenon which Chrysippus describes by means of the king-messenger metaphor: "Für sie [die hellenistische Zeit] war es selbstverständlicher Erfahrungssatz, dass die Brücke zum Verständnis der Welt nur über die sinnliche Wahrnehmung führe und es keine von dieser unabhängige Erkenntnis geben könne. Dass aber die Sinne zuverlässige Zeugen sein müssten, war gedankliches Postulat, weil nur in diesem Falle die feste Grundlage für die praktische Lebensführung gewahrleistet war, die man unbedingt brauchte" (op. cit., Vol. I, p. 54). The senses were not regarded, as has been seen, by Chrysippus as being absolutely trustworthy. In terms of his king-messenger figure, the king does not trust the messenger implicitly, but examines carefully everything reported by him.

[2] In the case of vision the contact is usually mediated by the surrounding air (SVF II 867). Presumably Chrysippus gave a similar account of hearing.

[3] SVF II 882. Interestingly enough Chrysippus' doctrine of the manner in which objects set up motions in the sense organs and of the transmission of these motions to a central organ could have almost been a model for Hobbes, who about nineteen centuries later wrote, "The cause of Sense, is the External Body, or Object, which presseth the organ proper to each Sense, either immediately, as in the Taste and Touch; or mediately, as in Seeing, Hearing, and Smelling; which pressure by the mediation of Nerves, and other strings, and membranes of the body, continued inwards to the Brain, and Heart, causeth there...." Leviathan, Pt. I, Chap. 1. The point at which I terminate the Hobbes' passage is, of course, the point at which the accounts of Chrysippus and Hobbes begin to diverge radically.

This initial step in the apprehension of the external world can also be described in terms of Chrysippus' doctrine of presentations and such description will in addition make more evident than I have done so far how in Chrysippus' epistemology the soul functions as a single corporeal unit.

Zeno had defined a "presentation" as an impression on the soul.[1] He apparently did not state, however, what he meant by "impression", as is evidenced by the controversy which erupted between Cleanthes and Chrysippus about the meaning of that expression.[2] Cleanthes takes the view that an object impresses itself upon the soul just as a signet ring is impressed into wax [3]—a model reminiscent of the memory device discussed in the *Theaetetus*.[4] Chrysippus deemed this an absurd view, for if the soul, he argued (II 56), is like a piece of wax with one surface exposed (and apparently this is the model Cleanthes had in mind), it could receive only one impression at a time and even that one would be obliterated by the next impression; but, in fact, the soul, according to Chrysippus,

---

[1] *SVF* I 58. *Cf.* Max Pohlenz, "Zenon und Chrysipp", (*Nachrichten aus der Altertumswissenschaft*, Philologisch-Historische Klasse, Neue Folge, Fachgruppe 1, 1936-38. Göttingen: Vandenhoeck & Ruprecht, 1938; pp. 173-210), p. 175. For an excellent discussion of ways in which Plato and Aristotle employed the term, φαντασία, here translated "presentation", see Donald Dudley, *A History of Cynicism* (London: Methuem & Co., 1937), Appendix II, pp. 216-220.

[2] A. C. Pearson, *The Fragments of Zeno and Cleanthes* (London: C. J. Clay and Sons, 1891), p. 61.

[3] *SVF* II 56. Descartes, for purposes of imagining how the faculties function in their apprehension of the truth, thinks the ring/wax—object/perception analogy too *weak* an expression of what happens when the senses are affected by an external object: "...all our external senses, insofar as they are part of the body, and despite the fact that we direct them towards objects, so manifesting activity, *viz.*, a movement in space, nevertheless properly speaking perceive in virtue of passivity alone, just in the way that wax receives an impression from a seal. And it should not be thought that all we mean to assert is an analogy between the two. We ought to believe that the sentient body is really modified by the object, as that in which the shape of the surface of the wax is altered by the seal." From Rule XII of *Rules for The Direction of the Mind*. Hume, in his well-known note," ...By the term of impression I would not be understood to express the manner, in which our lively perceptions are produced in the soul, but merely the perceptions themselves...." forestalled any discussions of *how* impressions occur in the soul.

[4] 191c8-e1. Plato, like Spinoza after him (*Ethica* II, Prop. XXV), held that an object which affects the body in some way engenders thereby an image which is *not* like the external object. Therefore, for both of them, sensation as a basis of knowledge was either rejected outright (Plato) or rated as the lowest form of knowledge (Spinoza).

receives many impressions simultaneously and, in fact, it retains impressions received while taking on still others. An impression, then, is not a scooping out and elevation of a portion of the soul's "surface." Rather an impression is a modification or alteration (ἑτεροίωσις) of the soul.[1]

Instead of the wax tablet model, Chrysippus used the air, which, he maintains (II 56), undergoes a great many alterations simultaneously when the persons in a room are all speaking at one time. The soul is like air in that it, too, may be altered in many ways. Indeed, the soul is a kind of air, for, as we have seen, it, in Chrysippus' view, is pneuma.[2] And herein lies the point of Chrysippus' interpretation of Zeno's "impression." It is misleading to suppose that this is Chrysippus' way of attenuating Cleanthes' excessive materialism.[3] The pneuma is as bodily as would be the hypothetical wax tablet. Chrysippus' substitution of the air model for the wax tablet model is a brilliant endeavor to make Stoic epistemology more tenable without abandoning its materialistic premises. And who can deny that Chrysippus has chosen an extremely happy model, for certainly the alterations the air undergoes in a conversation-filled room form a model more analogous to the changes a soul undergoes (if the soul be conceived as a body) in its relation to external objects than does that of the wax-signet ring. Chrysippus improves and makes palatable the Stoa's psychological materialism; but he does not thin it out or weaken it. He wishes to give a plausible account of the retention of presentations—as has been noted one function of the soul is to remember what is no longer present—and, in view of the obvious weakness of the wax tablet model, he substitutes another which, in his view, is devoid of those weaknesses and which, in addition, is consonant with his view of the soul as a

---

[1] *SVF* II 56. It seems that Cleanthes is a more faithful expounder of Zeno on this point than is Chrysippus; see Pearson, *op. cit.*, p. 61. *Cf.* Pohlenz, "Zenon und Chrysipp", p. 176.

[2] The doctrine of the *tabula rasa*, made famous for modern readers by Locke, perhaps, as Festa suggests, has more affinities with Cleanthes' model of the wax tablet than with Chrysippus' model of the air (*I Frammenti degli Stoici Antichi*. 2 vols. (Bari: Gius. Laterza & Figli, 1935), Vol. II, p. 99, note b). For an ascription of the *tabula rasa* doctrine to "the Stoics", see *SVF* II 83: "Whenever a man is born, he has the ruling part of his soul well-formed like papyrus for being written upon."

[3] A supposition made by Festa,"...Crisippo...all 'eccessivo materialismo di Cleante reagi' con la sua dottrina della fantasia come 'alterazione dell' intelletto.' " *Op. cit.*, Vol. II, p. 100.

unified substance. When the soul is affected by an external object, it suffers a modification; it becomes something else; it changes its condition or state.[1]

If a presentation is defined by Zeno in terms of an impression, and an impression, in Chrysippus' view, is a modification of the soul, then he must have regarded a presentation as a modification of the soul. And, in fact, one fragment (II 54) which preserves Chrysippus' definition of "presentation" contains the phrase, "modification coming about in the soul." "A presentation is a modification coming about in the soul and revealing in itself also that which has caused it." It is the phrase, "revealing in itself also that which has caused it", which is of special significance, because it leads to a further clarification of Chrysippus' epistemological stand.

The soul, now functioning as a messenger (to use Chrysippus' graphic figure), relays movements (pneumatic currents) engendered in the sense organs by an impinging object [2] to the soul, now functioning as ruler, and there (the locus of the ruling aspect of the soul, it will be remembered, is the heart) deposits its reports as presentations or modifications of that ruling principle.[3] Chrysippus, himself, gives an illuminating illustration of this process as it occurs with respect to one of the senses, or as he might say, one of the soul's messengers: "For example, when through the power of sight we see white, that which comes about in the soul through the act of seeing is a modification. And on the basis of this modification we are able to say that the white which is affecting us exists" (II 54). "Presentation" (φαντασία), Chrysippus maintains, is from the term "light" (φῶς) because the presentation reveals both itself and that which caused it (II 54). In fact, the terminology Chrysippus uses in this fragment is an extension of that used specifically for seeing. There he goes on to speak of a "real object"; the term which I so

---

[1] *SVF* III 471a where Chrysippus speaks of the soul being in this or that condition.

[2] "And this Zeno and Chrysippus together with all their adherents believe, namely, that the movement occurring in a part of the body from an object which has impinged upon it from outside is carried into the ruling part of the soul so that perception comes about in the living being" (*SVF* II 882).

[3] "...For just as the air, when many people are talking at the same time, receiving in one moment an untold number and great variety of impacts, forthwith undergoes many alterations, so also the ruling part of the soul, when subject to a variety of presentations, will be affected in a way similar to this" (*SVF* II 56).

translate is φανταστόν and is literally "that which is capable of being seen." But for Chrysippus φανταστόν is anything which is capable of affecting the soul and thereby producing a φαντασία in it—for example, something white, something cold, or something perfumed.[1] Recall the Chalcidius passage quoted above: "It is the peculiar function of inner deliberation and reflection to observe the *affection of each sense.* ..."

So far Chrysippus' account of the presentation has been clear and self-consistent, but it also raises some difficulties and it is no good pretending that they do not exist.

In the particularly rich fragment (II 54), to which I have already made allusion, Chrysippus distinguishes a presentation from an illusory affection. One of the hallmarks of the illusory affection is that no real object "lies under it" (ὑπόκειται).[2] It is a "vacuous attraction" and occurs, for example, in the minds of mad people, like Orestes, who see things which are not there. This fragment, taken by itself, might lead to the belief that a presentation is by definition produced in the soul by a real object, so that a person, aware of the presentation in himself, is by that fact itself entitled to infer that there is an object existing outside himself. However, in addition to the illusory affections discussed here, Chrysippus elsewhere (II 994; III 177) talks about *false* presentations.[3] This species of presentation is mentioned in connection with the topic of assent and the two can profitably be discussed together. Such a discussion will, in addition, lead naturally to a consideration of the second function of the soul in knowing, described in the Chalcidius fragment above, the deliberative and reflective side of the soul's activity, and, specifically, that mode of its activity which infers from the data reported to what the object present is.

The reports which come to the soul from the external world,

---

[1] *SVF* II 54. The last example is, however, from *SVF* II 879.

[2] Chrysippus is induced, I believe, by the correlative distinction, presentation-real object, to make a corresponding correlation between the illusory affection and the illusory object. Since there is no real object underlying the illusory affection, there is no object at all underlying it; if anything, Chrysippus means by "an illusory object" the content of the illusory affection, for example, "the blood-stained and dragon-like maidens" Orestes thinks he sees.

[3] We also possess a vexingly brief report (*SVF* II 927) in which Fulgentius tells us *en passant* that Chrysippus says in his *On Fate* that error arises among human sensations when "impulses are turned about by uncertain and fleeting compulsations."

brought by the senses acting as messengers, are not accepted by the ruling element of the soul uncritically. And, in the light of what Chrysippus tells us about illusory affections, it is permissible to infer that when the ruling part of the soul makes a judgment on sensory reports received, its aim is to distinguish presentations from illusory affections. But there are also false presentations. Wise men (and God) can produce or inculcate false presentations in others. Now I assume that what Chrysippus calls "illusory affections" in one context he calls "false presentations" in another.[1] Consequently the cognitive function of the dominant element in the soul could equally well be described as that of distinguishing false presentations from genuine or true presentations. And the *terminus technicus* for designating the fact that the soul has decided, rightly or wrongly, that a given image is a true presentation is *assent*.

The power of assent, Chrysippus says in one text (II 991), is one of the powers which has been given by fate to the living being. A presentation is a necessary though not a sufficient condition of assent.[2] To underscore this fact Chrysippus introduces his striking figure of the cylinder (II 974, 1000). A cylinder requires an external thrust to initiate its movement (he is obviously thinking of a cylinder at rest on a slightly inclined ground), but once it begins to roll it does so on its own power. In the same way "a presentation, when it has impinged, will certainly impress itself and, as it were, trace its appearance upon the mind; however, our assent will be in our power, and as has been said in the case of the cylinder, though pushed from without—what has to be considered in addition—it will move by its own force and nature" (II 974). Chrysippus insists that the mere presence of a presentation is not sufficient to cause assent, and in his argument against those who take the contrary position, a feature in his doctrine of assent comes to the fore which will be helpful when we consider the obvious problem which arose for him, namely, how one determines to which (or from which)

---

[1] In *SVF* II 54 the writer is reporting from a context in which the exclusive purpose of Chrysippus' discussion is to distinguish certain kinds of mental phenomena, or more specifically, to differentiate veridical and non-veridical images. In *SVF* II 994 and III 177 such precise differentiation is not to the point; Chrysippus there calls *false presentations* the mental phenomenon he had in the first context described as an illusory affection.

[2] *SVF* II 974. Chrysippus says a presentation is an "auxiliary and proximate" cause, not a "perfect and original" cause. It becomes clear from the fragment cited that these expressions mark the distinction between a necessary and a sufficient condition.

presentations one ought to give (or withhold) assent, or, in terms of the Chalcidius report, how the ruling function of the soul apprehends if there is an object present and, if so, what it is.

It is apparent (III 177) that the Academics had charged the Stoics with having made of man's actions consequences determined exclusively by presentations. Chrysippus denies this flatly, says the Academics are fighting a straw man, and presents his view, already discussed, that assenting (or refraining to assent) to his presentations is in man's power (III 177). In a passage (III 177), which troubles me as much as it did Plutarch, Chrysippus says that God and wise men produce false presentations in men, not requiring that they assent to them, but that they act with reference to that which appears (τὸ φαινόμενον).[1] Plutarch's objection is that this makes God or the wise man a voluntary cause of sinful action in the case of those men who assent to presentations which do not convey a direct apprehension of the object. But leaving aside the roles of God and the wise man here, this passage yields a term which will contribute to the formulation of the next step in my enquiry, for it appears that the distinction between presentations which do and presentations which do not convey a direct apprehension of the object is exactly that between "true" presentations and "false" presentations or between "presentation" and "illusory affections."[2] I shall henceforth call a presentation which conveys a direct apprehension of the object a CDA presentation.

---

[1] A conjecture: God produced the images of the "blood-stained and dragon-like maidens" in the mind of Orestes not with the requirement that Orestes assent to the proposition that those maidens were there about to attack him, but with the intention that he flee. The difficulty, of course, is that one hardly understands how the second could take place without the first. Dream imagery would be a cardinal example of presentations which do not require assent, but which are placed in the mind for a very definite purpose—a purpose which can be unfolded by an interpreter of dreams. Cf. SVF II 1202 and 1205.

[2] "The earlier Stoics say that the καταληπτική presentation is the criterion of the truth." Sextus Empiricus, adv. math. vii. 253. See Pearson (op. cit., pp. 62, 63) for a review of the views of Stein, Zeller, Hirzel on the meaning of this term. Pearson thinks it was Zeno's invention. I do not choose to enter the controversy. In the Chrysippean fragments there is no conclusive evidence that the presentation conveying a direct apprehension of an object was Chrysippus' criterion of the truth, that is, his invention. In view of the language used in the Plutarch fragment, discussed in the text above, I believe that the discussion can be conducted in terms of those presentations which reflect the existing object, thereby permitting apprehensions of it, and those which do not so permit.

The problem Chrysippus had to resolve, especially in answer to the attacks of the Academy, was: How does one distinguish between a CDA presentation and a non-CDA presentation. The basis of such a distinction would, of course, also be the basis on which one would give or withhold assent to a given presentation. The evidence on which I try to reconstruct Chrysippus' resolution of this problem, though extremely scanty, is highly suggestive, but it requires that I make a brief *excursus* into his metaphysics.

Chrysippus is a thoroughgoing monist. Everything that exists is material or corporeal (II 469). But the corporeal has two sides, an active and a passive (II 300). The manifold variety in the world is explained by reference to these two features of the corporeal. The active principle is the pneuma (reason or god); the passive principle is unqualified substance. Individual things having qualities arise from the penetration of unqualified substance by the pneuma; this pneuma constantly molds and forms that substance *from within* (II 413, 449). The point pertinent for our present discussion is that, in Chrysippus' view, this process gives rise to the existence of individuals only. Every existing thing has qualities and relations which distinguish it from every other existing thing (II 473, 397). The peculiar combination of qualities that an individual thing manifests are the *effects* of pneuma active in a particular region of unqualified substance. Consequently, the way to define a thing is to give an account of that peculiar blend of qualities and relations which it manifests.

It will be recalled that, according to the Chalcidius fragment (II 879), each of the senses reports some quality ingredient in the composite object impinging upon them. The ruling part of the soul, in determining what that object is, sums up these qualities and concludes that the object is something which possesses *just that* blend of qualities. But it must also be noted that the soul remembers things that are no longer present. Now it is plain that if no presently existing object is exactly like another presently existing object, then no memory of a presently existing object is exactly like the memory of another presently existing object. This does not exclude, however, the existence of similarities among objects (and among the memories of them). And it is my view that Chrysippus, when he ascribed the power of memory to the soul, must have assumed the memory to function somewhat as follows: it collects together in groups or families those presentations or impressions of existing

objects which are similar to one another. Each of these families of remembered presentations is what he meant by a *common notion*. It is on this basis that one can account for the manner in which the ruling part of the soul distinguishes CDA from non-CDA presentations.

Chrysippus nowhere in the extant material defines experience (ἐμπειρία), but he employs the term once where he admonishes students to withhold judgment about matters which require *experience* and investigation (II 763). He defines art as "an aggregate of apprehensions" (II 56). In another passage (II 81) still Chrysippus is reported to have held that sweetness is generically an object of thought (νοητόν); in its specific character and as immediately impinging on the sense organ sweetness is an object of sense (αἰσθητόν). In one passage, to which I shall recur shortly, Alexander, speaking of Chrysippus, says that he tries to persuade men by means of "common notions" (II 473). There are no fragments in which there appears a full-blown discussion of these terms. I nevertheless hazard the conjecture that Chrysippus adhered to a view about the development of art (or science) from sensory experience similar in some respects to that of Aristotle described in the *Posterior Analytics* (ii. 19) and the *Metaphysics* (A. 1.). The Stagirite put the matter in this way: "Memory comes from sensation, and from memory of the same thing occurring many times comes experience. Many memories of the same thing constitute one experience. From experience or from every universal fixed in the soul, the one over against the many, which is one and the same for all of them, arises art ..." (*Post. An.* 100^{a}3-9). If "presentation" be substituted for "sensation" and "common notion", for "universal"; and "ruling part of the soul", for "soul", we should almost have, it is my conjecture, an expression of Chrysippus' view concerning the relation of presentations, memory, experience, common notions, and art. The crucial difference would be that, for Chrysippus, the common notion would *not* be "one over against the many"; rather it would be the "many" themselves collected together in virtue of their similarity. In short Chrysippus is a nominalist. Nothing in the extant material is contrary to such a reconstruction, and, as has been seen, the evidence preserved coheres with it.

One passage already alluded to (II 473) is particularly significant for an interpretation of the relation between common notions and presentations. Chrysippus is trying to prove that there exist several kinds of mixture. Alexander of Aphrodisias reports in this passage as follows:

> That these distinguishing characteristics belong to mixtures, he [Chrysippus] tries to prove by means of the common notions and he says that we receive these as the chief criteria of truth from nature. At least we have one presentation of bodies being compounded by junction and preserving their individuality, another of bodies being confused together and mutually destroyed, and another of bodies being blended together in a complete interpenetration in such way that each of them preserves its own nature. And we would not have this difference of presentations if all bodies, when compounded in some way, should lay adjacent by junction, that is, if there were only one kind of mixture.

Now it seems odd that Chrysippus should say in one place that a presentation [1] is the criterion of truth and in another that the common notions are "the chief criteria of truth"; but Alexander, in the passage quoted, relieves our perplexity somewhat when he, as an example of Chrysippus' proof by common notions, forthwith introduces the use of presentations. For if one proves something by means of a common notion he does not prove it by means of a presentation unless there is a very intimate relation between the two; and I suggest that, in Chrysippus' mind, there was such a relation. To be more specific, a presentation is a member of some family of similar presentations which constitute a common notion; it constitutes the material by which the common notion is, through memory and experience, engendered. And, once implanted in the mind, the common notion becomes the criterion by reference to which one determines whether or not a given presentation is conveying a direct apprehension.[2] Since the common notion is generated by the experience of several like presentations, one can say either that CDA presentations are the criteria of the truth or that common notions are the criteria of the truth, though Chrysippus' view is, I should hold, most accurately formulated in the passage where he is reported to have maintained that the common notions are the "chief criteria of the truth." For example, consider Orestes, who,

---

[1] We now know that he means a CDA presentation.

[2] And this is why one report (*SVF* II 105) has it that the criterion of the truth for Chrysippus is the CDA presentation.

in Chrysippus' view (II 54), when he saw the dragon-like maidens' was the victim of a vacuous attraction; the maidens were illusory objects or false presentations. And a man in his right mind would have adjudged them false. Why? Because they were not sufficiently like the family of presentations of young girls which he has stored away in his memory. No one of *them* has dragon-like features. It is this family of presentations or this common notion which exercises the decisive control, and this, I believe, is the reason why Chrysippus calls common notions the *chief criteria* of truth.

It is clear then that, for Chrysippus, a man has the power to assent or to refrain from assenting to presentations and that, in his doctrine, the man's assent ought to be given, though frequently it is not,[1] to those presentations alone which can be referred to some common notion.[2] The generation of such notions comes about when the soul, functioning deliberatively, remembers (and classifies) the things that are not present. These common notions, regarded as controls upon the presentations experienced at a given moment, explain, I believe, a fragment in which we are told that Chrysippus proposed another criterion of the truth.

Diogenes Laertius, in one passage (II 105), reports that Chrysippus contradicts himself; for, while stating in one place that the CDA presentation is the standard of truth, he says in another that those standards are sensation and "anticipation" (πρόληψις). Sensation offers no difficulty because, as has been seen, it is an element in the CDA presentation, but the term "anticipation" is not so readily explained.[3] It is likely that Chrysippus meant nothing more by anticipation than the common notions or, as I should say, general

---

[1] Interestingly enough Chrysippus holds that we assent to false presentations because we are bad and it is "by reason of our weakness that we assent to presentations of this kind" (*SVF* III 77).

[2] I agree, then, almost completely with Pohlenz when he says,"...die Phantasia sei die im Bewusstsein aufgenommene Aisthesis und werde kataleptische, wenn sie zu den vorher in uns gebildeten Allgemeinvorstellungen stimme." (*Op. cit.*, I, 62) My agreement is a qualified one, because Pohlenz implies that *every* presentation is a sensation; but the false presentations which wise men produce in others are not sensations. Presentations constitute a more extensive class of mental phenomena of which sensations are a sub-class.

[3] For a discussion of the meaning of this term in Epicurus, the inventor of the term according to Cicero, see Cyril Bailey, *The Greek Atomists and Epicurus* (Oxford: The Clarendon Press, 1928) pp. 245-248 and Appendix II; and H. M. Currie, "Epicurean Prolepsis", *Phronesis*, VI (1961), p. 82.

ideas (in the Berkeleyian sense).[1] But why then does he call them "anticipations"? He does so, I conjecture, to call attention to a special function which the common notions have. Considered as stored experience, as the collections of remembered similar presentations, these general concepts are called "common notions." Looked at from the point of view of their function, that of "anticipating what will happen" by providing criteria to which new presentations can be referred for assessment, these common notions are called "anticipations".

Now this conjecture is one which can, to a degree, be tested, for there exist four Chrysippean fragments in which "anticipations" are mentioned. The first is the fragment (II 105) alluded to above, Laertius' report that Chrysippus makes of the anticipation a criterion of truth. The common notions, as we now know, are for Chrysippus the chief criteria of truth; and if "anticipation" is the name given to a common notion when regarded from a certain point of view, there is no reason why one should not say that *it* is the criterion of truth.

The second of the four fragments in which anticipations are mentioned is one (II 33) in which Chrysippus is said to have resolved the difficulty concerning anticipations and notions (ἔννοιαι), to have set right each of them, and to have put each in its proper place. Chrysippus nowhere says explicitly what he means by the term ἔννοια which I render with "notion". I hold that if a common notion (κοινὴ ἔννοια) is a collection of remembered similar presentations, then a mere notion is a member of the collection; that is, a notion is any remembered presentation. The assessment of Chrysippus' contribution preserved in the fragment mentioned comes to this: Chrysippus resolved the difficulty concerning anticipations (προλήψεις) and notions (ἔννοιαι) by defining each clearly; and if "anticipation" is another name for a common notion, as I believe, then one can understand the significance of this commentary upon Chrysippus' work.

The third fragment (II 841) in which the term "anticipation" occurs is like the second in that here, too, anticipations and notions

---

[1] "Now if we will annex a meaning to our words, and speak only of what we can conceive, I believe we shall acknowledge, that an idea, which considered in itself is particular, becomes general, by being made to represent or stand for all other particular ideas of the *same sort.*" George Berkeley, *A Treatise Concerning the Principles of Human Knowledge*, Introduction, Section XII.

are mentioned together. Galen, in this fragment reports that, for Chrysippus, reason or the soul [1] is "a collection of anticipations and notions." In the same fragment Chrysippus is said to have held that anticipations and notions are functions or activities of the soul (ἐνέργειαι τῆς ψυχῆς). Now if a notion is a remembered presentation and an anticipation is a family of remembered and similar presentations with which new presentations are compared, it is readily apparent why one might describe the soul as a collection of notions and anticipations. And, since memory is involved in both anticipations and notions, it is not nonsensical to call these latter "functions" or "activities" of the soul.

A fourth fragment (III 69) tells us that Chrysippus maintained that his doctrine of good things and bad things is especially connected with the implanted (or engendered) anticipations (αἱ ἔμφυτοι προλήψεις). Even without an *excursus* into Chrysippus' moral philosophy it is clear that the common notions with which on my interpretation the anticipations are identical can accurately be described as having been "engendered" or "implanted" in the soul as a result of sensations, memory, and experience. The phrase does not necessarily connote innateness, and little in Chrysippus' philosophy would lend support to a theory of innate ideas.[2]

The four fragments, then, in which the term "anticipation" occurs tend either to confirm or not to refute our interpretation of that term, an interpretation which coheres with the epistemological fragments already discussed.[3]

---

[1] *SVF* II, p. 228, line 23; Galen is here taking Chrysippus to task for not saying that these are parts of reason rather than of soul, especially in view of the fact that Chrysippus had said the former in another book.

[2] Arnim, too, denies that there is a doctrine of innate ideas in Chrysippus' philosophy: "Denn wenn unsere Auffassung der πρόληψις richtig ist, so kann sie nicht als eine von der sinnlichen Erfahrung unabhängige und ihr gleichberechtigte Erkenntnisquelle gelten." "Chrysippos", *Realencyclopädie*, col. 2508. *SVF* II 83 would rule out innate ideas altogether for the Stoics generally.

[3] Bréhier's explanation of anticipation is a very general statement and is true as far as it goes ("la sensation et la prénotion [Bréhier's translation of πρόληψις] de Chrysippe ne sont d'autre part que deux espèces de compréhensions." *Chrysippe*, p. 102), but he cites as evidence a passage in Arnim (*SVF* II, p. 27, line 10) in which Chrysippus' name does not appear at all, and he says nothing of the other three Chrysippean fragments in which the term "anticipation" appears. Pohlenz' interpretation is puzzling; he sets out as if to explain Laertius' report, but then does not tell us in what way the distinction he introduces explains "anticipation", though we are inclined

To summarize, Chrysippus endeavored to answer in the following way the question, "What is the standard by which one may know that a thing or things exist?" An existing object signals its existence and character by affecting the sense organs; pneumatic currents transmit the movements in the sense organs to the ruling part of the soul, situated in the heart, and there they change into images of the external objects, or to use the Chrysippean language, pneumatic currents cause a modification in the ruling part of the soul such that its state or condition is changed; it becomes in some way like the object which engendered those pneumatic movements. But images which do *not* derive from existing objects—dream imagery, illusory affections, false presentations—appear there also. Therefore the regent part of the soul, functioning deliberatively, has to distinguish between presentations which do and those which do not convey a direct apprehension of the objects. Such deliberation ought to precede, but frequently does not, assent to a given presentation or action upon a given presentation as if it were veridical. Chrysippus means by this deliberative process a comparing of a given presentation with some common notion, a product of memory and experience in the Aristotelian sense, in such way that a high degree of similarity of the two issues is an assent to the veridical character of the presentation. The anticipations are not innate ideas but rather are just the common notions themselves when viewed in their function as controls on new presentations.

I have not yet discussed what, according to the Chalcidius report, is, from Chrysippus' point of view, a fourth function of the soul in cognition, namely, that of foreseeing things which will happen. What Chrysippus means is that, on the basis of what one learns (and remembers) concerning the properties of existing objects, one is able, when one has CDA presentations of some of those qualities, to predict that other properties are present, too, in spite of the fact that one may not be in a position to have CDA presentations of them. For example,[1] suppose that a physician notes that Philo has a viscid bronchial discharge and then discovers that he has a wound in his lungs; he notes (and remembers) the same two phenomena in

---

to agree with his conclusion, "Für sich genommen konnte die Prolepsis in seinen Augen sowenig selbständiges Kriterium sein wie die Aisthesis." *Op. cit.*, I, 62.

[1] Examples similar to these appear in Sextus Empiricus, *adv. math.*, viii. 254, though he is not illustrating the phenomenon which I try to illustrate with them.

Diogenes, Aristippus, and Bachylides. Memory and experience induce him to conclude that these two properties are usually found together. And, if upon visiting Cleanthes, he notes a viscid bronchial discharge, he can predict that if he opens up Cleanthes' chest, he will find a wound in his lungs. The importance of this cognitive function of the soul is reflected in Chrysippus' concern with and interpretation of the truth standards of the conditional proposition.[1]

2. DIALECTIC

It is evident that, in Chrysippus' eyes, dialectic is a significant part of logic; and, if one considers the matter historically, it is somewhat surprising that Chrysippus attaches such importance to this branch of logic. To be sure, Plato had made much of dialectic; while his thinking about the kind of activity denoted by "dialectic" underwent considerable change and development,[2] he always believed that the dialectician was the philosopher and that philosophical activity was dialectic. In Aristotle's system, however, dialectic as a philosophical procedure undergoes a radical diminution in value. This depreciation of dialectic accompanies a changed concept of its nature. While for Plato "dialectic", whatever specific procedure it denotes in this or that dialogue, always names a truth-seeking process, for Aristotle it denotes a kind of reasoning from opinions generally accepted (*Topica* 100ᵃ30) and has its primary use in debating matches, equipping its practitioners to attack and to defend both sides of any question proposed.[3] For the Stoa,

---

[1] *Infra* pp. 72-82.

[2] Julius Stenzel, *Studien zur Entwicklung der Platonischen Dialektik von Sokrates zu Aristoteles* (dritte Auflage, unveränderter Nachdruck der zweiten, erweiterten Auflage von 1931; Stuttgart: B. J. Teubner, 1961), pp. 1-122. Richard Robinson, *Plato's Earlier Dialectic* (2nd edit. Oxford: The Clarendon Press, 1953), pp. 61-280.

[3] *Topica* i. 2. It is true that in this chapter Aristotle also cites two further uses of dialectic. One of them, which derives from the accomplished dialectician's ability to raise searching difficulties on each side of a question, is that of helping to decide what is true in particular problems which arise in the philosophical sciences (αἱ κατὰ φιλοσοφίαν ἐπιστῆμαι); the second of them, deriving from the dialectician's ability to argue from opinions generally accepted, is that of providing a basis for critical thinking about the first principles of each of the sciences, since that thinking cannot begin from those principles themselves. Nevertheless these two ends when attained are clearly only fringe benefits of dialectic and are parasitic upon the existence of special sciences which employ not dialectical reasoning, but demonstrative reasoning in their search for the truth. The whole of the *Topics* is,

dialectic, which Aristotle had devalued in the interests of demonstrative or scientific knowledge, regains its status as a science.[1] Chrysippus wrote a number of books dealing with dialectic (II 13), and, in one of them, *On Dialectic*, as if justifying the attention which he himself was paying to the subject, he cites (II 126) Socrates, Plato, and Aristotle, as having treated dialectic seriously and as having esteemed dialectic as one of the most highly requisite capacities in philosophy. What kind of activity has Chrysippus in mind when he uses the expression "dialectic", and why does he prize that activity so highly?

Bréhier maintained that the Stoics "seek to make a proof less in order to establish the validity of the thesis than to lead to a conviction which resists every opposed argument" and that for the Stoics "the aim of the dialectician is not really the invention, the discovery of new theses; all his efforts bear upon the discussion of theses which present themselves naturally to the human mind." [2] These assertions, no matter how much they may apply to some of the Stoics, most emphatically are not true of Chrysippus. Chrysippus says flatly—and this is a quotation from his book, *On the Use of Reason*— "It [the faculty of reason] must be used for the discovery of truths and for their organization, and not for the opposite ends, though this is what many people do" (II 129).[3] Admittedly, unless one can connect Chrysippus' view on the use of reason with his conception of dialectic, this passage does not take one very far, but, as will be seen shortly from Chrysippus' account of argument, which is one of the major products of reason and a principal ingredient in the subject matter of dialectic, the passage just quoted about "the faculty of reason" could apply equally well to dialectic. The passage ought to be read together with another Chrysippean quotation preserved by Plutarch: the practice of arguing on opposing sides of a question "is appropriate for men who advocate suspense of judgment with respect to all subjects ... but for the men who wish to produce knowledge in us, in accordance with which we shall live consistently, the contrary is appropriate, namely, to teach fundamental principles and to instruct the

---

in fact, a handbook—albeit an incredibly rich manual filled with many subtle observations on the uses of language—on how to become a successful debater.

[1] "Mais le trait propre de la logique stoïcienne est d'avoir fait de la dialectique une science." Émile Bréhier, *Chrysippe...*, p. 62.

[2] Émile Bréhier, *op. cit.*, pp. 63, 64.

[3] I am indebted to Dr. Harold Cherniss for this rendering of the passage.

beginners in the rudiments from start to finish. And in those cases
in which it is opportune to mention the opposing arguments as
well, it is fitting that they as in courts of justice destroy their
plausibility" (II 127). Here we see how far the Chrysippean conception of dialectic is from that of Aristotle; dialectic in the
Aristotelian vein, conceived, that is, as the art of arguing well on
opposite sides of the same question, is appropriate for sceptics, not
for those who aim to discover the truth. Dialectic was for Chrysippus
what demonstrative reasoning was for Aristotle inasmuch as
dialectical arguments could be used to demonstrate the connections
of things in nature.

According to Chrysippus, dialectic deals with things which
signify (σημαίνοντα) and things which are signified (σημαινόμενα)
(II 122). It was a Stoic doctrine that

> three things are linked together, that which is signified, that
> which signifies, and the external reality; of these the articulate
> sound, for example, "Dion", is that which signifies; the entity
> itself, which is disclosed by this [the articulate sound] and
> which we grasp as standing in close conjunction with our
> thought, is that which is signified; and strangers do not under-
> stand [that which is signified], although they hear the articulate
> sound; the externally subsisting object, e.g., Dion himself, is
> the external reality (II 166).

I conjecture that this was Chrysippus' view,[1] and that we may
therefore conclude that for him dialectic is concerned with articulate
sounds and the things signified by articulate sounds; and the latter
are not to be confused with externally existing objects.[2]

There is ample evidence that Chrysippus was deeply interested
in articulate sounds and in the structure and function of language
generally. This interest surfaces in such reports as that by Varro
(II 143), according to which Chrysippus denied that a person who
merely utters words is speaking; unless he puts each word in its
place, he, when he utters words, is doing something like speaking,

---

[1] Notice that to base this conjecture on II 166, a fragment which does
not contain Chrysippus' name, is not to contravene the methodological
principle stated on p. 1.

[2] For an excellent discussion of the distinctions drawn here, see Mates,
op. cit., pp. 11-19.

but he is not speaking.[1] Opposing Diodorus Cronus' view, Chrysippus held that every word is naturally ambiguous on the ground that the same person may understand a word spoken to him in two or more ways (II 152). Chrysippus' interest in language is further evidenced by the report that he recognized five parts of discourse; the two lists of them which have reached us, however, are not in complete agreement (II 147, II 148). One contains the proper noun, the common noun, the verb, the conjunction, and the article; in the other there appear the proper noun, the preposition, the verb, the conjunction, and the article. We may give more credence to the list preserved in Diocles Magnes' account (II 147) of Stoic logic, the list which contains the common noun, not only because to give an account of the parts of discourse is Diocles' main task in that passage,[2] but also because Chrysippus wrote a book about common nouns,[3] and because there exists another fragment (II 174) reporting Chrysippus' opinion that common nouns have contraries while definitions do not.

If we were able to reconstruct completely Chrysippus' view of the nature and the extent of the things signified by articulate sounds, we should be well on our way towards an insight into his semantics for ordinary language. It is regrettable that the material for such a reconstruction is so sparse. We do, however, have several rich fragments reporting the views of Chrysippus on propositions and arguments. And we know that for "the Stoa" the proposition is an example of the thing signified (II 166). I shall then first describe Chrysippus' positions on the proposition and the argument. Once his thinking on these subjects has been brought into full view, a picture of his semantics will begin to emerge.

2a. Propositions

Chrysippus says in his Dialectical Definitions (II 193) that a proposition is "that which is capable of being denied or affirmed

---

[1] Chrysippus apparently expressed this succinctly at some point, saying that the bust of a man is not the man (II 143).

[2] Galen, on the other hand, gives the list merely to illustrate a point in Plato's physics (II 148).

[3] II 13 (Diogenes Laertius vii. 192). The fact that "proper nouns" are distinguished from "common nouns" in Diocles' report would suggest that Hicks' translation of Περὶ τῶν προσηγορικῶν ("On Proper Nouns") is mistaken; Hicks himself translates Diocles' προσηγορία with "common noun." Cf. Liddell and Scott, s.v.

as it is in itself." And, as examples of propositions, he gives "it is day" and "Dion is walking.' 'The remainder of the fragment in which this description of a proposition appears contains two further points about Chrysippus' conception of a proposition.

The first is that the proposition is identical neither with the words which express it nor with the fact which it expresses. This feature of the proposition is made clear in Chrysippus' attempt to explain the derivation of the term "proposition" (ἀξίωμα); it is, he says, derived from the verb ἀξιοῦν which means "to think fit" and, in this case, to think fit "to accept" or "to reject." For he who says "it is day" seems to judge that the thought (idea, notion) [1] that it is day is fit to accept. His saying it is not the same thing as his acceptance (or rejection) of the thought; so the words are not identical with that thought but an expression of it. Nor is the thought that it is day identical with its being day. If the thought that it is day and its being day were the same, then one could never think it is day when, in fact, it is night; or, to generalize, there could be no such thing as a false proposition. The second feature about propositions which this fragment reveals is that, in Chrysippus' view, a proposition is true when the corresponding fact exists and otherwise, false. "It is day" is true just in case it is day; otherwise the proposition is false. Furthermore every proposition is either true or false. [2]

As for kinds of propositions, Chrysippus believed that there were two types: they are, in modern terms, the atomic and the molecular

---

[1] It is difficult to find a suitable expression to name the entity that is a proposition. It lies somewhere (?) between words and facts or events, and perhaps, in the absence of another expression, "thought" will have to do the job. For a brilliant discussion of a notion like that of Chrysippus, see Gottlob Frege, "The Thought: a Logical Inquiry", *Mind*, Vol. 65 (1956), pp. 289-311 (also appears in *Philosophical Logic* (ed. by P. F. Strawson. Oxford: Oxford University Press, 1967), pp. 17-38; I shall quote from this one). Frege writes in one place (p. 38), "Thoughts are by no means unreal but their reality is of quite a different kind from that of things. And their effect is brought about by an act of the thinker without which they would be ineffective, at least as far as we can see. And yet the thinker does not create them but must take them as they are. They can be true without being apprehended by a thinker and are not wholly unreal even then, at least if they could be apprehended and by this means be brought into operation."

[2] "Chrysippus exerts all his powers in order to convince us that every proposition is either true or false" (II 952). As will be seen in the following chapter where Chrysippus' doctrine of causation is discussed, Chrysippus' defense of the *tertium non datur* is the premise from which he argues that every motion has an efficient cause.

(II 203). An atomic proposition is one which is not duplicated, as for example, "it is day"; a molecular proposition is one consisting of two occurrences of an atomic proposition or two different atomic propositions, for example, "if it is day, then it is day" or "if it is day, there is light." (As will become apparent shortly, the truth condition described above applies to the atomic-type proposition only.)

Though it is not made clear in this fragment, it does become evident in another report (II 207) that the atomic propositions, which are elements of molecular propositions, are not merely placed side by side or uttered one behind the other; rather they are linked by some one of a number of possible connective particles. There are, according to Chrysippus (II 207), five kinds of molecular propositions, each being distinguished by the connective which links its constituent atomic propositions. One kind is the conditional, its connective being "if", and an example of which is, "if it is day, it is light." A second kind is the conjunctive, its connective being "and", and an example of which is "it is day and it is light." A third kind of molecular proposition, according to Chrysippus, is the exclusive disjunctive proposition, its connective being "either-or", and an example of which is "either it is day or it is night." A fourth type is the causal proposition, its connective being "because", and an example of which is "because it is day, it is light." The fifth kind of molecular proposition has not a name, but its connective is "more likely ... than" (or "less likely ... than"), and an example of it is "more likely it is day than it is night."

What are the conditions for the truth of the five kinds of molecular propositions, according to Chrysippus? With respect to the "more likely ... than" nameless type and the causal type, there is not an iota of information in the extant Chrysippean fragments.

We can elicit the truth conditions of the three remaining kinds of molecular proposition on the basis of direct and indirect evidence. The truth value of an exclusive disjunctive proposition, as Chrysippus believed (II 207), is a function of the truth values of its component propositions. The disjunctive connective signifies that one of the components is false. And, from the last of the five indemonstrable argument forms, described in another fragment [1] and discussed below, we may infer that the disjunctive connective signifies also

---

[1] II 241. Chrysippus says that from $p \vee q$ and $-p$ one may infer q. This shows that, for him, one proposition in a disjunctive proposition must be true.

that one of the atomic propositions in a disjunctive proposition is true (for which reason the disjunctive proposition, for Chrysippus, must be adjudged to be of the exclusive type). Therefore we may conclude that, for Chrysippus, a disjunctive proposition is true when one of its components is true while the other is false. The truth value of a conjunction is also a function of the truth values of its ingredient propositions. And we may infer from the third of Chrysippus' indemonstrable argument forms [1] that the connective "and" in a true conjunctive proposition signifies that the two propositions linked by it are true; and this is to say that, for Chrysippus, a conjunctive proposition is true when all of its component propositions are true.

It is not an easy task to determine which, from Chrysippus' point of view, are the criteria for the truth of a conditional proposition. Such a task requires that we review a Hellenistic classification of conditional propositions, a classification preserved for us by Sextus Empiricus whose account of Stoic logic is as reliable as that of Diocles Magnes and has the additional merit of being longer.[2] Chrysippus' name is not explicitly associated with any of these classifications, but we, on the basis of indirect evidence, are able to elicit and clarify the nature of Chrysippean implication.

Sextus Empiricus, in some well-known passages,[3] reports four different criteria for the truth of conditional propositions, each of which was adopted by one or more dialecticians in antiquity. Sextus tells us [4] that the dialecticians agreed that "a conditional proposition is true (ὑγιές) when its consequent follows upon its antecedent. But as to when and how it follows upon the antecedent they disagree with one another." The dialecticians recommend conflicting criteria of following upon (κριτήρια τῆς ἀκολουθίας).

Philo [5] maintained that the conditional proposition is true, or that "following upon" may be truly said to be the relation between propositions, in all instances except those in which the antecedent is true while the consequent is false. For example, given that it is

---

[1] *Ibid.* Chrysippus argues from -(p . q) and p to q. This presupposes that for (p . q) to be true, both p and q must be true .That is, q could not be the logical conclusion in Chrysippus' argument form if (p . q) were true when both p and q are false or when one is true and the other is false.

[2] *Adv. Math.*, viii. 112. *Cf.* Mates, *op. cit.*, p. 33.

[3] P.H. ii. 110-112; *Adv. Math.* viii. 112-117.

[4] *Adv. Math.* viii. 112.

[5] Sextus Emp. P.H. ii. 110ff.

day and that I am conversing, the following conditional propositions are, according to Philo, true: (i) if it is day, I am conversing; (ii) if it is not day, I am conversing; and (iii) if it is not day, I am not conversing; while, given the same circumstances, it is false, by Philo's definition of "follow upon", that if it is day, I am not conversing. In other words, Philo made "follow upon" the relation that is now called "material implication." [1]

Diodorus held any conditional proposition to be true if, beginning from a true antecedent, it could not have terminated and cannot terminate in a false consequent. [2] For Diodorus, then, each of the four propositions formulated above as examples of Philonian true and false conditionals is false. For Diodorus would deny that "if it is day, I am conversing" is a true conditional proposition, because if I cease conversing before nightfall the proposition will then have a true antecedent and a false consequent, and any conditional which admits such a combination of propositions is false. As Mates has clearly shown, a conditional proposition "holds in the Diodorean sense if and only if it holds at all times in the Philonian sense." [3] Sextus gives as an example [4] of a Diodorean true conditional proposition "if atomic elements of things do not exist, atomic elements exist." For, since the antecedent is always false, this conditional can never contain a true antecedent and a false consequent. Therefore it is Diodorean true. As Mates observes, [5] this example shows that the ancients were aware of the paradox in Diodorean implication, that an always false proposition implies any proposition whatsoever, even its own negation.

Sextus next describes [6] two other criteria of true conditional propositions, conflicting with those already presented as well as with one another. Unlike his descriptions of the two former views, the ones he now brings forward have no philosophers' names attached to them. Some men, Sextus says, maintain that a conditional proposition is true when the contradictory of its consequent is incompatible (μάχηται) with its antecedent; these are holders of the sunartesis (συνάρτησις) or connection theory. From the example

---

[1] C. I. Lewis and C. H. Langford, *Symbolic Logic* (2nd ed. Dover Publications, Inc., 1959, f.p. 1932), p. 136. *Cf.* Benson Mates, *op. cit.*, p. 44.

[2] Sextus Emp. *Adv. Math.* viii. 115.

[3] Mates, *op. cit.*, pp. 44-47 and, in particular, p. 45, note 20.

[4] Sextus Emp. P.H. ii. 111.

[5] Mates, *op. cit.*, p. 48.

[6] Sextus Emp. P.H. ii. 111.

furnished by Sextus, "incompatible" appears to mean logically incompatible; that is, the conjunction of the antecedent and the contradictory of the consequent would be logically false.[1] This third criterion of "following upon" is even stronger than the previous two and, judged by it, none of the three propositions illustrative of Philo's criterion, nor the one presented as an example of a true conditional proposition for Diodorus, is a true conditional. The criterion for the truth of a conditional proposition demanded by the third view is satisfied in such a proposition as "if it is day, it is day." A fourth group of persons, referred to by Sextus as "those who judge by way of implication" (οἱ τῇ ἐμφάσει κρίνοντες),[2] held the view that that conditional proposition is true, the consequent of which is potentially included by its antecedent. No example is given of a conditional proposition true by this standard. It was believed by the proponents of this view, however, that, because nothing at all could be included in itself, no proposition could be included in itself; and, therefore, the conditional proposition, "if it is day, it is day", must be judged false.[3]

Such are four conflicting definitions of the "follow upon" relation required for a true conditional proposition, current in the time of Chrysippus. They, as we have seen, were set forth as ways in which "follow upon" is to be understood in the assertion that a conditional proposition is true when its consequent follows upon its antecedent.

Chrysippus, reputed in antiquity to have been among the greatest of dialecticians (II 1), must have avowed—indeed, he may have produced—one of these theories about true conditional propositions. We have some evidence for excluding the first two from his authorship, for, as Cicero reports (II 285), Diodorus, Philo, and Chrysippus held differing views on the problem. There is no direct evidence that any of these forms of implication is peculiarly Chrysippean, but modern scholars, with varying degrees of certitude, have decided on the basis of indirect evidence to attach the third of these forms of implication to Chrysippus' name. Zeller [4] makes

---

[1] Mates writes, "Judging from the position of this type in the list, which was obviously intended to proceed from weakest to strongest, we are led to suppose that 'incompatible' is used in its ordinary sense, according to which incompatible propositions cannot both be true, i.e., their conjunction is logically false. The example bears out this interpretation." *Op. cit.*, p. 48.

[2] Sextus Emp. P.H. ii. 112.

[3] *Ibid.*

[4] Eduard Zeller, *Die Philosophie der Griechen in ihrer geschichtlichen*

the unsubstantiated assertion that Chrysippus established the third kind of implication reported by Sextus. Victor Brochard [1] also believes this to be the Chrysippean form. A. Schmekel [2] argues that the third type of implication is "without a doubt" the theory of Chrysippus. Mates is ambivalent; in one passage [3] he says that he "cannot find much evidence one way or the other." But in another place,[4] he calls the third type of implication "Chrysippean implication." Martha Kneale thinks that a passage in Cicero (*De Fato*, 12), which we shall examine shortly, "suggests" that the third view may be that of Chrysippus.[5] With the exception of Kneale the scholars alluded to have either given no evidence at all for their judgments on this matter, or they have cited evidence which is not merely not conclusive but evidence which lends no weight at all to their conclusions.[6]

Entwicklung. (Dritter Teil. Erste Hälfte. 6. unveränderte Auflage. Darmstadt, Wissenschaftliche Buchgesellschaft, 1963), pp. 108-109, note 5.

[1] Victor Brochard, "Sur la Logique des Stoiciens", (*Archiv für Geschichte der Philosophie* (Vol. 5, 1892), pp. 449-468), pp. 459, 460.

[2] A. Schmekel, *Die positive Philosophie in ihrer geschichtlichen Entwicklung.* (Erster Band, Berlin, 1938), p. 524, note 6.

[3] Mates, *op. cit.*, p. 48, note 26.

[4] *Ibid.*, p. 49.

[5] William Kneale and Martha Kneale, *The Development of Logic* (Oxford, 1962), p. 129. For an earlier expression of this view by Kneale (née Hurst), see Martha Hurst, "Implication in the Fourth Century B. C." *Mind*, 44, 1935, pp. 484-495), p. 495, note 1.

[6] Zeller, as was remarked, simply asserts, "Die erste von diesen Bestimmungen [the third in Sextus' list], welche auch Diog. 73 allein als die stoische Schullehre aufführt, hatte Chrysippus aufgestellt"; *Phil. d. Griech.*, p. 109, note 5. Zeller himself, however, although he doesn't use the *De Fato* passage as evidence that Chrysippus established the συνάρτησις form of implication, does cite it for the contention that Chrysippus, because he had established this form, would not tolerate propositions which violated it to be expressed in conditional form.

Brochard holds that Chrysippus rejected Diodorus' criterion of a true conditional, because Chrysippus thought it a consequence of Diodorus' (to him) unacceptable doctrine of possibility, a doctrine which makes reality and possibility indistinguishable; and Brochard thinks that "telle doctrine menait droit à la négation de toute liberté: et c'est pourquoi Chrysippe l'a combattue" (*op. cit.*, p. 458.) Brochard holds that, since Chrysippus rejected the Diodorean doctrine which entails Diodorean criterion, he must have authored the third or fourth criterion presented by Sextus, but Brochard gives no positive evidence for the association of Chrysippus' name with either of these criteria.

Schmekel's argument is vitiated by two circumstances, the first of which is that he cites as evidence for Chrysippean doctrine passages which do not contain Chrysippus' name. For example, he (*Die pos. Philos.*, p. 524) attributes the doctrine concerning conclusive and inconclusive propositions,

I believe that the passage from Cicero's *De Fato* (II 954) cited by Kneale, rightly interpreted, yields something stronger than a suggestion that the third form of implication described by Sextus is that of Chrysippus; if this ascription, however, is accurate, it compels us to conceive the incompatibility (μάχηται) alluded to in Sextus' description as empirical rather than logical. Let us take up these points in turn.

A proper understanding of the Ciceronian passage requires that we touch upon Chrysippus' doctrine of causation and his attitude towards divination. Chrysippus held that all things occur in accordance with fate, and he describes fate as the causal chain running through all things (II 915). He maintained that one does violence to nature when one introduces an uncaused phenomenon into one's explanation (II 973). And from Chrysippus' *On Fate*, the same book mentioned by Diogenes Laertius in the first of the two fragments cited, Diogenianus quotes Chrysippus as saying, "the prophecies of the diviners would not be true if all things were not encompassed

---

reported in *D.L.* vii. 78, to Chrysippus in spite of the fact that Chrysippus' name does not appear in the passage. But, a second and graver weakness of Schmekel's argument is his assumption that Chrysippus' indemonstrable argument forms (SVF II 245) have their basis in sunartesis as described by P.H. ii. 111; he makes such an assumption in order to conclude therefrom that the Chrysippean theory of implication is sunartesis. Sextus says in the passage cited: "Those who introduce sunartesis say that the connection in a conditional proposition is sound when the opposite of the consequent in it contradicts the antecedent in it." Now Chrysippus' second indemonstrable argument form (SVF II 245) contains as its first premise a conditional proposition and as its second premise "the opposite" of a consequent in the conditional, and it indeed concludes to the opposite of the antecedent in the conditional. But one cannot argue, as Schmekel does, that the person who propounds such an argument form is *ipso facto* committed to the sunartesis theory of implication. For the argument form would work for each of the four kinds of implication described by Sextus. The theory of implication one adopts determines what kinds of propositions he will admit as true conditionals; it does not (at least in the case of the four theories of implication described by Sextus) determine whether or not conditional propositions, true on the adopted theory, can be used in, say, the *modus tollens* argument. For example, strictly implied conditional propositions as well as materially implied conditional propositions function in a *modus tollens* argument. Therefore one could not infer from a person's endorsement of such a form of argument that he was a holder of, say, the material implication theory of conditional propositions. Similarly, Schmekel cannot legitimately infer from Chrysippus' undemonstrated argument forms that Chrysippus favored the sunartesis theory of implication.

Mates gives no evidence at all for calling the third form "Chrysippean implication." *Op. cit.*, p. 49.

by fate" (II 939). In other words Chrysippus' belief that all things are causally determined (under the surface of whatever appears to be fortuitous one will always find hidden causes (II 973)) provided the basis for his belief in divination. Chrysippus, we are told by Laertius (II 1191), maintained in his book *On Divination* that divination is a science.

Artificial or inductive divination, "divination from inference based on signs and events in the physical surroundings, in animal life, etc.," [1] was of great importance in Stoic epistemology. Cicero defines inductive divination as "the art of those who follow up new things by inference, having learned the old ones by observation." [2] And if we are to derive from the passage we are about to examine the Chrysippean criterion of truth for a conditional proposition, we must bear in mind that, as Professor Sambursky has expressed it, the Stoic school stresses again and again "the empirical basis of divination which was established through long continued and repeated observation of signs." [3] Predetermined events are unfolded in the course of time and "as certain combinations and constellations of events repeat themselves continually, careful study of their nexus can furnish means of knowing the future." [4]

Now let us return to the passage in question. Cicero has just pointed out[5] to his friend, Hirtius, that if fate is proven to exist on the grounds that divination functions successfully, then will, effort, and training will be destroyed. He then gives as an example of the "rules" (θεωρήματα, *praecepta*) which astrologers use, the following proposition: "if anyone is born at the rising of the dogstar, he will not die at sea." It is to be noted that the proposition is cast in conditional form. Cicero admonishes Chrysippus not to abandon his position in the dispute with Diodorus.

The issue between Chrysippus and Diodorus alluded to is this: Diodorus maintained that the possible is either what is true or what will be true.[6] It if will not be true, it is impossible. Chrysippus, on the other hand, maintained that, even though something is not

---

[1] S. Sambursky, *Physics of the Stoics* (London: Routledge and Kegan Paul, 1959), p. 66. Sambursky (pp. 65-71) gives a very informative account of the relation between divination and induction in Stoic philosophy.

[2] Cicero *De divinatione* i. 34 (Sambursky's trans.).

[3] Sambursky, *op cit.*, p. 67.

[4] *Ibid.*

[5] *De Fato* v. ii.

[6] *De Fato* vii. 13.

true and may never be true, it may nevertheless be possible.[1] Diodorus and Chrysippus were in agreement that everything true as an event in the past is necessary.[2] When Cicero, having introduced the θεώρημα in the form of a conditional proposition (given above), urges Chrysippus not to give up his side of the dispute with Diodorus, it is as if he were saying, "Chrysippus finds it difficult to reconcile this kind of implication with his doctrine of possibility."[3] For, when he tries to show that Chrysippus holds two incompatible doctrines, he begins by saying (II 954), "If that is *true* which *is connected* as follows, if anyone was born at the rising of the dogstar, he will not die at sea, *then* . . . that which is asserted falsely about the future is impossible" (italics my own). And here he appears to me to be supposing that this kind of conditional proposition is one which satisfies a criterion of truth approved by Chrysippus, for, if this were not the case, it would be quite pointless to try to show, as Cicero does (though unsuccessfully[4]), that this proposition entails a conclusion repugnant to Chrysippus' doctrine of possibility. We conclude, therefore, that whatever criterion of truth this proposition satisfies, that criterion of truth was the one approved by Chrysippus. Let us now try to determine what that criterion is.

Cicero's argument (II 954) can be set forth as follows:

(1) If the proposition, "if anyone is born at the rising of the dogstar, he will not die at sea", is true, then

(2) the proposition, "if Fabius is born at the rising of the dogstar, Fabius will not die at sea", is true. And, therefore,

(3) "Fabius was born at the rising of the dogstar" and "Fabius will die at sea" are incompatible. And this assertion, combined with "Fabius was born at the rising of the dogstar", enables us to infer that

(4) "Fabius lives" and "Fabius will die at sea" are incompatible propositions. Therefore

(5) "Fabius lives and Fabius will die at sea" is an impossible conjunction. But since "Fabius lives" is true,

---

[1] Epictetus *Discourses* ii. 19.

[2] *Ibid.*

[3] And this is born out by the upshot of the argument. Cicero informs us that Chrysippus asks the astrologers to put this conditional proposition in the form of a conjunction; had the proposition not satisfied the truth condition approved by Chrysippus, he could have said so and gotten out of his embarrassment in that way.

[4] *Infra*, pp. 79-80.

(6) "Fabius will die at sea" belongs to a class of impossible proposi-
     tions; and, from this, it may be concluded that
(7) that which is asserted falsely about the future is impossible.

It ought to be observed, however, that step (6) can be inferred from
step (5) only if Diodorus' doctrine concerning false propositions
about the future is presupposed. The truth, that is, of "Fabius lives"
together with the negation of the conjunction, "Fabius lives and
Fabius will die at sea" entails the falsity of "Fabius will die at sea",
but not the impossibility of Fabius' dying at sea one day, unless
the doctrine disavowed by Chrysippus, what will never be true is
impossible, be presupposed. Step (6), then, ought to read, " 'Fabius
will die at sea' is a false proposition." And, since false propositions
about the future are impossible propositions (i.e., the states of
affairs they describe cannot occur), and since "Fabius will die at
sea" refers to a future event, it follows that step (7) in the argument
ought to be "it is impossible for Fabius to die at sea." Step (7)
above in Cicero's argumentation as I have schematized it would
drop out because it is, as we have shown, not a conclusion, but a
premise in the argument.

   This restoration of the correct form of the argument also shows
how Chrysippus would have resolved the dilemma with which he
is allegedly saddled. He would have replied, "I agree that the argument leads to the conclusion that 'Fabius will die at sea' is false. I
deny, however, that it describes a state of affairs which cannot
possibly exist; for I do not agree with Diodorus that false propositions about the future are impossible propositions." But Cicero's
garbling of the argument [1] at the end and the fact that Chrysippus
could have defended himself against the imputation contained in
it do not mean that the argument no longer throws light on the
meaning of Chrysippean implication. The point still remains that
Cicero must have used a conditional proposition true in the Chrysippean sense if it was his purpose, as it appears to have been, to show
the incompatibility between Chrysippus' theory of implication, on

---

[1] It is not clear whether Cicero garbled the argument because he mis-
construed material he found in the handbooks or because it would satisfy a
polemical intent to show that Chrysippus was inconsistent. If the latter
were his motive, Cicero's is not an isolated case. The whole of Plutarch's
De Stoicorum Repugnantiis is a collection of summaries and quotations out
of context designed to show that Chrysippus and other Stoics were guilty
of self-contradiction.

the one hand, and his doctrine of possibility, on the other. What does this argument, then, tell us about Chrysippean implication?

We infer from (3) that, in Chrysippus' view, a conditional proposition is true when the negation of its consequent is incompatible (pugnant ... inter se) with its antecedent.[1] But it does not appear that logical incompatibility is intended here. There is, that is, nothing logically unsound about the conjunction, "Fabius was born at the rising of the dogstar and Fabius will die at sea." The incompatibility is rather of an empirical nature. The astrologers, having observed that a number of persons born under the dogstar did not perish at sea in spite of having been in situations likely to bring about this result, generalized on the evidence and concluded that if anyone was born under the dogstar, he would not die at sea. The denial of the consequent entails the denial of the antecedent (that is, the antecedent and the negation of the consequent cannot both be true), because the two facts of being born under the dogstar and not dying at sea, insofar as known, are so related that, having denied the consequent in the proposition, not to deny the antecedent would be to do violence to those facts. To put the matter in another way: for Chrysippus, a conditional proposition is true if the conjunction of its antecedent and negation of its consequent is impossible, but impossible in what Lewis calls [2] the "relative" sense, not in the "absolute" sense. "Impossible" here means "not consistent with the data, or with what is known";[3] it does not mean logically incompatible.

I should emphasize that Chrysippean implication differs from Philonian implication. For Philo any two propositions can compose a true conditional unless the first (antecedent) is, as a matter of fact, true while the second (consequent) is false. Such a conditional does not express connections in nature. For example, "if the sun shines, John will write letters" is a Philonian true conditional if and only if John does not, as a matter of fact, fail to write letters at a given period of sunshine. But there need not be a natural connection between the sun's shining and John's epistolary habits.

---

[1] Martha Kneale (*supra*, note 5, p. 75), alone of the scholars mentioned in the text above, has seen this. She did not, however, go on to note that *pugnant inter se* could hardly have meant logical incompatibility.

[2] Clarence I. Lewis and Cooper H. Langford, *op. cit.*, p. 161. It thus becomes apparent that, in our view, Chrysippean implication is not Lewis's strict implication.

[3] *Ibid.*, p. 161.

If there were and it were of the sort described above, John could not, as a matter of fact, fail to write letters when the sun shines. And it is this kind of connection—connections between objects in nature —that Chrysippean implication is designed to express. This is the case because for Chrysippus, as we have seen, two propositions can compose a true conditional only if it is impossible, as a matter of fact, for the first (antecedent) to be true while the second (consequent) is false.

We are not unaware that our interpretation confronts us with a difficulty. For it begins to appear that Chrysippean implication does not differ from that of Diodorus, because we take Chrysippean conditionals to be expressive of natural laws,[1] that is, to be stating that, as the actual world is (insofar as we know), it is impossible, so long as that world does not change, for the consequent of a true conditional proposition to be false while its antecedent is true. How, then, do we explain Cicero's report (II 285), in which he explicitly states that Diodorus and Chrysippus held different views about the criterion of truth of a conditional proposition?

A possible solution to our problem is that the kind of implication described above may have been regarded, in some extended sense of the term, as analytic, that is, the third type of implication in Sextus' classification. This appears to be the view of Brochard, who says, "It is credible, then, that Chrysippus has decided for the coherence theory [the third view reported by Sextus and called above by us the connection theory], understood in a broad sense. A conditional proposition is true when the consequent is implicitly contained in the antecedent. And we know that it is implicitly contained either when it is identical or from experience, and above all, accumulated experience ... because experience has taught us this connection." [2] The unhappy feature of Brochard's solution, of course, is that it means we must foist upon the minds of logicians in antiquity a confusion of empirical impossibility and logical impossibility. Of course, it may be the case that this distinction had not, as a matter of fact, been discerned in the Hellenistic age.[3]

---

[1] See Mates, *op. cit.*, p. 48, for an implicit identification of Diodorean implication with a conditional which expresses a natural law.

[2] Victor Brochard, *op. cit.*, pp. 459-460.

[3] "It is the more important to understand the distinction of those two meanings of 'possible', 'impossible', and 'necessary', because frequently they are confused, even by logicians, with consequences which are fatal to the understanding of logical principles." Lewis and Langford, *op. cit.*, p. 161.

We do not investigate that possibility here. However the case may have been with respect to this problem, it seems to me that the evidence that I have adduced is sufficient to enable us to give a true characterization of Chrysippean implication.

2b. *Undemonstrated argument forms*

As our discussion of Chrysippus' treatment of propositions may have indicated and as his exposition of arguments, about to be considered, will make obvious, the essential difference in Chrysippean logic and Aristotelian logic is that, while the latter is a logic of classes, the former is a logic of propositions. In Aristotle's formulation of the schemata for the figures and moods of the categorical syllogism [1] the substituends [2] for the variables are names of classes. That is, these variables take classes as their values. For example, the schema for syllogisms of the Barbara form as articulated by Aristotle is, "If A is predicated of all B, and B of all C, A must be predicated of all C." [3] The substituends for the variables in this schema are the names of classes having at least one member. To make use of examples of the sort Aristotle himself uses to illustrate invalid syllogisms, [4] we can in the Barbara schema above substitute 'mortal things' for A, 'animals' for B, and 'men' for C. In the Chrysippean argument schemata, as will become evident, the substituends for the variables are not the names of classes of individuals, but words constituting entire sentences. The variables in the Chrysippean argument schemata take as values not classes, but propositions. None of the preserved material in any way suggests that Chrysippus intended that propositional logic replace the class logic of Aristotle. It rather represents a brilliant extension of the scope of logic. We are not saying that Chrysippus *invented* propositional logic. The Megarians, Diodorus and Philo, had already

---

[1] *Prior Analytics* 25ᵇ 26-43ᵃ 19.

[2] "There are two questions, however, that one should be ready to answer whenever a variable is to be employed, namely, what are its *substituends* and what are its *values* (where the substituends are all those expressions that may be meaningfully substituted for the variable, and the values include all objects named by substituends)." Benson Mates, *Elementary Logic* (New York: Oxford University Press, 1965), p. 21.

[3] *Prior Analytics* 25ᵇ 38-40. Oxford trans. Lukasiewicz (*Aristotle's Syllogistic*, Oxford: The Clarendon Press, 1951, pp. 7, 8) rightly calls attention to the fact that this introduction of variables into logic was "one of Aristotle's greatest inventions."

[4] *Ibid.* 26ᵃ 6-10. He uses no concrete terms to illustrate the valid schemata.

begun work in this field when Chrysippus began to do philosophy. But Chrysippus was certainly the first Stoic to recognize the import of the new logic, and it may well be that he was the first philosopher to formulate the argument schemata to an examination of which we now turn.[1]

We have several rich accounts [2] of certain undemonstrated argument forms propounded by Chrysippus. They were called "undemonstrated" because it was not thought that any demonstration of their validity was required, since "it is immediately evident with respect to them that they yield a conclusion." [3] They are most frequently called "the undemonstrated", no substantive at all appearing in the Greek; but it is clear in each of our fragments that the author intends the adjective "undemonstrated" to qualify what we today call "argument forms."[4] A high degree of generality was achieved by using as elements in the forms the expressions "the first" and "the second", each of which is a variable, which takes as its value not a class, but a proposition.

The argument forms are as follows (II 245):

First argument form:
 If the first, the second.
 The first.
 Therefore, the second.
Second argument form:
 If the first, the second.
 Not the second.
 Therefore, not the first.

---

[1] *Cf.* I. M. Bochénski, *A History of Formal Logic*, (South Bend, Indiana: Univ. of Notre Dame Press, 1961), pp. 107-109. Mates, *op. cit.*, pp. 5-8.

[2] (II 241).

(II 242). It is not clear why Sextus does not, as Galen does, give the schemata for all five argument forms, but for three of them only. In another place (*P.H.* ii. 157, 158) he explicitly recognizes all five forms and gives examples of each.

(II 244).
(II 245).
(II 246).

[3] (II 242). This might be compared with Aristotle's "for the starting-point of demonstration is not demonstration." *Meta.* 1011[a] 13.

[4] "We define an *argument form* as any sequence of symbols containing statement variables but no statements, such that when the statement variables are replaced by statements—the same statements replacing the same statement variable throughout—the result is an argument." Irving M. Copi, *Introduction to Logic* (Second edit., New York: The MacMillan Company, 1961), pp. 254, 255.

Third argument form:
    Not both the first and the second.
    The first.
    Therefore, not the second.
Fourth argument form:
    Either the first or the second.
    The first.
    Therefore, not the second.
Fifth argument form:
    Either the first or the second.
    Not the first.
    Therefore, the second.

Examples of these forms, or what we should today call substitution instances, are given by Diocles Magnes in Diogenes Laertius (II 241) and by Sextus Empiricus (II 242). They are:

First argument form:
    If it is day, there is light.
    It is day.
    Therefore, there is light.
Second argument form:
    If it is day, there is light.
    There is not light.
    Therefore, it is not day.[1]
Third argument form:
    It is not the case both that it is day and it is night.
    It is day.
    Therefore, it is not night.
Fourth argument form:
    (no example given by our sources for Chrysippus;
    one of our own follows)
    Either Plato is in Athens or he is in Syracuse.
    Plato is not in Syracuse.
    Therefore, he is in Athens.

---

[1] (II 242). This is the way in which the example in Diogenes (II 241) should have read; as it stands, it goes
    If it is day, there is light.
    It is night.
    Therefore, it is not day.
It is very likely that Diogenes, while copying from Diocles Magnes, glanced at an example illustrating *another* form when he was copying out the minor premise in *this* illustrative case.

Fifth argument form:
  Either it is day or it is night.
  It is not night.
  Therefore it is day.[1]

Aristotle's few references [2] to argument ἐξ ὑποθέσεως show clearly, as Ross [3] has observed, that this kind of argument played no great role in his logical theory. And even for his followers, Theophrastus and Eudemus, inferences depending on conditional propositions continued to bear a "dialectical" character [4]; that is, the antecedent in the conditional proposition is accepted because certain parties *agree* to accept it as true.[5] For Chrysippus, however, the conditional proposition was an expression of the irrefragable connections of phenomena in nature. It provided an instrument for dealing with empirical facts and for making inferences from them to unobserved facts.[6]

Sextus also reports (II 242) that from these simple argument forms non-simple forms can be constructed and such non-simple forms "still require analysis into those [of a simple form] in order that it may be known that they, too, yield conclusions." There are two classes of the non-simple type, one consisting of homogeneous elements, two argument forms of the first kind or two of the second; this class, then, appears to be the hypothetical syllogism. The second kind of the non-simple type is that which contains heterogeneous elements, for example, the first and fifth argument forms. Fortunately we possess a fragment (II 1192) in which Chrysippus makes use of a non-simple argument containing heterogeneous elements to prove that the gods give signs of future events. We quote it here in full, giving to each of its atomic propositions a capital letter, so that we may then show the structure of the argument in symbolic form:

---

  [1] (II 241). This, in the absence of a law of commutation, is not a substitution instance of the fifth undemonstrated argument form. We assume that some such rule existed.

  [2] *Prior Analytics* 41ᵃ 37-ᵇ1, 45ᵇ 15-20, 50ᵃ 16-ᵇ4.

  [3] W. D. Ross, *Aristotle's Prior and Posterior Analytics* (Oxford: The Clarendon Press, 1949), pp. 31, 32.

  [4] Pohlenz, *op. cit.*, I, 49.

  [5] *Prior Analytics* 41ᵃ 37-ᵇ1; *cf.* the note on this passage in the Oxford translation.

  [6] *Supra*, pp. 79-82. *Cf.* Pohlenz' discussion of the nature of Stoic logic in general regarding this point, *op. cit.*, pp. 49, 50.

If (A) the gods exist, and (B) they do not declare to men before-hand what future events will be, then either (C) they do not love men, or (D) they do not know what future events will be, or (E) they judge that it is of no importance to men to know what the future will be, or (F) they think it is not consonant with their dignity to preannounce to men what future events will be, or (G) the gods, though they be gods, cannot reveal what future events will be. But (-C) it is not the case that they do not love us, for they are beneficent friends of the human race, (-D) nor is it the case that they are ignorant of the things which they themselves form and design; (-E) nor is it of no importance for us to know those things which will happen in the future, for we shall be more careful if we know; (-F) nor does giving signs of the future comport badly with their dignity, for there is nothing more excellent than kindness; (-G) nor is it the case that they cannot reveal what future events will be. Therefore it is not true that (A) there are gods and that (B) they do not give signs of future events. But (A) there are gods. Therefore, (-B) they do give signs.

This non-simple argument containing heterogeneous elements has the following structure:

(1) $(A . B) \rightarrow (C \vee D \vee E \vee F \vee G)$
(2) $(-C . -D . -E . -F . -G)$
(3) $-(C \vee D \vee E \vee F \vee G)$
(4) $-(A . B)$
(5) A
(6) $\therefore -B$

And it makes use of the second and third argument forms. Step (3) denies the consequent of the conditional stated in (1) and step (5) asserts that one of the conjuncts in a negated conjunction, step (4), is true, thereby giving as conclusion, step (6), the negate of the other conjunct.

There is another lesson to be learned from this fragment. Chrysippus, though direct evidence be lacking, must have had some notion about the interdefinability of the connectives. Without one of the laws, later formulated by DeMorgan,[1] he could not have gotten

---

[1] $-(p \vee q) \equiv (-p . -q)$.

from step (2) to step (3). And, in a fragment already discussed (II 954), it becomes apparent that Chrysippus believed a conditional proposition was equivalent to the negation of a conjunction of its antecedent and the negate of its consequent. For there Cicero, in an argument, which presumably adheres to the Chrysippean norms of logical validity, infers from "if Fabius is born at the rising of the dogstar, he will not die at sea" to the incompatibility of "Fabius is born at the rising of the dogstar and he will die at sea."

2c. *Opposites and paradoxes*

Chrysippus' interest in "things signified" other than propositions and arguments is evidenced by several brief fragments dealing with opposites and paradoxes. Simplicius, reporting on Stoic doctrine, observes in one place (II 173) that "generally contraries are thought to be in the class of entities" (ἐν τοῖς πράγμασι); and since 'τὰ πράγματα' was the quasi-technical term used by the Stoics for "things signified" (II 166), it is reasonable to suppose that the Stoics placed contraries in the class of things signified. If we may go one step further and assume that opposites generally were regarded as things signified, we might then say that Chrysippus' interest in this particular species of things signified ranged over at least the following questions: (1) Since it is possible "to say" the same thing with a simple expression and with a definition (i.e., a complex expression), are there contraries for each of these modes of expression (II 174) ? (2) What are the different forms of privation and possession, one of the modes of opposition described by Aristotle ? [1] There are, after all, contexts in which we should wish to say that a shoeless person was suffering a privation; but we should not wish to say this of a person having a bath (Chrysippus' example) (II 177); (3) With respect to natural possession and privation, Aristotle had held that a person once in possession could be deprived, but once deprived (for example, of his sight) could not regain possession; but, Chrysippus asks, what about the man with cataracts who regains his vision after submitting to an operation (II 178) ? Isn't this a counter example to the Aristotelian view?

---

[1] *Categories* 11^{b}17-14^{a}25. And Simplicius reports (II 172) that the Stoics followed in Aristotle's footsteps, he having given them the starting points for a discussion of opposites, which they then developed in their own books on the subject.

Chrysippus wrote a book about privations (II 177) in which a number of other questions of this sort were probably raised.

Several fragments (II 270, 271, 277, 278, 279, 280, 281-285, 287) make evident Chrysippus' interest in paradoxes, some of which—for example, the Liar, about which Chrysippus wrote a book (II 280)—have since become classical and have provoked much fruitful philosophical discussion. The fragments available are so niggardly in their reports that it is difficult to make out how in general Chrysippus viewed such paradoxes as the Liar. He was obviously worried by it; he apparently noted that, put in one way, it had the same form as his first undemonstrated argument schema,[1] and if Cicero's report which follows is accurate, he was unable to resolve the paradox:

> In what way, then, do you judge the following to have been argued: "If you say that it is light now and speak truly, then it is light; but you do say that it is light now and you do speak truly; therefore, it is light"? You certainly accept this kind of argument and affirm that it has been constructed with the utmost validity, so that in teaching you treat it as the primary mode of argument. Either, then, you, will approve whatever is argued in this way, or an art of this kind will not exist. Consider therefore if you are going to accept the following conclusion: "If you say that you are lying and speak truly, then you lie; but you do say that you are lying and you do speak truly; therefore, you are lying." How can you not accept this when you have approved the one above of the same form? These are Chrysippean [paradoxes], resolved not even by himself (II 282).

Chrysippus' preoccupation with semantical paradoxes exhibits a level of philosophical sophistication conspicuously absent in the late Stoa as exemplified, to take only one instance, in the bewildered Epictetus' remark, "I wish to know what Chrysippus means in the books of his *On the Liar*" (II 280).

3. RHETORIC

Quintilian reports (II 292) that Chrysippus defined rhetoric as "the science of speaking properly", and Plutarch records (II 297)

---

[1] *Supra*, p. 83.

another definition. We are told by him that, for Chrysippus, the rhetorical art "is that which concerns the embellishment and order of a set speech." Unfortunately, because of the scantiness of the material, we are unable to comment on the role that rhetoric played in Chrysippus' logic. We do know that for "the Stoics" it constituted one of the two major subdivisions of logic.[1]

Cicero's harsh judgment on Chrysippus' one work on rhetoric —he said it would be appropriate for anyone who might wish to remain mute (II 288)—may, if one bears in mind how, for Cicero, rhetoric is a rich discipline having several divisions,[2] be due to his opinion that Chrysippus conceived rhetoric in a too narrow way.

4. SUMMARY

In this attempt to reconstruct Chrysippus' logic I have tried to show that theory of knowledge and dialectic are two of the main topics dealt with by Chrysippus in this domain of philosophy. And, despite my adherence to the rather rigorous methodological principle formulated in the first chapter, I have, I trust, characterized rather fully several features of Chrysippus' logical theory.

Chrysippus believed that men can know that things exist and that they can know the nature of these objects. The soul of an individual, which is a detached fragment of the soul of the universe, is a uniform material substance possessing different functions. One of its functions is to report things that are present and these reports consist of presentations or images of those things which, in substance, are modifications of the soul itself. Another of the soul's functions is that of distinguishing the veridical from the non-veridical presentations. It does this by making use of "common notions" or families of similar presentations which it has the capacity to remember. The soul also possesses the power to assent or to refrain from assenting to a given presentation; to assent to it is to act upon it as if it were veridical. To deliberate about its veridical character is to compare it with some common notion and to determine whether or not it is similar to that notion. If the presentation one is now having of a chair is like one's common notion of a chair, one assents to its veridical character, and he may indicate his assent in some one of a variety of ways—for example, by sitting in the chair.

---

[1] Diogenes Laertius vii. 41. The other was dialectic.
[2] de Oratore i. 137-143.

It should be plain by now that Chrysippus' theory of knowledge is thoroughly empirical. The senses, functions of the soul, constitute man's messengers from the external world; and their reports are controlled by referring them, not to transcendental entities such as ideas or universals, but by determining how they compare with other reports which the soul, functioning naturally, has classified and stored away. Another of the soul's functions is to foresee what will happen, and it does so by making use of reports about the connections of things in nature. The generalizations made on individual presentations of these connections can be expressed in the form of Chrysippean conditional propositions. The function of distinguishing veridical from non-veridical presentations which involves memory, classification and comparison, and the function of foreseeing what will happen, are active powers of the soul or what we might call the soul's inner sense in contrast to its functioning through the senses as a messenger from the external world, which we might call its external sense. If such terminology be understood, one may describe Chrysippus' empirical bent in theory of knowledge by saying that, in his view, there is nothing in the mind which was not first present to the external and the internal senses.

Dialectic was conceived quite broadly by Chrysippus. Its aim is the knowledge of truths and their organization, and its material comprises things which signify and things signified. The former are articulate sounds and the latter are the meanings of these sounds, which are entities in addition to the sounds themselves and externally subsisting objects. Of things signified we examined chiefly propositions and arguments.

In his treatment of propositions, Chrysippus distinguished two groups of them, the atomic and the molecular, and he formulated the truth conditions for each type. Chrysippus, according to the preserved material, given his theory of knowledge and his doctrines of causation and divination, regarded a true conditional proposition as a general statement about the connections of things in nature. Therefore, if the proposition is true, it is *empirically* impossible for its consequent to be false while its antecedent is true. Chrysippus believed there were five fundamental kinds of valid inference or argument forms, and he gave a schema for each of them. Other more complicated modes of inference can be validated by reference to these, and we presented one of Chrysippus' own arguments which exhibits one of these non-simple modes of inference.

The attested material regarding Chrysippus' theory of opposites, his treatment of paradoxes, and the role rhetoric played in his logic, is so scarce that it is hardly necessary to summarize our exposition of them.

This latter remark provides the occasion for saying once again that our interpretation, since it restricts itself to evidence explicitly attested as Chrysippean, of course, can in no way give a complete picture of Chrysippus' logic. As we observed at the outset, to judge from the titles and number of his logical treatises and from the fact that he was hailed in antiquity as the greatest of dialecticians, his logic must have constituted an impressive edifice of acute thought. Our study, we believe, has laid bare but a few of the stones in that edifice.

CHAPTER FIVE

NATURAL PHILOSOPHY

Chrysippus takes his place in the tradition of philosophers who have sought to give a rational account of the universe. "To give a rational account of the universe", from Thales to Epicurus, had meant to designate that element or those elements in the universe which were permanent—indeed, eternal—and which in some way explained all the elements and occurrences in it which were transitory. And a portion of such an account was then dedicated to an exposition of the way in which the cosmos and its contents arose from or evolved out of its allegedly primordial elements.

Aristotle was the first to write a history of these accounts,[1] and, while, on one hand, there are good reasons to question the historicity of Aristotle's representations,[2] there is, on the other, no room for doubting that here and in his writings generally he provided the language for the later philosophical discussion of the problem.[3] What we have denominated "primordial elements" he, in his history, calls indiscriminately "cause" (αἴτιον), "principle" (ἀρχή), and "element" (στοιχεῖον).[4] Chrysippus uses the same language and, as I hope to make evident in the course of this chapter, he was familiar with the attempts of his predecessors rationally "to describe the nature of the world." [5] But, though he borrowed from some of them freely, his own account is not a mere *pasticcio*. His view of the universe, taken in its entirety, represents something genuinely new in Greek philosophy.

His natural philosophy will be dealt with under five heads: (1) fundamental doctrines in his physics; (2) the Universe; (3) the Soul; (4) Fate; (5) God. In order that one may more readily under-

---

[1] *Physica*, Book I.

[2] Harold Cherniss, *Aristotle's Criticism of Presocratic Philosophy* (Baltimore: The Johns Hopkins Press, 1935).

[3] John Burnet, *Early Greek Philosophy* (4th edit., London: Adam and Charles Black, 1930), p. 11.

[4] *Physica* 184ᵃ 11, 184ᵇ 15, 25. Cf. *Timaeus* 48ᵇ 7, 8 for use of ἀρχή and στοιχεῖον in this sense.

[5] This is Professor Kirk's expression, used in an account of the origins of this tradition. G. E. Kirk and J. E. Raven, *The Presocratic Philosophers* (Cambridge: The University Press, 1957), p. 73.

stand the motivations and nature of Chrysippus' account of the world, pertinent doctrines belonging to his predecessors, particularly Aristotle, Epicurus, Zeno, and Cleanthes, will be taken into account in the analysis of the fragments.

1. FUNDAMENTAL DOCTRINES IN HIS PHYSICS

In this section we deal with those topics which were most basic in Chrysippus' account of the nature and origin of the cosmos: (a) the two "principles" of the universe; (b) pneuma; (c) the categories; (d) materialism; (e) mixture; (f) motion, place, time, and the infinite.

1a. *The two "principles" of the universe*

We possess three fragments (II 300, 316, 317) which contain direct reports about "the principles of the universe", as Chrysippus viewed them. In his book, *On Substance* (II 300), he had expounded the view that these principles are two: one, the passive, is unqualified substance or matter; the other, the active, is god or reason, which is eternal and creates each thing throughout all the matter. He also believed (II 316) that the term "substance" (or "matter") has two senses: it may be used to designate the matter of the whole or universal matter (ἡ ὕλη τῶν παντῶν), and it also may signify the matter of the parts (ἡ ὕλη τῶν ἐπὶ μέρους) of the whole. The matter of the whole neither increases nor diminishes, while the matter of the parts may change in quantity. The first two of these reports are meagre, indeed, but fortunately they can be made to yield more information by comparing them with what is known about Zeno and Cleanthes, for Chrysippus in these essential doctrines agrees with his predecessors; and, by setting the view against its historical background, the teaching of Plato, Aristotle, and Epicurus, it should be possible to bring out clearly the peculiarity of the fundamental position of the Stoa.

Plato, in his "probable account" of the universe, rejects a view held by the Milesian thinkers,[1] the view, namely, that there is some single kind of matter which is the reservoir from which all other things arose and is the permanent ground underlying all change. He also refuses assent to the doctrines of the pluralist natural philosophers who, in reaction to Parmenides, explained existing

---

[1] For a general characterization of these views, see Aristotle, *Metaphysics* 983[b] 6-27, especially 983[b] 8-11.

things and change in terms of the regrouping in space of other things which exist eternally.[1] The "eternal principles" which Plato invokes [2] to explain the cosmos and its constituents are the Forms, the Receptacle or Space, and the Demiurge.[3] The receptacle or space, in which things come to be and pass away, is itself invisible and characterless.[4] Those combinations of qualities in space which we call bodies are copies of the independently existing Forms.[5] While the receptacle provides a place in which these copies may appear and the Forms provide the models of which the things that come into being and pass away are copies, the Demiurge [6] is the moving cause, the cause which brings it about that things "be by nature as excellent and perfect as possible." [7]

Aristotle, too, holds that, for an explanation of existing objects and the changes they undergo, three principles are required—a pair of contraries and a substratum.[8] He, too, rejects the view that the All is identical with some one nature such as fire, earth, air or water.[9] Each of these elements is already involved with a pair of

---

[1] They were the four "elements" for Empedocles; for Anaxagoras, the "seeds"; for Leucippus and Democritus, the atoms. For Plato's rejection of these doctrines and those of the Milesians, see Francis M. Cornford, *Plato's Cosmology* (The *Timaeus* of Plato translated with a running commentary; New York: The Liberal Arts Press, 1957), p. 178; also *Timaeus* 47[b].

[2] It must be remembered that Plato is somewhat sceptical about the possibility of physics. He thinks a probable account only is possible concerning the "principles" of things. "We are not now to speak of the "first principle" or "principles"—or whatever name men choose to employ—of all things, if only on account of the difficulty of explaining what we think by our present method of exposition. You, then, must not demand the explanation of me; nor could I persuade myself that I should be right in taking upon myself so great a task; but holding fast to what I said at the outset—the worth of a probable account—I will try to give an explanation of all these matters in detail. . . ." *Timaeus* 48[c-] wf. Cornford translation.

[3] *Timaeus* 51[e]-52[d] and Cornford, *op. cit.*, p. 197. In the former we learn that the Forms are "unchanging", "ungenerated and indestructible"; and that Space is "everlasting, not admitting destruction."

[4] *Timaeus* 50[e]-51[a].

[5] ". . . by nature it [the receptacle] is there as a matrix for everything, changed and diversified by the things that enter it, and on their account it *appears* to have different qualities at different times; while the things that pass in and out are to be called copies of the eternal things, impressions taken from them in a strange manner that is hard to express. . . ." *Timaeus* 50[c]. *Cf.* Cornford, *op. cit.*, pp. 189-191.

[6] Perhaps a mythical cloak for the Reason in the World-soul, as Cornford (*op. cit.*, p. 197) suggests.

[7] *Timaeus* 30[b]. Cornford translation.

[8] *Physica* 191[a] 4, 5; 20-22,

[9] *Ibid.*, 189[b] 1-3.

contraries.[1] Aristotle's explanatory principles are the substratum, form, and privation.[2] Every existing object is some matter having some form—bronze having the form of a statue or wood having the form of a bed.[3] It is in accounting for its change that Aristotle introduces the third principle, privation; for change is a displacement in the subject of one form by another which is its opposite or one which is in a range between the original form and its opposite. To use one of Aristotle's own examples, a man from being unmusical becomes musical.[4] The form "unmusical" is displaced by that of "musical" while the substratum, the man, endures throughout the change.[5] It is worthy of note that, for Aristotle, a substance (οὐσία) is a unity involving a group of qualities or forms and a substratum or what he calls "matter".[6] In addition to these three internal principles of existence and change Aristotle, in his *Metaphysics*,[7] discusses three external causes: the proximate moving cause—art in the case of artistic production and the male parent in the case of natural generation;[8] the remote and common cause in natural generation—that is, the sun and its oblique course;[9] the ultimate or first moving cause which, itself unmoved, moves by being desired.[10]

Epicurus, as we have seen,[11] invokes two principles on the basis of which he gives an account of the universe and its contents: the void and atoms. All the individual objects in this world and, indeed, the existence of an infinite number of worlds, can be explained by

---

[1] *Ibid.*

[2] *Ibid.*, 190ᵇ 23-27. Substratum (τὸ ὑποκείμενον), or matter (ἡ ὕλη), privation (ἡ στέρησις), and form (τὸ εἶδος). It is well-known that in Book I Aristotle develops his own view through a dialectical consideration of the doctrines of his predecessors. We do not review that dialectical treatment here, for it is not essential for a general characterization of Aristotle's principles of explanation.

[3] *Ibid.*, 191ᵃ 8-10.

[4] *Ibid.*, 190ᵇ 20-25.

[5] *Ibid.*, 190ᵃ 30-34.

[6] Sir William David Ross, *Aristotle* (Fifth edit., New York: Barnes and Noble, 1949) p. 166. *Cf. Physica* 191ᵃ 8-12. "For as the bronze is to the statue, the wood to the bed, or the matter and the formless before receiving form to anything which has form, so is the underlying nature (ἡ ὑποκειμένη φύσις) to substance (οὐσία), i.e., the 'this' or existent."

[7] Book Λ.

[8] 1071ᵃ 13-17; Ross, *op. cit.*, p. 175.

[9] *Meta.* 1071ᵃ 13-17.

[10] 1071ᵇ 35; 1072ᵃ 26; Ross, *op. cit.*, p. 175.

[11] *Supra*, p. 29.

reference to the size, shape, and arrangement of atoms in the void. Here there is neither a demiurge nor a final moving cause directing the course of the atoms. The three parameters which alone determine their movements are weight, impact, and spontaneous swerve.

Zeno, like Epicurus, lays down two principles in his account of the universe: all phenomena may be explained, according to him, by "that which acts" (τὸ ποιοῦν) and "that which is acted upon" (τὸ πάσχον) (*SVF* I 85). Whereas in Epicurus the forming principle and formed matter of Aristotle had dropped out altogether, in Zeno they are reinstated, though they are now conceived materialistically. That which is acted upon is unqualified substance or matter.[1] In three places (I 86, 87) it is called "primary matter". We are also told (I 87) that the term "substance" has two senses in one of which it signifies the matter of all things, and in the other of which it means the matter of the parts. Though substance is very summarily characterized in the sources that have survived, enough is said of it to make apparent its affinity with Plato's receptacle and Aristotle's primary matter. Like them it is eternal (I 85). It shares with them the characteristic of being without form (I 85); in fact, in language reminiscent of that in which Plato described the Receptacle,[2] Chalcidius reports (I 88) Zeno's belief that the primary matter, like wax which can be molded into innumerable forms, has no quality peculiarly its own. We indicated earlier that rational accounts of the universe, as we find them in Greek philosophy, are usually attempts to explain what is transient in terms of what is eternal, and, accordingly, we find that Zeno's substance or primary matter is everlasting, as is his other principle, the active power in the universe (I 85).

Recurring to Zeno's two senses of "substance" or "matter", it ought to be noted that he lays the foundation for a monistic view of the universe, a view which Chrysippus accentuates to the extent that it becomes the cardinal characteristic of his way of looking at things. We, according to Zeno, may use "matter" in one of its senses to designate copper, gold, and other things of this sort as the matter of the things which are made from them.[3] But these

---

[1] I 85. Chalcidius (*SVF* I 86) renders Zeno's οὐσία one time with "essentia" and another with "substantia."

[2] *Timaeus* 50ᵃ 5-ᶜ6. *Cf.* Aristotle *Physica* 207ᵃ 26: εἶδος γὰρ οὐκ ἔχει ἡ ὕλη.

[3] I 86, 87—With respect to terms the testimonies conflict here. Chalcidius (I 86) reports that the proximate matter for making things, for example, copper and gold, is matter (*silva*) and not *essentia* (οὐσία); Diogenes Laertius

things which do not always remain the same are said to be *parts* of matter in the other sense of that term, that is, the first matter or substance of all existing things, the matter which neither increases nor diminishes.

Zeno's second principle, the "that which acts" reminds us, terminologically at least, of the movent power in Plato's account of the universe, for Zeno's active power is said to create (δημιουργεῖν) each thing in the passive matter (I 85). The descriptions of this active power, both the direct and the analogical, which the tradition has preserved, give us our first insight into the dynamism of the Stoic universe.[1] The reason "runs to and fro" through the substance (I 87); it is like "sperm in the womb" (I 87); it passes through the substance like "semen through the genital organs" (I 87); it is an inseparable quality of the matter (I 87) and it gives life to the sensible world, endowing it with all the beauty which it now possesses (I 88). It moves the matter rationally—sometimes the whole, sometimes the part—and it is the cause of the numerous and vehement changes in the universe (I 88). The picture we get from these reports is of a universe vibrating with forces working *from within* and causing all the manifold occurrences in it. Each physical object and the changes it undergoes is explained by reference to a force moving in a region of matter. There is no demiurge outside *this* universe producing copies *in* it of forms *outside* it. There is no god situated at the periphery of *this* universe bringing about change in it through being desired. *This* universe is not just a colossal accident resulting from the random clashing of atoms in the void. The god of this universe is *within* it, extending right through every portion of it, moving it rationally and imbuing it with all the character it has.

Cleanthes, too, adhered to the view that the two principles in terms of which the universe can be described are the active and the passive, reason and unqualified substance, god and matter.[2]

The foregoing has shown, I trust, how Chrysippus' explanatory principles are related to those of his predecessors in the Stoa and

---

(I 87), on the other hand, says that οὐσία is used both for the matter of the whole and the matter of the parts.

[1] For a modern appreciation of this dynamism in Stoic philosophy, see Chapters I and II of S. Sambursky, *Physics of the Stoics* (London: Routledge and Kegan Paul, 1959).

[2] I 493, 494—the reports in which these principles are most richly characterized have Zeno as their subject.

how they compare with analogous principles held by other philosophers. A peculiar feature in Chrysippus' position is the way in which he regards so-called individual substances not as discrete units of matter, but rather as "parts" of one primary matter or substance. For example, he holds that "our natures are parts of the nature of the universe" (III 4). He maintains (II 317) that there is a primary matter which underlies things having qualities; this primary matter, we are told, admits of separation and fusion by way of its parts (κατὰ μέρη), and we take this to mean that the manifold of "individual objects" changes in innumerable ways—some of them becoming larger or smaller, for example—while the underlying substance or primary matter remains quantitatively constant.

Moreover in other fragments which are not immediately concerned with Chrysippus' δύο ἀρχαί we find material with the aid of which we are not only able to characterize Chrysippus' position more fully, but through which we can show how Chrysippus developed and supplied a theoretical foundation for Zeno's views.

Chalcidius reports in one passage that, for "the Stoics" "god is matter or an inseparable quality of matter." [1] It appears to have been Chrysippus' view also that unqualified matter is only an analytical category; that is, Chrysippus, like Aristotle, seems to take the view that unqualified matter does not, *in fact*, ever have a separate existence, but is always bound up with at least one quality. We have to use "appears" and "seems" in our account because we find nowhere in the fragments a statement quite so definite as that of Aristotle [2] with respect to the notion that unqualified matter never exists just by itself. However, we are told in one passage (II 596), in which the periodic destruction of the world is being discussed, that the world is always destroyed into fire, as into seed, from which the world is again generated. This would suggest, though it by no means proves, that the primary matter is never without *some* form. As the substratum of the formed world, the matter is, of course, molded in a manifold variety of ways. If we should expect ever to find it in its primordial state, it would be after the destruction of the world, but *even then*, we are told, it possesses the form of fire. Another fragment (II 581) lends strength to this interpretation; in this passage Diogenes Laertius is giving Chrysippus' view concerning the origin of the

---

[1] "...silva sit vel etiam qualitatem inseparabilem deum silvae...." I 87.
[2] Aristotle *de gen. et corr.* 329ª 25ff.

universe and he says, "The universe comes into being when the substance changes from fire through air into moisture. ... Now unless the substance is initially qualified as being fire, then a step in the process whereby the universe comes into being has been left out, namely, the passage from unqualified substance to fire substance. But if, in Chrysippus' view, there were such a phase, surely Laertius would have reported it in a passage in which it is his object to deal with each of the phases in the development of the universe out of the primordial substance. That Diogenes did not report it is indicative of its non-existence in Chrysippus' mind and this means that, for Chrysippus, before the universe came into being the primordial substance was already in a formed state, specifically, the state of fire.[1] And since each thing in the substance is created by god or the logos in it, we must assume that the logos has always been present in the substance. What is this logos or reason and what is its mode of existence in substance? The answer to this question leads us to a consideration of *pneuma* in Chrysippus' philosophy.

1b. *Pneuma*

There was current in the fourth century a widespread belief that life is bound up with warmth and that the material support of this warmth circulating in the body, is breath.[2] The view perhaps originated in Greek medicine, for the Hippocratic treatise on epilepsy develops the doctrine that the air breathed into the body provides it with life, motion, and consciousness; in short, the author [3] of

---

[1] It is true that in one Chrysippean fragment (II 580) we are told flatly that the four elements together constitute unqualified substance or matter, but, as I shall try to show when I deal with "the four elements", Diogenes can only mean that the unqualified substance, initially fire, *becomes* all four elements. Pohlenz, speaking of this subject and the ancient Stoa, says, "Der Urgrund, aus dem sich unsere Welt entwickelt, ist nicht die nur in gedanklicher Abstraktion bestehende qualitätslose Hyle, sondern die Materie, die bereits durch den Logos ihre erste, ursprüngliche Qualifizierung erhalten hat, die durch und durch feurige Ursubstanz." *Op. cit.*, I, 78.

[2] Pohlenz, *op. cit.*, I, pp. 73, 74.

[3] "Dass Hippokrates, selbst von Diogenes von Apollonia beeinflusst, der Begründer der Pneumalehre geworden ist, habe ich in meinem Buche 'Hippokrates und die Begründung der wissenschaftlichen Medizin' erwiesen (bes. S. 38ff. 84)." Pohlenz, *op. cit.*, Vol. II, p. 42. In spite of this I say merely "the author" because, as Edelstein, in his review of Pohlenz' book, has pointed out, "There is no book among the so-called Hippocratic writings which can be ascribed to Hippocrates himself." *American Journal of Philology* (Vol. LXI, April, 1940), p. 229. See also L. Edelstein, "The Genuine Works of Hippocrates", *Bulletin of the History of Medicine* (VII, 1939), pp. 236-248.

this treatise holds that breath is the soul of the organism. Aristotle probably derived his concept of the innate pneuma from the Sicilian medical school.[1] The doctrine of pneuma exercised the minds of the Peripatetics generally; it was, for example, the fundamental idea in the physiology and pathology of Diocles of Carystos.[2] Zeno explicitly formulated the argument that the entity upon whose exit life ceases must be the soul, and that since this thing is the warmth-maintaining pneuma, pneuma itself must be the soul (I 137, 138). Chrysippus takes over the doctrine from Zeno and Cleanthes, but extends the functions of the pneuma.[3]

What do the extant fragments tell us about Chrysippus' conception of pneuma? In the first place the pneuma, for Chrysippus, is composed of two substances, fire and air, and consequently is a mixture of hot and cold.[4] Secondly, the pneuma, in his view, is a binding agent; penetrating the whole material universe it unifies it; by means of this pneuma the universe holds together and its parts interact. (II 413). The fundamental unity of the primordial substance, which is characteristic of the monistic tendency in Stoicism is described by Alexander of Aphrodisias who reports that Chrysippus "assumes the whole of substance is unified by a certain pneuma which extends throughout it and by means of which it is held together and remains together and by which the whole is in sympathy with itself (συμπαθές ἐστιν αὐτῷ τὸ πᾶν)."[5] How this character of unity is preserved in the universe which evolves out of that substance will be shown below.[6] But I should note here that

---

[1] de gen. an. 736ᵇ 30ff. Solmsen, "Greek Philosophy and the Discovery of the Nerves", p. 174. For a discussion of a source more proximate than the Sicilian medical school, see Harald A. T. Reiche, *Empedocles' Mixture, Eudoxan Astronomy and Aristotle's Connate Pneuma* (Amsterdam: Adolf M. Hakkert, 1959), pp. 84-100.

[2] Werner Jaegar, "Das Pneuma im Lykeion", *Hermes* (vol. xlviii), pp. 29 ff. *Diokles von Karystos. Die griechische Medizin und die Schule des Aristoteles.* Berlin: W. de Gruyter & Co., 1938.

[3] "Wenn Kleanthes in seinem Hymnus (v. 9ff.) das Blitzfeuer preist, das durch alles hindurchgeht und überall Leben spendet, so wird seit Chrysipp das Gleiche vom Pneuma ausgesagt. Selbst die Gottheit, die Zenon als das schöpferische Feuer bestimmt hatte, wird jetzt lieber als das vernünftige Pneuma bezeichnet." Pohlenz, *op. cit.*, Vol. I, p. 74.

[4] 89 (II 841). See also 20 (II 471) where we are told that air in motion is like ether, so that they fall into a common category.

[5] II 473. *Cf.* II 912 where the universe is said to be animated by one mind (σύμπνουν) and coherent or "in sympathy with" (συμπαθῆ) itself.

[6] *Infra*, pp. 119ff.

Chrysippus clearly is a representative of the theory of cosmic sympathy.[1] Unfortunately there are no fragments setting forth the meaning and implications of this theory in Chrysippus' philosophy. But one may infer something about Chrysippus' doctrine of cosmic sympathy from his adherence to a monistic view of the cosmos and from his theory about the mixture of pneuma with all other things; for these doctrines together seem to imply at least that an occurrence of change in one part of the universe had an effect upon all the other parts of the universe, though neighboring parts were probably the ones affected immediately and perhaps those affected most acutely. This might very well be the meaning lying back of of the words, 'the whole is in sympathy with itself'. An example of sympathy cited in a fragment (II 1013), which is not explicitly Chrysippean, is that of the cut finger in whose condition the whole body shares.

Thirdly, the pneuma provides otherwise formless and motionless matter with qualities; in fact the qualities in any given object may be regarded as diversifications of pneuma, as air-like tensions in it (II 449). These give form to the material in which they are present. Fourthly, the pneuma, we are told (II 471), in words that remind us of the upward and downward movement of Heraclitus' fire "moves itself towards itself and away from itself or forwards and backwards." This is probably Chrysippus' version of Cleanthes' vibrant fire or vital tension.[2]

Finally just as pneuma is the power giving quality and shape to

---

[1] Cf. note 5, p. 100 above. Reinhardt, in his latest discussions of the doctrine of sympathy in Posidonius' philosophy ("Poseidonios", *Realencyclopädie*, cols. 653-656), also cites the passage we have quoted in the text above, but contends that here it "is something other than a doctrine of sympathy." (653). This is so, Reinhardt maintains, because "Bei Chrysipp ist es ein materieller Lebensträger, das Pneuma, das die gesamte Materie durchdringt und mit sich selbst kommunizierend macht." (654). But in Posidonius, Reinhardt argues, "wurde die Sympathie zur weltdurchdringenden Allkraft, zur Erklärung der Welträtsel, die auf einen verborgenen Zusammenhang aller Dingen wiesen." (cols. 654, 655). Reinhardt's reasoning strikes us as being lame. For he does not explain why Posidonius' substitution of an "Allkraft" for Chrysippus' material pneuma—both function as forces unifying the world and placing its parts in "sympathetic relations" with one another—entitles us to ascribe a "theory of sympathy" to Posidonius, but proscribes our ascription of such a theory to Chrysippus. Chrysippus, too, by the way, believed that there is a connection of all things with one another; where this connection is not conspicuous it is merely "verborgen". (II 973)

[2] I 563. Cf. Arnim, "Kleanthes", *Realencyclopädie*, cols. 565-566.

inert matter, it is the life-giving force in man; it is soul (II 879). Chrysippus' argument for this conclusion is similar to that of Zeno: we live and breath by the same thing; we breath by means of pneuma; therefore we live by pneuma; but that by which we live is soul. Therefore the soul is pneuma (II 879). As we have already seen, a contemporary school of medicine was holding "that psychic pneuma constitutes the 'vital principle' or soul in the living creature." [1] Chrysippus adds to the doctrine his view that the psychic pneuma splinters itself into pneumata or air currents having specialized functions.[2]

Most striking of all these descriptions is the third, for it attributes to the pneuma a function similar, if not identical, to that assigned to the active power, logos, or god. For, just as the active power creates each thing in the formless matter, the pneuma provides otherwise formless and motionless matter with qualities. And this dynamic character of pneuma, contraposed as it is here to the inert matter without quality, probably led Chrysippus to assume that the pneuma and the active power in the universe were one and the same thing. But none of the extant fragments makes such an identification explicit.

To summarize what has been said, there is an unqualified matter or substance through which a pneumatic current pulsates, and though these two elements can be separated in thought, they, in fact, do not exist independently. They are so closely wed and inter-penetrate to such a degree that they are, as it were, the two aspects, the passive and the active, of an eternal, unified mass, in terms of which the cycles, the ever recurring life and death of the universe and all that occurs in it, can be explained. If fire is the minimal qualification of the formless matter; that is, if substance when nearest to existing as unqualified, exists as fire, then the first quality which the pneuma induces by its vibratory movement through the substance, must be heat; or rather heat is the quality which the pneuma produces in the substance even when it is without all other qualities. To put this in another way, there never is a moment in the duration of substance when *no* quality at all is being produced in it by the active power of pneuma.

---

[1] *Supra*, p. 99. Pohlenz (*op. cit.*, I, 74) says it was a "volkstümlicher Schluss."

[2] *Infra*, pp. 129-130.

1c. *The categories*

It is appropriate at this juncture, before we go on to consider how, in Chrysippus' mind, the universe evolves out of this primordial fiery mass of substance, that we attempt to set forth the way in which he conceived the relation between substance and the changes it undergoes.

The two categories which he employs most frequently in this context are those of substance and quality. As we have already seen, he thinks of the pneuma as producing *qualities* in the otherwise formless *substance* (II 449). Also (II 316) he uses "substance" to describe not only the universal matter but particular matter or parts of the universal matter. And when he discusses individual or particular substances, he continues to make use of the substance-quality categories. In a long fragment (II 473) dealing with the kinds of mixture, to be discussed presently, Chrysippus uses the locutions, "substances and the qualities in them", "its own substance and the qualities in it", and "bodies and their own qualities".[1] And, just as the substance-quality relation is exemplified both on the macrocosmic level of the primordial substance and on the microcosmic level of individual substances, so is the pneuma present both in the universal substance as a whole and in the individual substances.[2]

Now, while we nowhere get a full-blown discussion of these individual substances, the language in several fragments is such as to lead to the conclusion that, for Chrysippus, every substance has a peculiar character which distinguishes it from every other substance. The matter of every individual substance is, to be sure, a "part" of the primordial substance or matter, but, by virtue of its qualities, each particular substance is a distinct individual.

That such was Chrysippus' view is already suggested in the fragment on mixture (II 473) just referred to. In this passage, wholly dedicated to an analysis of this doctrine, we are told that the bodies in a blend can be separated from one another "just because the mixed bodies in the blend preserve their own natures (τὰς αὐτῶν φύσεις)." Again, "the soul, having its own substantial existence (ἰδίαν ὑπόστασιν ἔχουσαν), like the body which contains

---

[1] τῶν τε οὐσιῶν καὶ τῶν ἐν αὐταῖς ποιοτήτων. τήν τε οἰκείαν οὐσίαν καὶ τὰς ἐν αὐτῇ ποιότητας. πολλὰ τῶν σωμάτων σώζειν τὰς ἑαυτῶν ποιότητας

[2] II 879. Where the pneuma is said to be present in the human body as soul.

it, preserves its own proper substance (τὴν οἰκείαν οὐσίαν).'' And of iron heated in a fire, Chrysippus held that ''each of them (the fire and the iron) preserves its own proper substance (τὴν οἰκείαν οὐσίαν).'' That each substance has distinctive qualities seems also to explain the terminology used in another fragment about mixture (II 481): each of the bodies which has been mixed is able to retain its own distinction or appearance (τὴν οἰκείαν ἐπιφάνιαν). Finally, we possess one ethical fragment (III 259) in which a similar locution is used. Believing that the virtues were qualities of the soul,[1] Chrysippus says in the fragment cited that the number of virtues ''depends on the peculiar nature of the substances as modified by the qualities.'' [2]

If the fragments thus far quoted make it already more than probable that Chrysippus regarded every particular substance as having its own individual character, one other fragment (II 397), a quotation from one of Chrysippus' books, sets forth this doctrine in almost explicit language—set forth though, to be sure, in a strange way, perhaps the more so because the report is taken from Plutarch who writes with a polemical intent and hence chooses from Chrysippus' text what suits his purposes.

''Two individuating qualities (δύο ἰδίως ποιοί),'' he says, ''cannot exist in the same substratum.'' As an illustration of his doctrine, he wants us to consider the case of two men, one whole in body and the other, missing a foot. If the first has his foot amputated, then the second perishes, because it is impossible for two individuating qualities to be present in the same substratum. When asked why the second perishes rather than the first, who after all had just had a foot amputated, Chrysippus replies, ''It is as it ought to be, for Dion, having had his foot amputated, reverts to the imperfect substance of Theon.''

To raise this point first, is Chrysippus here really answering the question asked or another, namely, why must *either* of the men perish? For Chrysippus actually seems to argue that if two individuating qualities cannot exist in the same substance, and if a man having only one foot, for the sake of example, be taken as this quality, then there cannot be two such men. Consequently one *or* the other must perish. He does not, in fact, explain why Theon rather than Dion must perish or the converse. The argument, there-

---

[1] III 255, 256.
[2] SVF II 259 — ἐν ταῖς οἰκείαις ὑπαλλαττομέναις κατὰ τὰς ποιότητας.

fore, is not to the point. But this is probably Plutarch's fault. As is his practice, he has here taken from Chrysippus' text only the portion that served his purpose and, in doing so, he has probably garbled the original sequence of the argument.

In any event the really important feature of the fragment is the Chrysippean doctrine that two individuating qualities—and from the example he uses it is obvious that he means two identical individuating qualities—cannot exist in the same substance. Obviously Chrysippus is here thinking of substance in its universal sense and of Dion and Theon as being separate qualifications of that substance. And what he appears to be saying is that every qualification of that primordial substance must have its own individual character. The case of Theon and Dion exemplifies the doctrine that if, in some area of the primordial substance, the same two individuating qualities exist, then that area will not be differentiated. But we must remember that such areas or parts of the primordial substance are themselves individual substances; it follows that each of them contains an individuating quality which differentiates it from every other individual substance, for no two individuating qualities can be identical.[1]

---

[1] Zeller also interpreted the ἰδίως ποιός in this way: "Da der ἰδίως ποιός ein Ding von allen anderen unterscheidet, versteht es sich von selbst, dass, wie Chrysippus bei Philo aetern. m. 951, B (501M.c. 9 Bern.) sagt, δύο εἰδοποιούς (was = ἰδίως ποιούς) ἐπὶ τῆς αὐτῆς οὐσίας ἀμήχανον συστῆναι." (III¹, 5th edit., p. 100 in note 2 which begins on p. 99). F. H. Coulson discusses the passage in an appendix to the Loeb Library edition of Philo which he translated (*Philo*, IX, Cambridge: Harvard Univ. Press, 1954) pp. 528, 529. Coulson says that Zeller's rendition of ἰδίως ποιός as "distinctive form" conveys to him no clear meaning, but, he himself goes on to say that, for Zeller, the ἰδίως ποιός distinguishes a thing from every other." This seems eminently intelligible to me. I cannot discern why Coulson (who does not state the reasons for his perplexity) is troubled by Zeller's interpretation. Professor Reesor has, admitting the "extremely difficult" nature of the passage, in her article, "The Stoic Concept of Quality" (*American Journal of Philology*, Vol. LXXV (January 1954), pp. 40-58) interpreted it in the following way: She, in what appears to be a highly-misleading way, renders ἰδίως ποιός with "qualified object" (the whole point of the ἰδίως is to signify that the substance so qualified has an individual or distinctive character; it is not just qualified; it is *peculiarly* qualified or qualified in a way that no other substance is). She then says, "...we may observe that Dion and Theon were at first one substance (man), but two qualified objects, whole-limbed and footless." (*op. cit.*, p. 47). This is only half right. Dion and Theon are, throughout their respective careers, one substance in the *universal* sense of that term, but that sense is *not* the generic sense, *man*, as Professor Reesor suggests. Chrysippus nowhere intimates that he believes in the existence of such generic substances. "Substance" in his philosophy is

If our interpretation be correct, the fragment confirms Chrysippus' thoroughgoing nominalism apparent in his logical theories. Every individual substance, though a "part" of the universal substance, has a quality which really individuates it and distinguishes it from every other.[1] Moreover, the fragment shows that it was right to interpret the common notions of Chrysippus in the sense of Berkeley's general ideas rather than of Locke's abstract ideas. If everything which exists has its own individual flavor, then one can speak of similarities among existing things (and presentations or images of them), but not meaningfully of a concept which, in some way, is like every member of some group of them.

In conclusion I should point out that Chrysippus nowhere outlines a systematic doctrine of the categories of being or of terms. This is a matter of decisive importance, for in the later Stoa the doctrine of categories is of great significance, and it has also been in the foreground of the most recent discussions, attempts having been made to trace it back to Chrysippus.[2]

---

used in two senses only, as I have tried to show in the text above: it signifies the universal, never increasing and never diminishing, primary, unqualified matter; and it signifies the parts of this matter, as qualified, and as undergoing change—in other words, what we call "individual things". The "imperfect substance" to which Dion reverts is the universal substance imperfectly or incompletely qualified in a certain way. And, since this universal substance cannot, in any portion of itself, have two (like) individuating qualities (for that portion would not, then, be differentiated), either Theon or Dion must perish. We agree with Professor Reesor when she says that, after Dion has undergone the amputation of his foot, he and Theon are "not one substance and two qualified objects, but one substance and one qualified object" (op. cit., p. 47), though she means by "substance" here "man" and we mean "universal substance" and though we would substitute for her "qualified object" (ἰδίως ποιός) "individuating quality".

[1] If our interpretation of Chrysippus on this point be correct, then it is certainly he who is the author of the following doctrine, set forth by Seneca (ep. 113, 16): "And no two living things are equal. Consider the bodies of all beings: every one has its particular colour, shape, and size. And among the other reasons for marvelling at the genius of the Divine Creator is, I believe, this—that amid all this abundance there is no repetition; even seemingly similar things are, on comparison, unlike. God has created all the great number of leaves that we behold: each, however, is stamped with its special pattern. All the many animals: none resembles another in size— always some difference!" (trans. by Richard M. Gummere, Loeb Library edit).

[2] Phillip De Lacy, "The Stoic Categories as Methodological Principles", *Proceedings of the American Philological Association* (Vol. LXXVI, 1945), pp. 246-263. Margaret E. Reesor, "The Stoic Categories", *American Journal of Philology*, Vol. LXXVIII (January, 1957), pp. 63-82. Pohlenz, *op. cit.*, *infra*, note 3, p. 107.

I do, of course, not mean to say that Chrysippus does not use any categories of being. Of the four categories usually attributed to the Stoa,[1] the first two, substance and quality, he employs often, as we have seen. The third, disposition (πὼς ἔχον), one might find alluded to in the fragment which reports that, in Chrysippus' view, virtue is a disposition, and that the emotions correspond to a state or disposition in the soul.[2] The fourth, relative disposition, appears in only one fragment (II 550).

But this material does not provide sufficient evidence for ascribing to Chrysippus a *doctrine* of categories. Rather does he seem to have employed them occasionally without giving them any special significance. The theories to the contrary are almost exclusively based on indirect evidence. This is true of Reesor and Pohlenz.[3] Since a full-fledged theory of the categories is attested only by the late authorities, Plotinus and Simplicius,[4] everything points to the conclusion that the systematization of these categories is post-Chrysippean.

1d. *Materialism*

One brief fragment (II 469) reports Chrysippus' affirmation that all things are bodies, and that body penetrates body. What Chrysippus means by "body" is not made clear, and no other fragment states it directly. However, the expression, "body penetrates body", suggests that he is thinking of primordial substance and pneuma, the second of which "penetrates" or "spreads through" the first.

Moreover, other Chrysippean fragments, compared with the doctrine of Zeno, indicate what he may have meant by "body". For Chrysippus, a cause[5] "has being and is a body", but that of which

---

[1] By Plotinus (II 371) and Simplicius (II 369): substratum (ὑποκείμενον), quality (ποιός), disposition (πὼς ἔχον), and relative disposition (πρός τί πως ἔχον).

[2] III 459. This is uncertain, however, because in this fragment the Greek term which I render "disposition" is διάθεσις.

[3] Reesor (*op. cit.*, p. 67) thinks, for example, the category of disposition was acknowledged by Chrysippus "since he described the soul as breath in a certain disposition." But the fragment she cites (II 806) does not contain Chrysippus' name. Pohlenz argues, partly on the basis of Chrysippus' conception of the soul, that this philosopher gave a deeper significance to the category of disposition (*op. cit.*, I, 70). He, too, cites a number of fragments as evidence (*op. cit.*, II, 40-41), which are not, in an obvious way, Chrysippean.

[4] *Supra*, note 1.

[5] In the section concerning Fate below Chrysippus' doctrine of causal chains is discussed more in detail.

it is the cause has neither being nor body (II 336). Zeno had held that that of which the cause is a cause is an "accident" (συμβεβηκός) or a "predicate" (κατηγόρημα); the cause is that through which something comes about; for example,[1] through wisdom "being wise" comes into being; through the soul, "living" comes into being; and through self-control, being self-controlled comes into existence. Now since Chrysippus, too, believed (II 336) that cause is the "that through which" something comes about, we may assume, I think, that he, too, would agree that self-control is that through which being self-controlled comes about. And on the basis of his other notions about cause, this would commit him to the view that self-control has being and is a body while the accident or predicate, "being self-controlled", neither has being nor body. Chrysippus, then, would say that a man's body, the pneuma coursing through it (his soul), and the qualities produced by that pneuma are corporeal, but that his particular acts, for example, being self-controlled on a given occasion, are incorporeal.

What, then, is the status of such acts? Is Chrysippus maintaining that they do not exist at all? On this question his view on time (II 509) throws some light. Past and future time, he says, in no way *exist* (ὑπαρχεῖν οὐδαμῶς); rather do they subsist (ὑφεστάναι), "just as predicates exist only when the acts (named by them) are taking place; for example, walking exists for me when I am walking, but does not exist when I am lying down or seated." The position which Chrysippus appears to maintain, then, is that the real existents in the world are bodies—the macrocosmic body of primordial substance, the microcosmic bodies which are "parts of" the primordial substance, the pneuma, and the qualities which the pneuma produces in substances, while events, the things that occur, or "predicates", as he and Zeno call them, are incorporeal and, as such, have an existence somewhere between non-being and bodies existing in the full sense of the word.

Chrysippus' affirmation of the corporeal nature of causes is a flat rejection of the incorporeal causes of Plato (the Ideas) and Aristotle (the unmoved mover). But a critique of the Platonic Ideas, as has already been indicated,[2] had been formulated before the time of the Stoics. Antisthenes, for example, had maintained that every existing thing is a body. And Zeno and Chrysippus, it is apparent,

---

[1] These examples appear in the Zeno fragment (I 89).
[2] *Supra*, pp. 23-24.

are continuing and systematizing that tradition.[1] The importance
of their materialism, as it developed for "the Stoics" generally,
lies in the attempt to fix body as the profound and real level of
being while maintaining another level of existence on the surface
of or at the periphery, as it were, of being, a level which comprises
happenings, acts, or events. At least the ground for such an interpretation can be found in the extant Zenonian and Chrysippean
fragments. It is no easy matter to judge how far it was carried by
them.[2]

1e. *Mixture*

Zeno had assumed (I 92) that bodies are thoroughly mixed
(δι' ὅλου κεκράννυσθαι); that is, two bodies so completely inter-
penetrate that both are present in the same place. If substance
and pneuma be taken as examples of bodies, how can the second
penetrate or spread through the first? There were within the Stoa
several views concerning this matter, but it was that of Chrysippus
which was most highly esteemed (II 470). He sought to solve this
paradox with his theory of "blending" (κρᾶσις), and perhaps it can
best be understood against the background of analogous theories
proposed by Aristotle and Epicurus.

Aristotle explained the "combination" (μίξις) of bodies by means
of his distinction between the potential and the actual.[3] It seemed
to him that "combination" had to be distinguished from juxtaposition, on one hand, and from a mere destruction of the constituents
in the compound, on the other. When two bodies "combine", they
are not simply set one beside the other, each persisting unaltered.
Nor is one of them destroyed, because then it would have ceased
to exist nor are both destroyed, because then neither would *be*, and
therefore, Aristotle implies, one could not continue meaningfully
to speak of them. The constituents in a compound body, he holds,
continue to exist because they can be separated out from the compound again, though they do not exist actually. And it is in this
sense that they exist potentially in the compound, *viz.*, that they
can be said not to have been destroyed upon their entry into it.[4]

---

[1] Plato, *Sophist* 246ªff. *Cf.* Karl Praechter, *Die Philosophie des Altertums*,
12th edit. (Berlin: S. Mittler & Sohn, 1926), p. 162.

[2] *Cf.* Émile Bréhier, *La Théorie des Incorporels dans L'Ancien Stoicisme*
(Paris: Librairie Alphonse Picard & Fils, 1908), especially pp. 10-13.

[3] *de gen. et corrupt.* 327ª 30ff.

[4] *Ibid.* 327ᵇ 23-33.

One further Aristotelian view is relevant to the interpretation of Chrysippus' doctrine. Aristotle held that some things which have the same matter are "such as to act upon one another and to suffer action from one another"; that is, they "reciprocate" (ἀντιστρέφει).[1] But if a large quantity of one of these reciprocating materials is brought together with a small quantity of another of them, the effect produced is not a combination but rather a transformation of the latter material into the former; there comes about "an increase of the dominant." Therefore, a drop of wine does not "combine" (οὐ μίγνυται) with ten thousand gallons of water, but is rather transformed into water.[2]

Epicurus, following Democritus,[3] held that compound bodies were generated not from a "mixture"[4] of the atoms, but either from their mere co-existence in the void even at a great distance or from their interlacing with one another.[5] As for the first possibility, rare compounds such as light and air are formed by those atoms which rebound to a great distance from one another.[6] As for the second, hard dense compounds, such as rock and iron, are formed by atoms which have become interlocked or entangled,[7] and liquids are formed by atoms enclosed in a sheath of entangled atoms.[8]

Chrysippus distinguished three ways in which bodies combine (II 473). The first two correspond to conventional types. One is juxtaposition (παράθεσις), or mechanical mixture, in which mode of combining each of the ingredients maintains its own qualities and individuality; an example of juxtaposition is the relation among the beans and grains of wheat in a heap. It is the kind of juxtaposition which Aristotle refused to call a combination or mixture

---

[1] *Ibid.* 328ᵃ 19-21.

[2] *Ibid.* 328ᵃ 23-28.

[3] And followed by Lucretius (*de rerum natura*) ii. 85-111. Bailey *op. cit.*, p. 339.

[4] Plutarch *adv. Colotem* 1112B, where Plutarch denies that what the Epicureans call coming to be (γένεσις) is either a mixture (μίξις) or a cohesion (κόλλησις).

[5] *Letter to Herodotus apud* D.L. X.43. Also Bailey, *op. cit.*, pp. 339-341.

[6] *Ibid.* Also Lucretius ii. 98, 107, 108, and 112-120 where he gives as examples the sun and light.

[7] τύχωσι τῇ περιπλοκῇ κεκλειμέναι *Letter to Herodotus apud* D. L. x. 43. Lucretius ii. 100-105 for examples.

[8] στεγαζόμενοι παρὰ τῶν πλεκτικῶν *Letter to Herodotus apud* D. L. x. 43. No examples provided, but see Bailey, *op. cit.*, pp. 340-341.

and the only kind Epicurus' premises permitted, [1] though Epicurus believed that new qualities might arise in the compound body, because the compound body is more than the aggregate of atoms constituting it.[2] The second mode of combining is that called "confusion" (σύγχυσις) by Chrysippus (II 473); the ingredients in a confused body are destroyed and a new body arises from their combining together in this way. The generic example of confused bodies cited by Chrysippus is the medical drug. Presumably, any chemical compound would be, in his terms, a confusion. Aristotle, it will be remembered, refused to give the name "combination" also to this kind of mixture.

It is the third kind of Chrysippean compound which is revolutionary in character. Chrysippus calls (II 475) it a blending (κρᾶσις) or a mixture (μίξις).[3] The ingredients in a blend or mixture completely interpenetrate one another in such way that each preserves its own substance and the qualities in it. A palmary example of such a blend, in Chrysippus' view, is the mixture of body and soul. That the category of "blending" was introduced to explain the manner in which pneuma penetrates bodies, providing them with cohesive force, and generating properties in them, is evidenced by Alexander's citing, in the same fragment (II 473) in which he describes Chrysippus' blend or mixture, examples of blends such as the soul's penetration of the body, the "nature" of plants and the "state" of inorganic bodies; the nature and state are to plants and inorganic bodies respectively what soul is to body, namely, forms of pneuma wholly penetrating matter without losing its qualities.

In order to prove the existence of these kinds of mixtures Chrysippus appeals to common notions [4] and he employs analogies to bolster his view that blendings occur. Just as we do things with the help of others which we cannot do by ourselves; and just as grapevines, which could not stand by themselves, do so by entwining with one another, so may certain bodies be unified by completely

---

[1] "Whatever Epicurus' conception of combination may be, it is of a purely mechanical union, in which each atom throughout retains its own individuality and may at any moment by means of the appropriate blow, be set free from the compound." Bailey *op. cit.*, p. 348.

[2] *Ibid.* p. 356.

[3] In one passage (II 471) we are told that *the Stoics* called this form of combining "blending" if the ingredients were liquid bodies and "mixing" if they were dry bodies.

[4] *Supra*, pp. 60-62.

interpenetrating throughout, while each preserves its own quality
(II 473). Again, there are compounds which can be broken down
into their ingredients; this, he says, could not be the case if the
ingredients had not preserved their own natures.[1] Such a separation
is effected, for example, in a blend of wine and water when an oiled
sponge is immersed in the blend and the water alone is absorbed
into the sponge (II 471). The most dramatic example of a blend is
that given by Chrysippus in explicit opposition to Aristotle. A drop
of wine, Chrysippus maintained (II 479), having been thrown into
the sea, "blends" with every part of it. And, in another passage
(II 480), he goes so far as to say that the drop of wine permeates
the whole universe!

The significance of the concept of blend is, of course, that it is
meant to explain the relation of body and soul.[2] The soul pneuma
is a body (II 790, 791) that penetrates every part of the animal body
(II 879). Sambursky has rightly suggested[3] that the example quoted
last was especially apt because the pneuma of the soul blended with
the body is regarded as a highly-rarified mixture. Remembering
that the soul is made up of air and fire, one may find that the example
of frankincense, which becomes highly rarified when burned and
yet preserves its qualities (II 473), is also a very decisive one.[4]

1f. *Motion, place, time, and the infinite*

Aristotle had maintained that there were four kinds of motion:
coming to be and passing away (with respect to substance); alteration (with respect to quality); increase and diminution (with respect
to quantity); and locomotion (with respect to place).[5] He employs
for all these kinds of motion the generic term "change" (μεταβολή),

---

[1] Alexander is incredulous on this point (II 481).

[2] Verbeke, too, points out that this was the problem for which the doctrine
of κρᾶσις was formulated as a solution. G. Verbeke, *L'Évolution de la
Doctrine du Pneuma* (Paris: Desclée de Brouwer, 1945), pp. 63, 66.

[3] Sambursky, *op. cit.*, pp. 15-16.

[4] Edelstein has reminded me that in the later discussions of the Stoic
concept of blend, the critics again and again harp on its paradoxical character,
and have no difficulty in branding it as logically unsound. One will perhaps
be less harsh in one's judgment if one recalls the fact which I have stressed,
namely, that this concept was mainly meant to explain the interrelation of
body and soul. It is a problem that has not proved to be less cumbersome
for other philosophers and has given rise to a number of theories no less
paradoxical than the Stoic one.

[5] *Physica* 201ᵃ 10-15. In the *Categories* (15ᵃ 13, 14) he considers each of
these separately and therefore concludes that there are six kinds of movement.

while "movement" (κίνησις) denotes all the forms of motion except that which takes place with respect to substance.[1] He defines motion as "the fulfillment of what exists potentially, insofar as it exists potentially."[2]

There is one fragment (II 492) in which Arius Didymus—no mean source—attempted to sum up Chrysippus' doctrine of motion. Because of its brevity and because of its terminology, which coincides in part with that of Aristotle, it is not easy to disentangle the various ideas and to recover their original context.[3] For Chrysippus, Arius says, "motion (κίνησις) is change (μεταβολή) with respect to place, either wholly or in part, or change (μεταλλαγή) from a place, either wholly or in part." Of the alternatives here proposed the second, "change from a place", probably is meant to state more specifically or precisely the first alternative, "change with respect to place." For "change with respect to place" (μεταβολὴ κατὰ τόπον) is exactly the expression Aristotle had used to designate *locomotion*.[4] And "change from a place", Chrysippus' phrase, is, I think, merely a more concrete description of locomotion than the Aristotelian "change with respect to place". But what about the words "either wholly or in part"? Are they to be interpreted: "with respect to the whole (universe) or with respect to a part (of the universe)"? It seems impossible to give a definite answer to this question.

So far Chrysippus has used "motion" to designate locomotion or change from one place to another, one aspect of the Aristotelian doctrine of motion. The immediately following terms show that he used the term also to denominate change with respect to form (σχῆμα). By "form" he apparently means the state or condition of a thing (σχέσις), for he maintains that there are two kinds of rest correlative with the two kinds of motion: "rest" means, on the one hand, absence of motion (locomotion) in a body and, on the other, it means that *the state* of the body (σώματος σχέσις) is the same at the present moment as it was before. As I have pointed out,[5] the pneuma induces a state or condition in a body and Chrysippus holds (III 459) that the virtues (qualities) of the soul correspond

---

[1] *Physica* 201ᵃ 8, 9 and the note on the passage in the Oxford translation.

[2] *Ibid.* 201ᵃ 10, 11.

[3] *Cf.* Pierre Duhem, *Le Système du Monde*. Histoire des doctrines cosmologiques de Platon à Copernic (Paris: Librairie Scientifique A. Hermann et Fils, 1913), Vol. I, p. 310.

[4] *Categories* 15ᵃ 14.

[5] *Supra*, pp. 100-102; 111.

to its state or condition. Probably, then, a body's state, for him, determines not only its qualities, but its quantity and its duration or its coming into being and passing away. That is, change with respect to state or condition would embrace all the Aristotelian forms of change or motion other than locomotion. If this is the correct interpretation, it would account for Chrysippus' silence with respect to the kind of change Aristotle called coming to be and passing away, alteration, and increase and dimunition.

In addition to these two kinds of motion, locomotion and change with respect to state or condition, there are, according to Arius, two primary motions (and here he must mean locomotion), namely, rectilinear and curvilinear, from which a great variety of motions can be compounded.[1]

Aristotle believes that if something is place it has the following five attributes: (i) it "is what contains that of which it is the place;" (ii) it "is no part of the thing"; (iii) it "is neither less nor greater than the thing" (occupying it); (iv) it "can be left behind the thing and is separable"; (v) it admits of the distinction of up and down, and each of the bodies is naturally carried to its appropriate place and rests there, and this makes the place either up or down." [2] Turning to Chrysippus' definition of place, we find that he defines (II 503) it as that which either is occupied by some existing thing or is capable of being so occupied. In other words, he ascribes to place one (the first) and possibly two (the fourth) of the characteristics assigned to it by Aristotle. The Aristotelian theory of place must have been very much in his mind, for the Stagirite had supposed that the place a thing occupies is neither less nor greater than the occupying thing (characteristic iii above), and in Arius' report (II 503) the question is raised, and abruptly dropped, concerning whether either is greater than the other.

As for time, Chrysippus defines (II 509) it as a dimension of movement insofar as it is said to be a measure of swiftness and

---

[1] II 492. These species of locomotion were known by Aristotle (*Physica* 261^b 28ff.) and Plato (*Timaeus* 34A; *Laws* 893^{c}ff.). *Cf.* Friedrich Solmsen, *Aristotle's System of the Physical World* (Ithaca, New York: Cornell University Press, 1960), p. 176.

[2] *Physica* 210^b 39-211^a 6 (Oxford trans.). Max Jammer, *Concepts of Space. The History of the Theories of Space in Physics* (New York: Harper & Brothers, 1960 (f.p. 1954)), pp. 15-24, for an excellent discussion of the relationship between Aristotle's "theory of place or a theory of positions in space" (*Ibid.*, p. 15) and the "Stoic" doctrine of space.

slowness, or it is a dimension corresponding to the movements of the heavens. Everything, the report continues, is moved and exists in time. It is infinite in each direction and since it is continuous, infinitely divisible. It follows that no time is completely present. One might say in a loose sense that a given moment of time is present by saying, for example, "It is *now* 10:30 a.m." But, strictly speaking, no moment is a present moment. If Chrysippus were to consider the minute between 10:30 and 10:31 as an instance of a "present moment", I suppose he would simply lop it into two parts, thirty seconds spilling over into the past, the other thirty backing up into the future.

In three reports by two writers[1] it is said that "past time and future time do not exist but subsist; only present time exists." The only clarification offered is in the form of an analogy (II 509). The present exists in the same way that predicates are truly applicable. Walking exists for me when I am walking; but if I am seated, it does not exist for me. But this is not helpful in showing us what is meant by "subsist", nor does it seem to say more about the existence of the present moment of time than that when it exists, it exists. Given Chrysippus' earlier admonition never to say, in strict parlance, that a moment of time is present, one may assume that whatever he now means by the *existence* of the present moment, as distinguished from the subsistence of the past and future, the locution itself is a loose one. I gather from Chrysippus' obvious sensitiveness to the continuous nature of time that he wishes to say that in any so-called moment of time, there is some past, some present, and some future. And, perhaps, this is what he intends also when, instead of altogether denying existence to the past and future while the present moment exists, he gives them a somewhat more substantial status by saying of them that they *subsist*.

This is not a very satisfactory definition of time, or rather, not a very fully developed one; but, even so, it is obvious that Chrysippus was troubled by what is vexatious in time—once one begins to ponder its nature.[2] These words of a contemporary philosopher

---

[1] II 509 — Stobaeus
II 517 — Plutarch
II 518 — Plutarch

[2] "Quid est tempus ? . . . si nemo ex me quaerat, scio; si quaerenti explicare uelem, nescio." St. Augustine, *Confessions*, xi. 14, 17.

would not have been meaningless for him: "Time always contains an element of non-existence, and yet it exists. . . . Where is the abyss of non-existence out of which emerges the present, and into which it sinks back again?"[1] Another factor to be born in mind is the following: though Aristotle raises the question—if there were no soul, would there be any time?[2]—it is nevertheless characteristic of the analyses of time in antiquity (and that of Chrysippus is no exception) that they restrict themselves to objective time, that is, to time as objectively determined by the revolution of the celestial spheres; the psychological analyses of time begin only with St. Augustine.[3]

Closely connected with the problem of time is that of infinity. We possess four fragments[4] in which something is reported about Chrysippus' view of the infinite. The first (II 482), as Arnim has constituted it, combines two seemingly incompatible reports. We are told by Stobaeus that, for Chrysippus, bodies, surfaces, lines, places, the void, and time are divisible *ad infinitum*. Diogenes, however, reports that Chrysippus did not speak of division *ad infinitum* but rather said that a body was "infinitely divisible". The reason for Chrysippus' preferring the latter way of talking, as Diogenes says, is because the process of division goes on without cessation; the expression, *"ad infinitum"* wrongly suggests that there is an infinite into which a body is divisible. Though one cannot speak with definiteness, Chrysippus appears to be taking Aristotle's stand [5] with respect to the infinite divisibility of spatial magnitudes: namely, that to say a body is infinitely divisible is to say that it is potentially infinite; that is, one may go on dividing it without end. It is likely that Stobaeus or his source has simply used the convenient rubric "divisibility *ad infinitum*" for purposes of classifying Chrysippus, without adding the qualification attaching to his doctrine.

The second (II 484) of the fragments contains a remarkable

---

[1] Erich Frank, *Philosophical Understanding and Religious Truth* (New York: Oxford University Press, 1945), p. 64.

[2] *Physica* 223ᵃ 22. *Cf.* John F. Callahan, *Four Views of Time in Ancient Philosophy* (Cambridge: Harvard University Press, 1948), pp. 75-76.

[3] Frank, *op. cit.*, Chapter III — "Creation and Time", and especially note #41.

[4] II 482, II 484, II 483, II 489.

[5] *Physica* 206ᵃ 16-36. *Cf. Aristotle's Physics* (ed. W. D. Ross, Oxford: Clarendon Press, 1936), Introduction, p. 50.

formulation of "the main characteristic of the infinite set".[1] That this is Chrysippus' formulation I conclude from the fact that to the problem raised here Plutarch gives Chrysippus' reply [2] in a fragment (II 483) which will be discussed presently. Its gist is that, since a man and his finger have an infinite number of parts as do the universe and a man, it cannot be said that a man has more parts than does his finger nor that the universe has more parts than a man. The missing premise in this enthymeme is that an infinite set is one having a subset whose members are as many as are the members of the set.[3]

In the third fragment of the series (III 483) Chrysippus maintains that the large macroscopic parts of the body—the head, the trunk, the legs—are countable. But he says, if we are asked about "the least (or extreme) parts" (τὰ ἔσχατα μέρη), "we are to deny that the body is composed of any number of parts, either an infinite or a finite number." Chrysippus here rejects the Epicurean doctrine (and that of Anaxagoras) that bodies are composed of indivisible particles. And since the body does not consist of an aggregate of small particles at all, there is no sense in which one could ask (or answer) whether the body's particles are finite or infinite. The body is a continuum, a part of substance bound together or unified by pneuma. And Chrysippus would probably hold that, like all continua, the body is infinitely divisible, though, as he here says, you cannot say that the body is composed by an infinite (or finite) number of microscopic parts. It does not consist of such parts at all, and therefore concepts applicable to countable aggregates are not applicable to it.[4]

In still another of the fragments (II 489) in this group Chrysippus is asked the question: if a cone is divided by a plane parallel to its base, are the surfaces of the segments equal or unequal? If they are equal, the cone becomes a cylinder; if they are unequal, the

---

[1] Sambursky, op. cit., p. 97.

[2] When Lamprias asks Diadumenus how the Stoics handled the problem, Diadumenus gives Chrysippus' reply (II 483).

[3] "This property of the infinite set was rediscovered after the Stoics by Galileo who shows the equivalence of the denumerable set of natural numbers and its subset of square numbers." Sambursky, op. cit., p. 97.

[4] If it seems that Chrysippus, in this fragment, contradicts his opinions as reported in fragment II 484 and discussed above, it may help to recall that there when the "parts" of the finger were mentioned, the author remarks parenthetically "for division increases bodies to an infinite number."

cone's surface becomes uneven like that of a washboard. Chrysippus replied that the surfaces are neither equal nor unequal.

Here Chrysippus is, in effect, negating the law of excluded middle with respect to the pair of qualities, equal and unequal. The same negation is presupposed in the first part of the same fragment where he implies that the sides of a pyramid are neither equal nor unequal. Luria calls this a "spezifisch stoische Annahme" and believes that the two examples taken together indicate that Chrysippus reviewed the atomistic theses and problems systematically and sought to solve them on Stoic principles.[1] Sambursky's convincing interpretation of the passage shows that Chrysippus' formula, "neither equal nor unequal", anticipated some of the notions of the infinitesimal calculus, namely, "the limit and the process of convergence towards a limit." [2] If this is the case, it is particularly regrettable that so little of the Chrysippean material in this sphere of investigation is extant. Nevertheless, it is adequate to show that the Stoa concerned itself not just with moral philosophy, but with topics somewhat removed from the problems of human conduct.

Here we conclude our account of the fundamental notions in Chrysippus' natural philosophy. We have discussed, as fully as the extant fragments permit, his doctrine concerning the two principles of the universe, pneuma, the categories, materialism, mixture, motion, place, time and the infinite. And we have tried to make clear to the reader that, by developing certain germs he found in Zeno's explanatory principles, he gave to Stoicism a strong monistic

---

[1] S. Luria, "Die Infinitesimaltheorie der antiken Atomisten", *Quellen und Studien zur Geschichte der Mathematik, Astronomie und Physik* (Berlin: Julius Springer, 1932, pp. 106-185), p. 171.

[2] Sambursky, *op. cit.*, p. 89. The following remarks by Sambursky constitute his interpretation of this passage: "Characteristically, the statement is given a form negating the law of the excluded middle. Indeed, this law is violated if the essentially static notions of equal and unequal are applied to the conception of a dynamic approach to zero. The surface of any section of the cone is either unequal to that of a given section if the distance between both is unequal to zero, or both surfaces are equal if the distance between the sections is zero—*tertium non datur*. However, if we consider the infinite series of sections which is approaching the given section when the distance between each member of the series and the fixed section is approaching zero, we have to discard the static concept of equal and unequal, taking into account that for each given difference in surfaces one can determine a distance which will yield a still smaller difference. This is what Chrysippos [sic] intended to express by the formula 'neither equal nor unequal'." pp. 93, 94.

flavor; and that his doctrine of the individuating quality furnishes the basis for the nominalistic tendency in his epistemology. His doctrine of blending was an attempt to explain the interaction of the two eternal "principles" which he had inherited from Zeno. We also introduced, with respect to some of the topics treated, analogous doctrines held by Plato and Aristotle in order to impress upon the reader that Chrysippus was a philosopher who reflected upon and attempted solutions for some of the same problems that had preoccupied two of the giants in the Greek philosophical tradition.

2. THE UNIVERSE

One might be inclined to use Democritean terms to describe Chrysippus' world and represent it as the void containing only one atom. Like Democritus' void, that in Chrysippus' world is infinite; like Democritus' atoms, the one atom forming the Chrysippean universe is a compact, unified, self-contained entity, having no vacuous interstices whatsoever. But there the illustrative value of atomistic notions breaks down. The heterogeneous and dynamic structure of Chrysippus' universe bears no likeness at all to the homogeneous and passive nature of an atom.

2a. *Its generation*

Like Zeno (I 102) and Cleanthes,[1] and before, even Aristotle,[2] Chrysippus recognized four basic elements out of which all other things are composed. The formation of these elements represents the intermediary phase through which the primordial fiery substance is converted into the universe. As Arius Didymus reports (II 413), Chrysippus uses the term "element" in a threefold way. In the first he applies it to fire, and here he undoubtedly means the primordial fiery substance, for it is this fire, we are told (II 413), from which the remaining elements derive their existence and it is into it that they are dissolved. Secondly, he applies it to all four elements—fire, air, water, and earth, for it is from them that all other things derive their existence. The formulation of the third sense of "element" is unfortunately missing in the text of Arius; the text resumes with the following words, which seem to describe

---

[1] Hans von Arnim, "Kleanthes", *Paulys Realencyclopädie der Classischen Altertumwissenschaft* (Stuttgart: Alfred Druckenmüller, 1921), col. 563.

[2] *de gen. et corrupt.* 330ᵃ 25-330ᵇ 2.

all over again the primordial fiery substance: "that which exists first in such way as to generate from itself in a methodical way up to the end and from there to receive the dissolution into itself in the same way."

Each of the Chrysippean elements, unlike those of Aristotle, has one primary property: fire is hot; air is cold; water is moist; earth is dry.[1] Fire changes into air, air into water, and water into earth, each change being effected by a change in the density of the element from which the change takes its start (II 413). All other things, plants, and animals are composed of these elements and are periodically dissolved into the basic elements, and the elements then, in turn, convert back into fire (II 413).

Fire and air are light and move upwards; water and earth are heavy and are born downwards (II 434, 555). What permanence the universe has is derived from the fact that the four elements equalize its weight (II 555). Fire is the highest of the elements and the sphere of the fixed stars is generated in it; next, working inwardly, comes the air, then the water, then the earth, "which is the center of all things".

In some of the Chrysippean fragments—most of them cosmological—the term which names Aristotle's fifth element, "ether," sometimes [2] occurs. In them it is used variously to signify highly rarified fire (II 579), the purest and most highly rarified part of the universe (II 527), god, reason, or the governing part of the universe (II 634, 642, 644). Chrysippus did not recognize a fifth element as such, and the doxographers are aware that he used the term interchangeably with "fire", the term which denotes the purest of the elements.[3]

---

[1] (II 580). I say "primary" because Arius makes his report using the definite article, i.e., fire is *the* hot element. Aristotle's elements have the following qualities: fire is hot and dry; air is hot and moist; water is cold and moist; earth is cold and dry. *de gen. et corrupt.* 330^{b} 5, 6.

[2] II 634, 642, 527, 1077.

[3] II 555, 580, 1067; but see also II 601 for the Stoa in general. Verbeke (*op. cit.*, p. 74) thinks that pneuma in Chrysippus' philosophy "est rebaissé au rang des quatre elements", while with Zeno, and particularly with Cleanthes, it had more the characteristic of Aristotle's fifth element. But, in the first place, Verbeke argues from a false premise, for he asserts that "Chrysippe ne parle pas d'un mouvement circulaire." But see II 492 and *supra*, p. 114. Secondly, Chrysippus has a tendency to give to the logos or pneumatic component in the primordial fiery substance the title "ether" and, since the four elements are derived from this, one cannot speak of a "depreciation" of the pneuma to the level of the elements in Chrysippus' system.

Chrysippus, like Zeno, believed that the many-named active principle in the universe—God, reason, fate, Zeus, the seminal reason of the universe, and pneuma, according to my inference—converted the whole substance (τὴν πᾶσαν οὐσίαν), which must have been in a fiery state, through air into water.[1] God, as seminal reason, remains in the water, "as the sperm wanders about in the womb", and he next produces the four elements. Here the difference between the Aristotelian and Chrysippean views begins to emerge, but a fuller discussion of it will be more appropriate at the conclusion of the following section.

2b. *Its nature*

Leaving aside the infinite void which surrounds it, the Chrysippean universe may be divided into two parts, one of which rotates around the other (II 527).[2] The rotating part is the ether or heaven, and in it the stars and planets are placed. An outermost sphere contains in its concave surface the fixed stars which are innumerable. Within this sphere are nine other concentric spheres, seven of which contain one planet each on their concave surfaces. From the outermost to the inmost, not counting the all-embracing sphere of the fixed stars, there come consecutively the spheres of Saturn, Jupiter, Mercury, Mars, Venus, the sun, the moon, the air, and finally, the sphere of water surrounding the earth. Visible are those portions of the earth which, being elevated sufficiently, protrude through the surrounding water. If small, these protrusions are called "islands", and, if large, they are named "continents" by men ignorant of the fact that they, too, are surrounded by water.

It is to be noted that, even though Chrysippus was clearly of the opinion that there existed outside the universe an infinite void, there is no evidence that he conceived this infinite void and the universe as being constituents of some larger unity. He is concerned merely with defining the universe as a composite whole of ether and

---

[1] II 580. Cleanthes deviates from both Zeno and Chrysippus on this point; he holds that not all the fiery substance is converted into water; an outer layer of the fiery substance is preserved. v. Arnim, "Kleanthes", *Realencyclopädie*, col. 564.

[2] For the similarity of this passage to the pseudo-Aristotelian *de mundo*, cf. Diels, *Doxographi Graeci*, p. 465. See also E. S. Forster's introduction to his translation of *de mundo* in the Oxford collection of Aristotle's works for a brief summary of Capelle's examination (*Neue Jahrbücher*, XV, 1905, pp. 529-68) of the treatise. Capelle concluded that *de mundo* was based on two works, *Meteorological Doctrine* and *On the Cosmos*, both by Posidonius.

earth and the creatures in them or as the composite whole of gods and men and the things that have been produced for them (II 527) and, in another breath, he says that it *is* god (II 636). It evolves into a unified living being by virtue of the reason or divine active element coursing through it. Chrysippus maintained that the universe was a living being, rational, and intellectual (II 633). It also becomes a self-sufficient being, and it is the only being which enjoys this most highly-prized of all qualities.[1] As he explains in his book, *On Providence*, "The universe alone is said to be self-sufficient, because it alone has in itself all the things which it needs. And it is nourished and increased from itself, while the other parts change into one another" (II 604). Thus the Chrysippean universe, being god, possesses the self-sufficiency which both Epicurus and Aristotle ascribed to their gods.[2]

That the universe must have a soul, Chrysippus argues (II 633) from the circumstance that each of our souls is a detached fragment of it. His argument (II 633) for the view that it is a living being is that nothing is better than the universe, and living beings are better than non-living beings. Moreover as the soul in man permeates every part of his body, so cosmic reason penetrates into every part of the universe; and just as one part of man's soul is the governing part, so the soul of the universe has its governing part, namely, the ether.[3] Reason, on the other hand, permeates some parts of the universe more; some parts, less (II 634). In the case of bones and sinews it is a disposition or a binding force and, in the ruling part of the whole, it is unalloyed reason.

Finally, the world is wise and divine (II 641), and Chrysippus employs an *a fortiori* argument to prove this. Man's nature is not perfect, and yet it exhibits virtue; "how much more easily is it

---

[1] Aristotle expresses the Greek view generally when he says, "the final good is thought to be self-sufficient" *EN* 1097ᵇ 6, 7. *Cf.* the Epicurean fragment, "Self-sufficiency is the greatest of all riches." Usener 474. Quoted by Bailey, *op. cit.*, p. 532.

[2] Aristotle, *Meta.* 1091ᵇ 6, 7. Epicurus nowhere explicitly attributes self-sufficiency to the gods, but that they possessed this quality can be inferred from a passage in Lucretius: "For it is essential to the very nature of deity that it should enjoy immortal existence in utter tranquillity, aloof and detached from our affairs. It is free from all pain and peril, strong in its own resources, exempt from any need of us, indifferent to our merits and immune from anger." ii. 646-651. Trans. by R. E. Latham.

[3] II 633, 642, 644. Cleanthes had held (I 499) that the governing part of the universe is the sun.

exhibited in the world" than which there is nothing more perfect (II 641). But if the world possesses virtue, it is wise and, consequently, divine (*ibid.*). It is interesting to note that, in preparing the ground for this argument, Chrysippus affirms (*ibid.*) the Aristotelian teleological principle that "all things are better in their perfect and mature forms." His examples are the horse, dog, man, all of whom are "better than" respectively the foal, pup, and boy.

Chrysippus is also at one with Aristotle in his doctrine that there is one universe in space and that there are no interstices in it. It is continuous throughout. Like Aristotle, he employs the four elements as building blocks, but in his system they play a somewhat less basic role inasmuch as they are periodically derived from and dissolved into a more fundamental substance. As we have seen our philosopher does not recognize Aristotle's ether as a distinct element.

Aristotle's "conviction that movement is an immanent tendency of nature and of natural objects" [1] approaches the dynamism which characterizes the Chrysippean universe, but the Stagirite's unmoved mover, which engenders movement by being desired, sharply distinguishes his cosmology from that of Chrysippus. The Stoic philosopher's god engenders movement and qualities by extending through the universe and by mixing with its parts. The biological simile used to express this relation—that of sperm or seed coursing through the womb—expresses the dynamic, intimate and constant character of the relation between the forming power and the matter formed in the Chrysippean cosmos. The relationship between an entity that desires and a desired object can be—though it is not so essentially—static, remote and interrupted.

2c. *The conflagration*

Chrysippus, and indeed the ancient Stoa generally,[2] held that periodically the universe changes into fiery ether; the period in which the conflagration occurs is called the Great Year (II 596). But Chrysippus insisted that what might appear to be a destruction was not that at all, but only a *change* of the universe into fire.[3] The universe's soul consumes itself, he holds; "one must not say that

---

[1] Friedrich Solmsen, *Aristotle's System of the Physical World*, p. 254.

[2] For the background in Greek physical speculation and Chaldean astrology, see Pierre Duhem, *op. cit.*, Vol. I, pp. 275-276.

[3] II 596. Though Philo reports (II 611) that Chrysippus held that the universe changed into bright light, and that it was Cleanthes who believed that it changed into fire.

the universe dies" (II 604). For the fire into which the universe changes contains the seeds of another universe; and the things in the new universe generated will not be specifically different from those in the universe which preceded it (II 624). Indeed, it is not impossible, according to Chrysippus, that we, after several cycles of life, shall get for ourselves "the same role in life which we have at present." [1] It may be that we shall have a mole on our eye which is not there now; but, as is evident from such incidental changes in one man's life, whom we do not call a different person because of them, we should not say or think that we were different persons.[2] A remark by Eudemus helps us to see the similarity of this view to a Pythagorean doctrine. He said, "If we are to believe the Pythagoreans, I shall once more gossip among you with this little staff in my hand, and again as now will ye be sitting before me, and likewise will it be with all the rest." [3] And Aristotle, in one place, considers [4] a view which appears to be an antecedent of that of Chrysippus.

The doctrine of recurrent cycles raises a number of questions, not the least interesting of which is the concept of history which it entails. The Chrysippean or Stoic doctrine of periodic conflagrations and regenerations of very similar worlds carries with it the corollary that the world has one all but closed history; once it were perfectly recorded, the only material with which historians might occupy themselves would be incidental novelties analogous to the appearance of a mole on Jones' eye. Logically, on this view, history cannot be regarded as "the progress of time, as a sequence of

----

[1] II 623. Shakespeare's comparisons of men's lives with actor's roles have their ancestors further back than Seneca, if, as we should conjecture, Seneca himself was influenced by Chrysippus in such passages as *Ep.* lxxvi. 31, 32; lxxx. 7-9. "To speak in Stoic categories, man in his life plays among other roles one which he adopts through his choice of work. In order to act well, he must be thoroughly acquainted with the character of his role, a character that varies with the various professions." p. 14—Ludwig Edelstein. "Motives and Incentives in Antiquity." Read at the Symposium on the History of Science, Oxford, England, 9-15 July, 1961. *Cf.* also by the same author "The Professional Ethics of the Greek Physician", *Bulletin of the History of Medicine,* XXX (1956), pp. 411 f.

[2] On the basis of such changes alone. We in all likelihood should think of ourselves as "different" since we could not *recall* our last appearance on stage!

[3] Quoted and commented upon by Gomperz in his *Greek Thinkers* (trans. by Laurie Magnus. London: John Murray, 1901), Vol. 1, p. 140.

[4] *Physica* 223^b 23-224^a 2 and Solmsen, *Aristotle's System of the Physical World,* p. 148, note 16, for an important observation concerning this passage.

moments in which something new happens." [1] However, there is no evidence that Chrysippus deduced this consequence from his doctrine. Another of the questions which his view raises is dealt with in the following section.

2d. *Why the universe and periodic conflagrations?*

Why, in Chrysippus' view, does god or reason convert the primordial fiery substance into a universe, and why does the universe periodically dissolve into the substance from which it arose? Plato, as is well-known,[2] answers a similar question by referring to the *goodness* of his Demiurge; being good, the Demiurge was not jealous, and therefore *could* not fail to construct a universe as rich in being as possible. Epicurus flatly rejected this teleology. Divine beings have nothing whatsoever to do with the original formation of the world nor with the phenomena that occur in it. This world and all worlds are colossal accidental aggregations of atoms. As Epicurus, in his *Letter to Herodotus*,[3] puts the matter, "Hence, where we find phenomena invariably recurring, the invariableness of the recurrence must be ascribed to the original interception and conglomeration of atoms whereby the world was formed." And as we have seen,[4] "the original interception and conglomeration of atoms" depend on weight, mechanical impact, and spontaneous swerve alone. But Chrysippus (and Cleanthes) clearly aligns himself with the Platonic view. For Chrysippus holds that the gods always take the course that is better. He is said to have maintained that providence or god (II 1150) "has overlooked nothing which is relevant to a highly reliable and advantageous deployment of things; because, if it were better for the goods of the world to be disposed in another way, in that way alone he would have undertaken to order them, inasmuch as nothing could occur to hinder god." It is true that Chrysippus, in this passage, is speaking of the administration of an already-formed universe and that we have extended the principle of benevolence enunciated here to embrace also the development of the universe out of substance and its dissolution into substance again. But there is some warrant for doing so, because, as we have

---

[1] Erich Frank, *op. cit.*, p. 70, and all of Chapter III for a comparison of Greek and Christian conceptions of time.

[2] *Timaeus* 29^{d}ff. and Chapter II of Arthur O. Lovejoy's *The Great Chain of Being* (New York: Harper Torchbooks, 1960, first published 1936).

[3] Diogenes Laertius x. 77. Hick's trans.

[4] *Supra*, pp. 29-30.

seen, Chrysippus holds that God or Reason is at work within the primordial substance when it is in its pristine fiery state. And, presumably, even then god was being guided by "what is better". [1]

3. THE SOUL

As we have already seen [2] the substance of the soul, in Chrysippus' view, is *pneuma*. Erasistratus, a physician and Chrysippus' contemporary who accepted some of the doctrines of "the pneumatic school of medicine", [3] believed that *pneuma* is breathed into the body from outside (there is no innate *pneuma*). It passes by the bronchi "and thence through the pulmonary vein to the left ventricle of the heart." [4] One report (II 897) shows that Chrysippus and Erasistratus were in disagreement on a detail: while Erasistratus held that the left cavity of the heart was filled with vital pneuma, Chrysippus maintained that the cavity contained psychic pneuma. As we shall see shortly, Chrysippus' position here coheres with his doctrine about the soul's locus in the body, a doctrine the plausibility of which he tried in a number of significant ways to establish.

We find what appears to be an anticipation of Chrysippus' view in a well-known fragment attributed to Anaximenes: "as our soul, being air, holds us together and controls us, so do wind [breath— (πνεῦμα)] and air enclose the whole world." [5] These words were commonly thought to be a direct quotation from Anaximenes, but Kirk, one of the most recent interpreters of the passage, argues convincingly [6] that these cannot be the words of Anaximenes himself. He concludes his account with a statement of the fact that "the

---

[1] *Infra*, pp. 156-157.

[2] *Supra*, p. 101.

[3] *Supra*, pp. 99-100. Galen, *On the Natural Faculties*, Loeb. ed. by Brock. Note 3 on pp. 186-187, pp. XXXIV-XXXV of Introduction.

[4] J. F. Dobson, "Erasistratus", *Proceedings of the Royal Society of Medicine* (Vol. XX, April, 1927, pp. 825-832), p. 828.

[5] Diels 13B2. I have used Kirk's translation (*The Presocratic Philosophers*, p. 158), though I have inserted a comma after the first "air".

[6] G. S. Kirk and J. E. Raven, *The Presocratic Philosophers* (Cambridge: The University Press, 1957) pp. 159-161. The sentence is not in Ionic, so, at the very least, it must have been reworded. "συγκρατεῖ" could not have been used by Anaximenes. "It is an unnatural compound which could only have occurred in the κοινή; it is really a compendium for συνέχειν καὶ κρατεῖν." (*Ibid.*, note 1, p. 159). κόσμον is unlikely to have been used by Anaximenes in this sense. While Kirk does not believe these to be Anaximenes' own words, he holds that the sentence does "represent some kind of reproduction of a statement by Anaximenes." (*Ibid.*, p. 159).

idea of the soul *holding together* the body has no other parallel in a Pre-socratic source, or indeed in any Greek source earlier than Stoic ones and some of the later Hippocratic works." [1] And, indeed, Zeno had held that the soul is warm pneuma.[2] That this pneuma was regarded as breath is seen in a fragment (I 141) in which Eusebius (or his source) finds an affinity between Zeno's doctrine and the allegedly Heraclitean view [3] that the soul is "sensitive exhalation" (αἰσθητικὴ ἀναθυμίασις), though Zeno, following contemporary medical theory, probably regarded psychic pneuma as being more intimately related to inhaled air than to that which is exhaled. According to Zeno (I 141), the soul is sensitive or sensible because, if it were not, it could not be molded by existing objects through the sense organs and receive impressions.

Chrysippus follows his predecessors not only in this one detail, so it will be necessary to say more about their whole view of the soul. In Zeno's opinion (I 143), it is distinguished into eight parts: the ruling element, the five senses, the faculty of speech, and the procreative faculty. The soul in its totality is mixed throughout all the body (I 145), a mixture that is dissolved upon the soul's "exodus". If we are to believe one of our reports (I 146), Zeno affirmed as positively as Aristotle that reason in men (ὁ νοῦς) is divine, and, therefore, immortal; soul is long-lived pneuma (πολυχρόνιον πνεῦμα) which is not wholly destructible. On the other hand, this reason (νοῦς or λόγος) [4] does not appear in a fully-developed form when the soul is born, but rather grows and attains its completion when the child reaches the age of seventeen (I 148).

---

[1] *Ibid.*, p. 160.

[2] I 135, 140. Cicero says that Zeno thought the soul to be constituted by fire. Since fire and air are the two components in *pneuma*, it is easy to imagine how this confusion came about in the mind of some writer of doxographical handbooks, one of which Cicero may have been working from.

[3] Heraclitus held, in fact, that the soul is made up of fire, that it comes to be out of water and that it perishes into water; he also maintained that the soul was a fragment of cosmic fire, just as Chrysippus held that individual souls are fragments of the soul of the universe. Kirk and Raven, *op. cit.*, p. 206. Burnet is sceptical about Heraclitus' use of the word ἀναθυμίασις. *EGP*[4], p. 151, note 2.

[4] Our reports use these terms interchangeably, and since none of them gives us direct quotations, we are unable to say if Zeno uses one or the other or both. These passages, by the way, seem to be exceptions to Pohlenz' observation that "Der Logos ist der Zentralbegriff der stoischen Philosophie, der den aristotelischen Nus in der Lehre wie in der Terminologie ganz zur Seite gedrängt hat." *Op. cit.*, I, 34.

(One fragment (I 149), reporting the "Stoic view" on this matter, has it that the λόγος, by dint of which we are called rational (λόγικοι), attains its complete development during the first seven years of the child's life.)

Cleanthes, like Zeno, held that the soul's substance is pneuma (I 521). According to him (I 522) all souls endure until the time of the conflagration. Apparently, like his teacher, he believed that reason was something which developed from within, attaining its completed state at a certain year in the child's life.[1] For he called (I 524) certain teeth "wisdom teeth" (σωφρονιστῆρας) because of the simultaneity of their appearance and reason's (νοῦς) attainment of soundness or self-control (τὸ σῶφρον).

Especially striking is the Cleanthean fragment (I 518) which contains two interesting arguments designed to show that the soul is corporeal. The first is that children resemble their parents, not just in physiognomy, but in their behavior, disposition, and inclinations—in their psychology, Cleanthes means. And, since resemblance and nonresemblance are attributes which apply to body alone, the soul must be a body. Secondly, unless the soul were corporeal, it could not share in movements with the body, for between what is corporeal and what is incorporeal there is no communication or transference of movement. But soul and body patently share one another's movements: the soul participates in the body's pain when it suffers a blow, is wounded, or has a sore; and the body "is sick along with" (coagrescit) the soul when the latter is afflicted with cares, anguish, or love; the body, on such occasions, generally suffers a loss of vigor and more particularly, blushing and growing pale attest the soul's shame and fear, respectively. It is of interest to note, incidentally, that Cleanthes thus anticipated some of the objections which an incorporeal soul/corporeal body dichotomy would invite.[2]

---

[1] Arnim thinks he certainly meant the twenty-first year. ("Kleanthes", Real-Encyclopädie, col. 566.). I 523 reports that Pythagoras, Anaxagoras, Plato, and Cleanthes hold that reason (λόγος) enters in from outside. Arnim observes that "he who said this appears to have incorrectly understood the philosopher." Arnim has included among the Zeno fragments concerning the soul one (I 149) which has it that, according to the Stoics, the reason (λόγος) is not implanted straightway, but is gathered together later from the senses and presentations at the age of fourteen.

[2] In one of the recent attacks on the "absurd" Cartesian dualism between a conscious mind and extended body, Gilbert Ryle (The Concept of Mind. New York: Barnes & Noble, Inc., 1949), puts the problem of their interaction

To return to Chrysippus, the information about his doctrine of the soul is abundant, and though most of it comes from Galen, an unsympathetic Platonist, it is our good fortune that he intersperses his critical comments with many quotations from Chrysippus' writings. These fragments, generally speaking, are concerned with two topics, the soul's nature and the locus of the soul's ruling part in the body. We begin with the former.

3a. *The nature of the soul*

Like Cleanthes, Chrysippus, too, held that the soul is a body, and his argument (II 790), somewhat similar to those of his teacher, is derived from the phenomenon of death and a consideration of the relation between the incorporeal and the corporeal. Death, he maintains, comes about when soul and body separate. But nothing incorporeal can be separated from something corporeal, because it could never have been attached to it. Therefore, the soul is a body. Again, it ought to be noted how one of the problems of modern philosophy, to wit, the interaction between non-extended mind and extended body, is here anticipated.

Following Zeno, Chrysippus (II 879) distinguishes eight parts of the soul, which are pneumatic currents originating from the heart: the ruling part, the five senses, the voice, and the power of procreation. These parts are also called "functions" or "powers" of the soul. And it becomes evident in another fragment (II 875) that Chrysippus regards seven of the so-called parts of the soul as functions of the eighth part, the soul's ruling or governing element. The senses, the genital organs, and the voice are extensions of this part of the soul, just as branches are extensions of a tree. In a telling simile,[1] Chrysip-

---

forcefully: "Even when 'inner' and 'outer' are construed as metaphors, the problem how a person's mind and body influence one another is notoriously charged with theoretical difficulties. What the mind wills, the legs, arms and the tongue execute; what affects the ear and the eye has something to do with what the mind perceives; grimaces and smiles betray the mind's moods and bodily castigations lead, it is hoped, to moral improvement. But the actual transactions between the episodes of the private history and those of the public history remain mysterious, since by definition they can belong to neither series." p. 12. Zeno, Cleanthes, and Chrysippus would have had no difficulty explaining this interaction, because, for them, it was an interaction between two bodies. *Cf.* Bréhier, *Théorie des Incorporels dans L'Ancien Stoicisme*, p. 9.

[1] Pohlenz, in his review of *Stoicorum Veterum Fragmenta* (*Berl. Phil. Wochenschrift*, August 1, 1903, p. 971) cites an unpublished mediaeval treatise by a certain, Hisdosus which contains the analogy of the soul and

pus (II 879) compares the "parts" of the soul, diffused through the whole body from the heart, to the threads in a spider's web which function as extensions of its legs. And, as we have seen,[1] the senses make their reports to the ruling element in the soul just as the movements of a spider's web indicate to the spider the presence of something in some part of the web.

Chrysippus, deviating from his teacher, Cleanthes, who had analyzed the act of walking as pneuma passing from the ruling part of the soul into the feet, says that walking may be described as the presence in the feet of the ruling part of the soul itself (II 836). This should perhaps be understood to mean that it is there through an extension of itself, just as the spider's web may be considered an artificial extension of the spider's legs.[2]

The parts of the soul are also described as qualities of *one* underlying substance, and the differences of the qualities, as functions of the different degrees of tension in the underlying pneumata or air-currents. This description, it is true, is assigned by Iamblichus to "the disciples of Chrysippus and Zeno". [3] Yet, as we know from our examination of Chrysippus' theory of knowledge,[4] the term "impression", according to his interpretation of it, signifies a changed state of the soul. A presentation is not something apart from the soul, but is a determinate condition of it. This view coheres with one part of the report on his disciples' views, which has it that the Stoics believed *presentation*, assent, impulse, and reason to be qualities of one underlying substance, the ruling part of the soul, just as sweetness of taste and sweetness of smell belong to an apple.

---

its senses to a spider and its web. Hisdosus cites *Heraclitus* as the author of the analogy.

[1] *Supra*, pp. 51-52.

[2] The objection to such a conjecture is, of course, that it is, then, difficult to see that Chrysippus and Cleanthes really had different analyses of the act of walking. Is not Chrysippus' extension of the ruling part of the soul effected through the pneuma which passes from the heart to the feet? The difference may be the subtle one that, for Cleanthes, the pneuma is sent out from the heart to the feet, analogously to a command, whereas for Chrysippus the pneuma is like a vehicle through which the ruling part itself passes to the foot. Such an interpretation is supported by his spider simile.

[3] II 826. And if we remember that Aristotle was a philosophical disciple of Plato, and Theophrastus, of Aristotle, we ought to hesitate, in the absence of independent evidence, to infer that a disciple's philosophical position *mirrors* that of his master. We should, of course, *not* hesitate to do so in the case of the Epicureans.

[4] *Supra*, pp. 53-54.

It may be the case that Chrysippus thought of all the qualities and activities of the soul as being states or conditions of the pneuma which is its substance, just as he regarded a presentation as an alteration of the soul's state. Pohlenz, in his review of Arnim's work,[1] blames him for omitting certain passages [2] which give "an integral representation absolutely necessary for the understanding of Chrysippus' psychology." But none of the passages contains Chrysippus' name. Each contains what appears to be an extension of the Chrysippean view that a presentation in the soul is, in fact, a modification of it, or that it *is* the soul in a determinate state.

Thus, in one passage, virtue is defined as "the soul in a certain condition." [3] In another [4] "justice" is defined in the same way and then Seneca adds that it (justice) is "a state (*habitus*), a kind of power (*quaedam vis*), of the soul." This sounds, indeed, very much like Chrysippus, who had described (III 384) endurance and continence as "states" ($\xi\xi\epsilon\iota\varsigma$) of the soul which follow upon reason. In another of the passages cited by Pohlenz [5] the soul or mind is described as not standing over against a passion but as itself transformed into the passion (*in adfectum ipse mutatur*). And in another [6] again all knowledge is said to be the governing part of the soul in a certain state ($\pi\tilde{\omega}\varsigma$ $\xi\chi$ον $\epsilon\sigma\tau\grave{\iota}\nu$ $\dot{\eta}\gamma\epsilon\mu\omicron\nu\iota\kappa\acute{o}\nu$). This, too, seems to have some affinity with Chrysippus' doctrine (III 471a) that "the beautiful or ugly soul depends upon its ruling part which is in this or that state $\xi\chi$ον $\omicron\check{\upsilon}\tau\omega\varsigma$ $\mathring{\eta}$ $\omicron\check{\upsilon}\tau\omega\varsigma$) by reason of its own divisions."

It cannot be affirmed with certainty that the psychology revealed in the fragments cited by Pohlenz is Chrysippean. Nevertheless on the basis of the genuinely Chrysippean fragments, it is clear that the view presented here is a generalized version of Chrysippus' concept of the soul as being in a certain state by dint of its presentations. And it may well be the case that Chrysippus himself was the author of the more general doctrine.

There are only two short fragments (II 811, 815) relevant to

---

[1] *Op. cit.*, pp. 966, 977.

[2] Parts of Seneca *ep.* 113; Sextus *adv. dogm.* i. 39; Alexander *de an. libri mantissa* p. 118, 6 and 35 Br.; Seneca *de ira* i., 8, 3. Sextus, *adv. dogm.* i. 237.

[3] Seneca *ep.* 113, 2 — "*animus quodammodo se habens*".

[4] *Ibid.* Sections 7 and 8. *Cf.* section 11 where "courage" is similarly described.

[5] Seneca, *de ira* i. 8, 2.

[6] Sextus, *adv. dogm.* i. 39.

Chrysippus' views on the immortality of the soul. Apparently he held that the souls of all except the wise were destroyed at the time of the death of the body and that even those of the wise perished at the time of the conflagration.

Perhaps the most radical feature in Chrysippus' psychology is its outright rejection of the Platonic (and Aristotelian) tripartite soul. In the *Republic* Plato overcomes the "excessive dualism" between mind and body, which the Phaedo strongly emphasizes,[1] and posits three parts in the soul analogous to the three classes in the ideal state, having earlier pointed out that goodness is the same in the individual and in the state. He reinforces this analogical argument with one based upon the phenomenon of conflict in the soul (439[e]) and the law of contradiction (436[b]). One of the parts of the soul is the rational (τὸ λογιστικόν), the one that reasons and calculates (439[d]); it is located in the head (*Timaeus* 69[c]). The second part of the soul is the spirited element (ὁ θυμός), or "the power of noble wrath" which is usually an ally of reason.[2] It is situated between the neck and the diaphragm. Anger, having received a command from reason, sends it out to the sentient parts of the body (*Timaeus* 70[a]) from the heart which functions as a kind of communications center. The third part is the irrational (ἀλόγιστον) or appetitive (ἐπιθυμητικόν), with which the soul "loves and experiences hunger, thirst, and the other desires" (439[d]). It is situated between the midriff and the navel (*Timaeus* 70[d], [e]). The rational part of the soul is divine while the appetitive element is brutish, despicable, and godless (*Rep.* 589[d], [e]). Moreover, being divine, the rational part of the soul is immortal, while the spirited and appetitive elements are mortal (*Timaeus* 69[d], [e]). The wise and happy man is he who strives to bring about a certain condition (ἕξις) in his soul. The brutish part is to be tamed; the spirited or ambitious part, to be sobered; and the rational part, to govern with wisdom. In brief, a harmonious condition of the soul is to be established.[3]

Chrysippus, following Zeno, denies that there is any such thing as "an irrational part" of the soul. What is called "the irrational part" by some is identical with the rational part (III 459); there is

---

[1] For an excellent account of Plato's view of the soul, as expressed in each of the pertinent dialogues, see G. M. A. Grube, *Plato's Thought* (Boston: Beacon Press, 1958 (first published in 1935)), Chapter IV.

[2] *Rep.* 439[e] and Shorey's note in the Loeb edition.

[3] *Rep.* 591[b]-592[a].

no irrational faculty (II 906). He does not, of course, deny the
existence of passions or emotions, but he explains them in terms of
a state of the governing part of the soul, all of which is rational,
rather than by finding in the soul some special faculty which can
function as the source and locus of the emotions. Chrysippus' account
of the emotions and the therapy for them must be postponed to the
chapter on moral philosophy. Here we wish to emphasize merely
his rejection of the Platonic tripartite soul or what has been called
his intellectualistic psychology [1]—his view that the ruling part of
the soul is through and through rational. For only if this is kept in
mind will we be able to discern the import of his arguments about
the bodily locus of the soul's ruling part and to understand that
Galen's attacks on those arguments, to a consideration of which we
now turn, are wrongly directed.

3b. *The locus of the soul's ruling part*

In agreement with the founder of the Stoa, Chrysippus affirms
that the heart is the seat of the ruling or governing part of the soul.[2]
Galen summarized and quoted many of Chrysippus' statements
made in defense of his points of view, for his criticism of Chrysippus
seemed to him to require the restatement or direct quotation of
the arguments given.[3] This is fortunate, indeed, for nowhere can
the modern reader descry so clearly one of Chrysippus' modes of
argumentation as in those fragments in which the topic under consideration appears.[4]

Galen's attack on Chrysippus is a two-pronged one: (i) Chrysippus' argument contains a presupposition for which he fails to formulate a proof (II 888); (ii) Chrysippus tries to establish his view
by means of "plausible dialectical arguments" (πιθανὰ ἐπιχειρήματα)
rather than by ones that are "scientific and demonstrative"
(ἐπιστημονικά τε καὶ ἀποδεικτικά).[5] I shall examine in turn the two
aspects of Galen's attack; for, by doing so, I hope not only to make

---

[1] Pohlenz, *op cit.*, I, 92. Bréhier, *Chrysippe*, p. 253.

[2] II 880, 885, 910. For Zeno's affirmation and the argument for it, see
I 148. *Cf.* Pearson's note on the passage (*op. cit.*, pp. 147-148).

[3] II 885 through II 909.

[4] In fact, Arnim tries (II 911) to fit together into a connected whole the
quotations preserved by Galen from the second part of Book I of Chrysippus'
de anima. Cf. also "De la partie hégémonique de l'âme", traduit du grec
par Georges Blin et Monette Keim, *Mesures* (15 avril 1939, pp. 163-174).

[5] *de Hipp. et Plat. Plac.* III 1 p. 254 (Mueller). This is a continuation of
Arnim's II 885.

plain how Galen failed to understand Chrysippus' monistic psychology, but also to make evident the manner in which, in the third
century B.C., one philosopher comes to approve the opinion of an
expert in a delimited area of investigation when that opinion is one
of several discordant views on the subject.

Since Chrysippus tries to prove that the ruling part of the soul
has its seat in the heart by showing that so-called irrational psychic
phenomena, such as anger, have their locus there, he, according
to Galen, is evidently presupposing that where the irrational parts
of the soul are, there the rational part is also (II 888, 890). And he,
Galen alleges, ought to have formulated a proof for this proposition
(II 888). But the second-century physician is simply being blinded
by his Platonistic psychology. What he here overlooks—and what
vitiates his whole criticism—is that, in Chrysippus' view, as we
have tried to show,[1] there is no irrational "part" of the soul. Irrational psychic phenomena—passions or emotions—were probably
regarded by Chrysippus, as we have seen,[2] as states of the ruling
part of the soul itself. Such a way of regarding them would readily
explain the aim of several of his arguments, for any reasoning which
proves the locus of "irrational" psychic phenomena to be the heart
would, on this view, *ipso facto* prove the heart to be the seat of the
governing part of the soul. And, *malgré* Galen, there is no burden
of proof on Chrysippus for the doctrine—where the "irrational
parts" of the soul are, there the rational part is also. This would
be the case only if Chrysippus were a Platonist. But he was not; and,
as it appears, in the third century B.C. it was hardly required of
any philosopher that he explain his reasons for not being a Platonist.

With respect to Galen's second objection, Chrysippus himself
makes some remarks about his own approach to the subject, and
their significance is heightened by the fact that they occur in a
passage (II 885) which Galen has lifted verbatim from one of our
philosopher's books. In the first place, Chrysippus observes that,
in regard to the seat of the ruling element in the soul, men—both
philosophers and physicians—disagree (διαφωνοῦσιν). Secondly, he
points out that the whereabouts of the soul's governing part is not
evident to sense, as is the case with respect to the remaining functions of the soul (it is sensibly apparent, for example, where in the
body the voice operates). Nor, he goes on, are there any demonstra-

---

[1] *Supra*, p. 132-133.
[2] *Supra*, pp. 130-131.

tive proofs by which one might draw conclusions about this subject. Having recognized (whether rightly or wrongly is not the point here) that the problem at hand is not amenable to a directly empirical solution and that demonstrative reasoning is not applicable to it, Chrysippus turned to less rigorous devices even though they, as he realizes full well, issue in probable conclusions only.[1] There is nothing methodologically naive about the cautious approach we find Chrysippus making here. He is not, as Galen would have us believe, unsophisticated about the methodological proprieties of his investigation. Before pointing out how he relates the results of his investigations to contemporary scientific views, I examine at close range some of the obviously inconclusive arguments which he employs.

There is first a group of such modes of reasoning which appeals to gestures, the belief of *hoi polloi*, idioms, etymologies, and general linguistic usage. That the ruling part of the soul is in the heart is revealed in our pointing to ourselves; for when we do so, we point to the chest (II 895). The fact that the many believe that the passions of the soul occur in the chest indicates that they do occur there (II 896). There are certain idioms, for example, "he swallows down the things said", "anger springs up in him", and "I made an impression on your heart", which suggest that the ruling part of the soul is in the heart (II 891, 901). The etymology of the word "heart" and an analysis of the way in which men use the term "heartless" (II 899, 902) constitute evidence for the same conclusion.

Moreover, Chrysippus inherited from Zeno (I 148) the following argument: the place from which discourse is emitted is the place where the reasoning element resides; discourse is emitted from the heart; therefore the heart is the locus of the rational element or the governing part of the soul (II 894). This is a syllogistic argument, but Chrysippus would probably deny that it was "demonstrative" on the ground that its second premise is not of the proper sort.[2] And, if this is so, he is not here adducing a kind of

---

[1] *Cf.* II 891 and 894 where Chrysippus employs the terms, εὔλογον and πιθανόν. And as one fragment (II 763) makes evident, Chrysippus was aware of the dangers of rash assertion in areas where experience and information are needed.

[2] That is, "true, primary, immediate, better known than and prior to the conclusion, which is further related to them as effect to cause." Aristotle, *Post. An.* 71[b] 20-22 (Oxford trans.). Whether or not Chrysippus believed that the premises in a demonstrative argument had to satisfy *just* these

argument which, as he has made a point of saying, is not available for this investigation.

Our philosopher also employs the verses of the poets as part of his argumentative weaponry.[1] For example, he cites (II 905) from Homer (*Il.* iv. 24), "But the heart of Hera could not contain her anger, and she spoke forth" and (II 906 - *Il.* x. 220), "Nestor, my own heart and my own proud spirit arouse me." Galen, on principle, objects to appeals to the poets as a mode of proof that the ruling part of the soul is in the heart: "For what the poets have said is of no importance, but rather what the truth is and what can be demonstrated" (II 906). But Chrysippus has prefaced his treatment of this subject by pointing out that it is not amenable to demonstration (nor to empirical investigation). Therefore one can either adduce not fully rigorous arguments, examples of which have been given here, which will bestow on their conclusions plausibility or probability, or one can suspend judgment altogether. Chrysippus chose the former course.

As he was well-aware, there was disagreement (ἀντιλογία) on this subject among the physicians (II 885). And this undoubtedly refers to the discordant views of Praxagoras, on one hand, and Herophilus and Erasistratus, on the other, regarding the place in the body where the nerves originate.[2] Above we discussed Chrysippus' use of Praxagoras' opinion and referred to Edelstein's study on the sciences in antiquity.[3] In the third century B.C. there was no established scientific school. When physicians, for example, disagreed, there was no basis on which one could argue that one of them was more, say, in the stream of "scientific progress" than the other.[4] Chrysippus, Galen tells us (II 897), placed Praxagoras' authority against those who held that the nerves had their origin in the head. We are now able to make clear why he did so. Chrysippus admits that he is not an expert in anatomy, so he cannot

---

conditions is not attested. I strongly suspect that Chrysippus knew Aristotle's "Analytics", but I cannot prove it.

[1] II 890, 904, 905, 906, and 907. "The fact that good poems express the truth gives these poems a place in philosophical discussions. Chrysippus was especially fond of quoting lines from the poets in support of some doctrine." Phillip De Lacy, "Stoic Views of Poetry", (*American Journal of Philology*, Vol. LXIX (July, 1948), pp. 241-271), p. 264.

[2] Pohlenz, *op. cit.*, I, 87. Solmsen, "Greek Philosophy and the Discovery of the Nerves", pp. 184-197.

[3] *Supra*, pp. 38-40.

[4] As Solmsen suggests; *supra*, note 3, p. 40.

adjudicate between the claims of Herophilus and Praxagoras on the basis of anything like professional training. There was no such institution as a Greek Academy of Science or a Greek Medical Association which might have endorsed the findings of one of these disagreeing physicians.[1] The only course, short of scepticism, which remained open to Chrysippus was to accept that opinion about the origin of the nerves which cohered best with his view about the locus of the ruling part of the soul. A whole battery of probabilistic-type arguments—and, to say it once more, the question, according to Chrysippus, is not soluble by any other kind of reasoning—points to the conclusion that its seat is the heart. Praxagoras' opinion that the nerves have their origin there seemed to Chrysippus to coincide with his own conclusions and it was, I believe, on this basis that he favored Praxagoras' view rather than that of Erasistratus or Herophilus.

If our interpretation be correct and if it can be generalized, we have, in this section, not only received further confirmation of Chrysippus' monistic psychology and witnessed how sensitive he is to methodological issues, but we have also gotten a glimpse of the relation, in one of its aspects, between philosophy and science in the third century B.C.

With respect to Chrysippus' own philosophy the most significant point that emerges from Galen's attack is our philosopher's (to Galen, incomprehensible) acceptance of the premise that "the place where the irrational passions occur is the locus of the ruling part of the soul." And this premise is based upon another which constitutes the cardinal feature of Chrysippus' psychology: the soul is a unified entity having diverse functions. Thus Chrysippus could not, like Plato, admit that one part of the soul is in the head; another, in the heart; another, in the midriff. Such an admission, for him, would have been tantamount to the denial of the soul's unity, an insistence upon which constitutes the fundamental doctrine in his psychology.

4. FATE

Chrysippus' doctrine of fate as a necessary causal chain will perhaps be more comprehensible if we precede our reconstruction

---

[1] Or, to put the matter in Kuhn's terms, Greek neurology had not yet a sufficient number of agreed-upon "paradigms" to constitute "normal" scientific research on its problems. Thomas Kuhn, *The Structure of Scientific Revolutions* (Chicago: The University of Chicago Press, 1964 (f.p. 1962), pp. 10-11.

of it with a brief discussion of necessity and contingency in the philosophies of Plato, Aristotle, and Epicurus, Zeno, and Cleanthes. An additional motive for such an introduction is that, seen against the background of earlier views of necessity, and particularly in contrast with that of Plato, the peculiarity of the Stoic and Chrysippean view, nearer the modern in one important respect, will come into sharper focus.

It is well-known that, in Plato's view, the generation of the universe is "a mixed result" of the combination of reason (νοῦς) and necessity (ἀνάγκη) (*Timaeus* 47ᵉ, 48ᵉ), or, as Plato also puts it, some things are fashioned by reason and some things come about through necessity (*Timaeus* 47ᵉ). In the first part of his discourse (29ᵈ) Timaeus had sought to state the purpose or reason why the universe had been created;[1] the answer is that the demiurge wanted things to be as good as possible. The reason why the demiurge can do things in a way that is only as good as possible,[2] and not perfect, is because the necessity in the world is never overruled with respect to *all* things.[3]

Plato calls (*Timaeus* 48ᵃ) this necessity, which is a factor in the generation of some things in the universe, an errant cause (πλανωμένη αἰτία). And this already suggests a certain random character with which he associates necessity—an association which appears strange to modern minds, accustomed as we are to associate necessity with order and intelligibility. In a passage in the *Laws* (891ᶜ - 892ᶜ), in which he discusses some earlier cosmogonies, necessity is linked with chance while what is lawful and ordered is associated with design.[4] Necessity for Plato means the very reverse of natural law; as Grote saw,[5] "necessity" in the *Timaeus* means "the indeterminate, the inconstant, the anomalous, that which can

---

[1] We agree with Cornford (*Plato's Cosmology*, p. 165) that Plato does not mean to suggest that the demiurge, like the God of Judaic-Christian thought, created the universe out of nothing. He fashioned or brought order into already-existing materials.

[2] *Timaeus* 30ᵇ 5, 6; 53ᵇ 5, 6.

[3] "Reason overruled Necessity by persuading her to guide the greatest part of the things that become towards what is best . . ." *Timaeus* 48ᵃ, Cornford's trans.

[4] Cornford, *Plato's Cosmology*, p. 167. I have profited greatly from Cornford's whole discussion (*op. cit.*, pp. 162-177) of reason and necessity in Plato.

[5] George Grote, *Plato and the Other Companions of Sokrates* (Three volumes, London: John Murray, 1865), Vol. III, p. 249.

be neither understood nor predicted." It is represented in a certain refractoriness of the material [1] and in disorderly motion (*Timaeus* 52[d], [e]). Plato, if we are to judge by the *Timaeus* myth, believed the universe to be shot through with design, order, or purpose; but this final cause, as Aristotle would call it, does not function universally and ineluctably; it is limited by irrational or spontaneous movements, which it is not always able to overrule by persuasion, and these movements, associated with necessity by Plato, are, paradoxically enough, responsible for the contingency [2] that exists in the Platonic universe.

Aristotle, though he believes nature is a final cause or "a cause that operates for a purpose", [3] is not a determinist. He believes that there is an element of contingency in nature, and this is most explicitly and most unambiguously [4] set forth in a passage [5] concerning the truth values of propositions about future events. There Aristotle argues that if the law of excluded middle embraces propositions containing predicates that relate to the futu.., then "everything takes place of necessity". If the proposition, "a sea-fight will take place tomorrow", is *now* either true or false, then it is necessary that it take place tomorrow or necessary that it not take place tomorrow. Because Aristotle discerned clearly that this is the case generally—that to maintain the universal applicability of the law of excluded middle is to commit oneself to a position of absolute determinism [6]—and because he rejects this determinism,

---

[1] For example, the impossibility of having bone which is both hard and non-brittle.

[2] I mean by "contingency" that reality is so constituted that some past and present events might not have occurred and that not all the events that will occur in the future are *bound* to occur.

[3] *Physica* 199[b] 32, 33.

[4] The upshot of the discussion of chance in Chapters 5 and 6 of Book II of the *Physics* is *not* that there is indeterminacy in the universe, for "chance" is merely the unexpected conjunction of two chains of rigorously caused events.

[5] *de inter.* 18[a] 27-19[b] 4. There is a significant body of contemporary literature on this passage, the interpretation of which (passage) is notoriously controversial. See, for example, *Aristotle's Categories and De Interpretatione* (Trans. with notes by J. L. Ackrill, Oxford: The Clarendon Press, 1963), pp. 132-142. G. E. M. Anscombe, "Aristotle and the Sea Battle", (*Mind*, LXV (1956), pp. 1-15). Jaakko Hintikka, "The Once and Future Sea Fight: Aristotle's Discussion of Future Contingents in *De Interpretatione* IX" (*Philosophical Review*, Vol. LXXIII (October, 1964), pp. 461-492.

[6] *Ibid.* 18[b] 26-31.

on the ground that deliberation would then be pointless,[1] he limits the law of excluded middle to propositions about the present and the past.[2]

The nearest Aristotle comes to a discussion of free will, in which he believes but which he never investigates at length, is in a passage in the *Nicomachean Ethics* [3] where he maintains that we are responsible for becoming the kind of men we are or for developing the kind of characters we develop. "Activities exercised on particular objects ... make the corresponding character," and men, before they become inured in vice, are responsible (αἴτιοι) for their activities and, consequently, for their characters.[4] They do not have to cheat for example; but, if they do, they become unjust. Since the final end of life is that by reference to which a man does everything else he does and since this end appears to each man in a form answering to his character, he cannot disavow responsibility for the way in which the final good appears to him, because he himself, in the ultimate analysis, determines what his character will be.

Epicurus, like Aristotle, perceived the consequences of admitting that *every* proposition is either true or false. For he is afraid "that if he admits this [every proposition is either true or false] he will also have to admit that all events whatever are caused by fate (on the ground that if either of two alternatives is true from all eternity, that alternative is also certain, and if it is certain it is also necessary)." [5] He rejects fate or necessity on grounds somewhat similar to those of Aristotle. If something happens in accordance with necessity, one can neither praise nor blame the agent, for necessity is not something that can be held accountable or responsible (ἀνυπεύθυνον); but our actions are not bound or governed by some master other than ourselves; praise and blame attach to them, and this, too, signifies that our action is free (ἀδέσποτον).[6]

And as is well-known, so strong was this wish to preserve freedom, Epicurus, deviating radically from Democritus,[7] laid the foundation

---

[1] "There would be no need to deliberate or to take trouble, on the supposition that if we should adopt a certain course, a certain result would follow, while, if we did not, the result would not follow." *de inter.* 18ᵇ 32-34.

[2] *Ibid.* 19ᵃ 35-19ᵇ 4.

[3] Book III, Chapter 5.

[4] *Ethica Nicomachea* 1114ᵃ 7.

[5] Cicero *de fato* x. 21. Loeb edit. (trans. by Rackham).

[6] D.L. x. 133.

[7] Cicero *de fato* x. 23. *Cf.* Bailey, *The Greek Atomists and Epicurus*, p. 321.

for freedom at the very core of his system by introducing as a movent force, in addition to weight and impact, a spontaneous or uncaused swerve of the atoms.[1] How such a swerve secures freedom of choice is clearly brought out by Lucretius at the conclusion of his discourse [2] on the subject: "but that the very mind feels not some necessity within in doing all things, and is not constrained like a conquered thing to bear and suffer, this is brought about by the tiny swerve of the first-beginnings in no determined direction of place at no determined time." [3] Moreover Epicurus said he would rather believe in the myths about the gods (which he abhorred) than submit to the "fate" (εἱμαρμένη) of the natural philosophers,[4] so much did he cherish freedom beyond any other thing. For he clearly assumed that without such freedom, moral philosophy would be pointless. Rather than relinquish it, as required by the premises of the atomistic materialism he had inherited from Democritus, he chose to make the system inconsistent by tacking onto it his doctrine of the swerve, thus introducing a flaw in a materialistic system, for it is an indirect admission that there are non-material causes or conditions.[5]

In principle the factor of swerve in the movements of the atom makes for contingency, not just in the behavior of high-grade organic bodies, but in all bodies throughout the world. But, although Epicurus and Lucretius explicitly recognize chance alongside necessity as the conditions of things which come to be,[6] neither of them relates chance happenings to the swerve in the atom. In other words, though the machinery for the explanation of contingency generally had been provided, no use was made of it except with regard to free choice.[7]

---

[1] Cicero de fato x. 22.

[2] ii. 251-293.

[3] ii. 289-293. Bailey's trans.

[4] D.L. x. 134.

[5] Bailey, op. cit., p. 321.

[6] D.L. x. 133.
   Letter to Pythocles, D.L. x. 89.
   Lucretius vi. 29.

[7] Bailey (op. cit., pp. 324-327) examines M. Guyau's thesis (La Morale d'Epicure, pp. 85-91) that the swerve in Epicurus' system accounts for a contingency throughout organic and inorganic nature, and concludes, "On the whole it seems safest to conclude that Epicurus did admit the element of contingency in the world, and may possibly have attributed it to the atomic 'swerve': most probably the brilliant idea devised by Guyau did not occur to him, but he would gladly have adopted it if it had."

When one now turns to the Stoic system, one is confronted by an entirely different view. This is seen already in three extant Zenonian fragments (I 175, 176, 177) on the subject, brief though they be. Zeno maintains in these fragments that (I 175) "fate is the chain-like cause of existing things or the reason (λόγος) in accordance with which they are ordered"; that fate (I 176) is "the moving power of matter according to identical rules and in the same way and it does not differ from providence and nature"; that (I 177) "some things are in our power (ἐφ'ἡμῖν) and some are not."

Cleanthes refuses to identify fate and providence as Zeno does.[1] A bad man's deed may have been fated; nevertheless it is not in accordance with Providence. In fact, as is made plain in his *Hymn to Zeus* (line 17), the acts of bad men constitute the one class of events which come about without Zeus' aid (σοῦ δίχα), though they are somehow absorbed into the order of the universe by Zeus.[2]

If asked to describe Chrysippus' position, in a preliminary way, in terms of those of his predecessors, it would not be inaccurate to say, first, that he accepts Zeno's view and seeks to amplify and defend it; and he rejects Cleanthes' doctrine concerning the non-identity of providence and fate. He wished to preserve the teleology of Plato and Aristotle.[3] And while he approved the Aristotelian doctrine that a man is responsible for the kind of character he has, he did not wish to commit the blunder of Epicurus and speak of an uncaused cause. Such an aggregate of views constitutes a thorny position, to say the least, and this explains perhaps the richness of our accounts of Chrysippus' views on this subject. We treat his doctrine of fate under three heads: what it is, how we know that it exists, and its relation to free will.

4a. *What it is*

In one passage Chrysippus describes fate as "everlasting movement, continuous and ordered" (II 916). This undoubtedly relates to the orderly movement of pneuma through the primordial substance; in his book, *On the Universe*, Chrysippus maintained that the substance of fate is "pneumatic power" (II 913). The characteristic of continuity in this movement is the ground of the Chrysippean

---

[1] Pearson, *op. cit.* Cleanthes' fragment #18.
[2] *Cf.* Arnim, "Kleanthes", *Real-encyclopädie*, col. 567.
[3] This we examine below in the section on God.

doctrine that the universe is coherent with itself or that its parts
are in sympathy with one another (II 912).

Chrysippus believed that there is necessity in all things (II 914);
and that which is necessitated (καταναγκασμένον) is identical with
fate (II 916). He held that *all* things happen in accordance with fate
(II 925, 997). Everything that has occurred, is occurring or will
occur is controlled unexceptionably by fate (II 913).[1] Fate is, in
one place (II 915), described as "the continuous causal chain of
the things that exist."

That this chain of causes is rigorously connected or that there
are no uncaused beginnings of motion, as in Epicurus' system, is
expressed in Chrysippus' definition of fate, given in his book, *On
Providence*. Fate, he says there, is "a certain natural order of all
things, following closely upon one another and moved in succession
from eternity, and their intertwining with one another is unalterable" (II 1000). The unalterable character of this succession
of events is again touched upon by Chrysippus when he explains
the names of the Fates; Atropos, he says, gets her name from the
fact that the distribution of lots to men "is immutable and un-
changed for eternity" (II 913, 914). And, denying Epicurus' thesis,
Chrysippus maintained that nothing comes about without a cause
(ἀναιτίως), or that nothing comes about except in accordance with
antecedent causes (προηγουμέναι αἰτίαι).

Cicero (II 137a) placed Chrysippus in the class of "those who
introduce an eternal series of causes". We have already discussed the
one fragment (II 336) in which Chrysippus says a cause is the "that
through which" or the "why" of the effect. He held that, for every
effect, one could, in principle, find a cause. What is uncaused and
spontaneous is non-existent. One who, like Epicurus, introduces an
uncaused phenomenon does violence to nature (II 973). Even in
situations which seem to be of a spontaneous or uncaused nature
"obscure causes are working under the surface" (II 973).

Chrysippus, then, appears to mean by fate a vast causal nexus
from which nothing that happens is excluded. For each particular

---

[1] In other words Chrysippus is here formulating what modern philosophers
would call the principle of causality. Hume says at the beginning of his
famous analysis of this principle, " 'Tis a general maxim in philosophy, that
*whatever begins to exist, must have a cause of existence." A Treatise of Human
Nature*, i. 3, 3. The maxim *became* general. It is Chrysippus' merit to have
been the first philosopher in the western tradition to have enunciated it.
Cf. Bréhier, *Chrysippe et l'Ancien Stoicisme*, p. 183.

occurrence there exist prior conditions which are sufficient to explain its emergence into reality and given which that particular could not be different from what it is. Though this group of fragments says nothing about particular links in the causal chain repeating themselves in such way that one could derive from them generalizations about causal connections in nature,[1] Crysippus must have thought that some such induction was possible, as we have seen from his interpretation of the conditional proposition, and as we shall see more clearly in his observations concerning divination.[2] Now that we know what he means by fate and what he intends when he says that *all* things are subject to fate, the question arises— how does Chrysippus try to prove its existence?

4b. *How we know that it exists*

In the extant fragments two proofs are preserved which Chrysippus formulated with a view to demonstrating that fate exists. In addition to such proofs in the usual sense he also relies on an etymological argument; the names of the fates, he believes, constitute strong evidence for the existence of fate.

Chrysippus' first argument for the existence of fate went as follows (II 939): if it were not the case that all things are encompassed by fate, then the prophecies of the diviners would not be true; but the prophecies of the diviners are true (this premise is suppressed but understood); therefore, all things are encompassed by fate. This argument, it ought to be noted, exemplifies the *modus tollens* argument form or Chrysippus' second undemonstrated argument form.[3] Moreover it is based upon the empirical evidence, namely, the efficaciousness of divination in which Chrysippus

---

[1] Such as is attributed to "the Stoics" by Alexander Aphrodisiensis in II 945: "Since there is a multiplicity of causes, they [the Stoics] say equally with respect to all of them that it is impossible that while the same conditions exist with respect to the cause and that on which it has an effect, that sometimes it should turn out one way and sometimes, another. For, if such were the case, it would result that there is an uncaused movement." *Cf.* Sambursky's ". . . it should be noted that the Stoic statement, which simply reads 'every time A is restored B must follow again', is the first statement on causality on record which introduces the element of recurrence and the idea of reproducibility of a situation B from a situation A. This implies the possibility of the prediction of events . . ." *Physics of the Stoics*, p. 54.

[2] *Infra*, p. 145.

[3] *Supra*, pp. 83-84.

believed. He wrote two books on divination [1] and he defined (II 1189) it as "the power of knowing, understanding, and explaining the signs, which are presaged by the gods for men."

The nature of the evidence requires some comment. Only if the prophecies of diviners are based upon the observation of unalterable connections in nature such that, after having experienced A followed by B, A_1 followed by B_1, A_2 followed by B_2, then observing A_3 and taking it to be a "sign" of B_3 can they predict that B_3 will occur. And these prophecies would not be successful unless such unalterable connections, that is, fate, did exist. Were this not Chrysippus' assumption it would be difficult to understand how he could have argued from divination to fate.

Diogenianus, an Epicurean,[2] attacked Chrysippus' argument on the ground that it was circular. He said Chrysippus tried to prove fate through divination and divination through fate. But we know, on the basis of another fragment (II 1192) that Chrysippus thought divination to be a science ($\tau\acute{\epsilon}\chi\nu\eta$), because its predictions or prophecies are fulfilled. His belief in divination, therefore, does not rest on his belief in fate, as Diogenianus suggests, but rather on a pragmatic consideration: its success in practice. Certainly Chrysippus would admit that fate is the *ratio essendi* of divination; he nowhere argues, however, as Diogenianus would have it, that fate is, in addition, the *ratio cognoscendi* of divination.

Diogenianus' second criticism of Chrysippus' attempt to link fate with the existence of successful divination is the following (II 939): if divination is useful, then fate does not exist; and if fate does exist, then divination is not useful. Apparently Diogenianus has in mind a situation of this sort: if a diviner usefully tells Jones that there is imminent danger for him so that he might avert it, then fate is not so all inclusive as to embrace Jones' will or his action; but if fate is absolutely comprehensive and determines even such events as Jones' not meeting with disaster, then the diviner's warning is useless or superfluous, and more generally, so is his art.

Chrysippus would probably have met this criticism with his doctrine of "condestinate"[3] facts (II 956). By such a fact he means a circumstance whose existence involves another fact. For example,

---

[1] II (1187), though II 1216 implies that he wrote only one book on the subject.

[2] Arnim, "Diogenianus", (3) *Realencyclopädie*, cols. 777, 778.

[3] I have adopted Rackham's translation (Loeb ed.) of *confatalia*.

"Oedipus being born to Laius" entails that Laius mate with a woman. "Milo wrestling at Olympia" entails that he have a wrestling partner. "A patient getting well" entails that he be attended by a physician (II 956). It follows that even if "disaster not overtaking Jones" has been fated, the fact, being a complex fact, entails that Jones be advised of the imminent danger and that he take appropriate steps to avoid it. That is, it is a fact which is destined to take place *in conjunction with* Jones' willing to avoid disaster and his taking steps to avert it. Therefore the diviner's art is not useless even in a universe in which fate prevails. This reply, however, raises a new problem: how to explain Jones' feeling that he himself decided to go to a diviner and the feeling that he, if he had wished, could have neglected going to a diviner? But this problem encroaches on the relation of fate to free will, which we shall examine in the following section.

Chrysippus' second proof that fate exists is built on a series of arguments which exemplify the first and second of his argument forms. He, like Aristotle and Epicurus, discerned that a universal application of the law of excluded middle to propositions makes it necessary that there are no uncaused movements (II 952); but, unlike them, he welcomed this consequence. On the contrary, as Cicero says (II 452), he "exerts all his powers in order to convince us that every proposition is either true or false." The first argument in the series to prove that fate exists, it will be noted, makes use of the law of excluded middle, unqualifiedly accepted with respect to propositions, as the second of its premises. For the series of arguments goes as follows (II 952):

> If any motion is without a cause, then not every proposition will be either true or false.
> Every proposition is either true or false.
> Therefore no motion is without a cause.

> If no motion is without a cause, all things which happen occur through antecedent causes.
> No motion is without a cause.
> Therefore, all things which happen occur through antecedent causes.

> If all things which happen occur through antecedent causes, all things take place through fate.

All things which happen occur through antecedent causes.
Therefore, *all things take place through fate.*

Chrysippus' affirmation of the law of excluded middle even with
respect to propositions about the future commits him to a scheme
of things in which there is no contingency; indeed, this is what a
fated course of events is. This means that there is no such thing
as possibility if we mean by that term something more than human
ignorance of the future. In fact the term "possible" for the "Stoics"
designated not an objective contingency in the nature of things,
but only a subjective category—ignorance about the future.[1] Every
proposition is, in principle, classifiable as necessary or impossible.[2]

In spite of the fact that the Stoics generally adopted the position
to which they were logically bound, Chrysippus, inexplicably,
maintained (II 954) that even if something never takes place, it is
still possible. Even if a jewel is never broken, it is still possible for
it to be broken. This is an explicit denial of Aristotle's contention
that "it cannot be true to say that a particular thing is possible,
but will not be." [3] It is also a position impossible to reconcile with
Chrysippus' doctrine of fate, as Plutarch saw (II 202). As Sambursky has pointed out,[4] the position Cicero ascribes to Chrysippus
(II 954) sounds much like that of Philo, but it does not appear
likely that Cicero has confused the two positions.[5] Rather could it
be the case that Chrysippus only intended to state what later
became the "Stoic" position: to say that the jewel may break even
though it never does break is a euphemistic way of affirming that,
from the point of view of our limited knowledge, it always seems
possible for the jewel to break, though, as a matter of fact, it never
breaks? Such a position, which admits as objective categories only

---

[1] Sambursky, *Physics of the Stoics*, pp. 75, 76 for references. *Cf.* August
Faust's "Innerhalb der Welt gibt es nach stoischer Ansicht gar nichts
bloss Mögliches, sondern nur Notwendiges; lediglich unser Möglichkeits-
begriff ist zu verteidigen, denn der besteht ausserhalb der Welt." *Der
Möglichkeitsgedanke*, Erster Teil (Heidelberg: Carl Winters Universitätsbuchhandlung, 1931), p. 271. Faust considers the Stoic unreal realm of λεκτά
to be "outside the world" (*op. cit.*, p. 272). This touches upon an interesting
problem which requires further investigation, namely, the relation between
ontology and cosmology in Stoic thought.

[2] Plutarch states this alternative well in (II 202).

[3] *Meta.* 1047[b] 4, 5.

[4] *Op. cit.*, p. 75.

[5] It is also ascribed to Chrysippus implicitly by Plutarch (II 202) and
by Epictetus (II 283). For Philo see Simplicius, Categ. 195, 31ff.

the necessary and the impossible and recognizes "possibility" merely as a name for human ignorance about the future, coheres logically with the conception of a universe governed by rigorous causality or fate. But to stress it once more, Chrysippus never says explicitly that this is what he means by "possible".

Nothing need be said about the etymological argument except perhaps that it was characteristic of Stoic philosophers to think such an argument could be used with force, because they believed that language is not conventional, but natural.[1] It is in this sense that Chrysippus takes comfort from the fact that Lachesis (Λάχεσις) is named from the assigning (λαγχάνειν) of his fate to each person; Atropos ("Ατροπος), from the unchangeable (ἄτρεπον) and immutable lot assigned to each; and Clotho (Κλώθω), from the fact that all things have been interwoven (συγκεκλῶσθαι) and connected together (II 914).

4c. *Its relation to free will*

Needless to say, Chrysippus' doctrine of fate provoked a great deal of controversy; and those who objected to it most violently were those who felt that Chrysippus' determinism did away with free will. An eternal series of causes binds man's mind with the necessity of fate and deprives it of free will (II 954). How can there be free will if nothing, not even the most minute thing, is moved other than by the reason of Zeus (II 997)? Aulus Gellius reports the reaction to Chrysippus' doctrine most precisely and vividly (II 1000): "If Chrysippus, they [holders of rival views] say, thinks that all things are moved and governed by fate and that the courses of fate and their turns cannot be changed or surmounted, then the faults and misdeeds of men ought not to cause anger or to be referred to themselves and their wills, but to a certain imperious necessity, which stems from fate; and this is the mistress and arbiter of all things, by which everything which will happen must happen; and for this reason punishments of criminals have been established by the law unjustly, if men do not come to their evil deeds willingly, but are led to them by fate." Epicurus, too, it will be remembered, objected to the doctrine of fate on the ground that it would make nonsense of praise and blame, which are so naturally attached to human actions.[2]

---

[1] Pohlenz, *op. cit.*, I. 42.
[2] D.L. x. 133.

But Chrysippus, though he would not in any way compromise his doctrine of fate, believed as wholeheartedly as did Epicurus and most men of common sense that criminals ought to be punished. And, according to Gellius (II 1000), he must have been somewhat bitter towards the wicked who thought that the Stoic doctrine of fate bestowed upon them the right to do evil deeds with impunity. Men, he maintained (II 1000) "who are dissolute, vile, harmful, or reckless ought not to be tolerated and heard out when they, having been caught in guilt and crime, have recourse to the necessity of fate, as if to some temple-asylum, and say that crimes of the worse sort which they have committed must be attributed not to their own foolhardiness, but to fate." Chrysippus' bitterness, however, was not mere moral indignation. Aware as he was of what a doctrine of fate could and did, in fact, mean for morality, he tried to work out a deterministic doctrine and at the same time make a place for human responsibility.[1] This he did by introducing two sets of distinctions (which turn out to be one in fact and two in terminology) —one between proximate causes and perfect causes; and the other between things that are "in our power" and things that are not. Let us see what these distinctions mean and how Chrysippus uses them in his attempt to reconcile fate and responsibility.

These distinctions are applied specifically (II 974) to the relation of an assent to a given presentation. The presentation, Chrysippus maintains, is an auxiliary or proximate cause of assent; it is a cause not under our control; but the perfect or original cause of assent to a presentation is in our power. A man may have a presentation of himself eating a huge and not very healthy dinner or one of himself having sexual relations with his neighbor's wife. And the *occurrence* of these presentations may well be something outside his control; but, in Chrysippus' view, it *is* "within his power" to assent or not to assent to these presentations—which, I take it, means to attempt to enact them or to make them become facts (or to refrain from doing so).

Chrysippus tries to illustrate what he has in mind (II 974) by the introduction of a cylinder simile; the initial force needed to

---

[1] Chrysippus here tries to reconcile determinism and the assignment of responsibility much in the way in which such soft determinists as David Hume and Charles Stevenson were later to do. And like them he, too, fails. Unless the will is free, there can be no assignment of responsibility and the will cannot be free if everything has antecedent causes. *Cf. infra* note 3, p. 152.

start a cylinder rolling down the slope on which it is resting corresponds to the proximate or auxiliary cause—in the example, to the appearance in the mind of some presentation; the cylinder's own form is responsible for its continued motion and corresponds to the perfect or original causes, the causes in our power—in the example, the decision to assent to or to refuse to assent to the presentation. And so far, Chrysippus' distinction appears eminently sensible; it is one to which not even Epicurus could object, for it *seems* to affirm the existence of freedom in decision making or, more generally, the existence of uncaused causes. But does Chrysippus really unsay his doctrine of fate in such radical fashion?

If we examine some of the remaining fragments, it begins to emerge that perfect or original causes, or causes "in our power" are themselves fated, too, as one would expect a philosopher to hold who asserted that "nothing, not even the most minute thing, rests or is moved other than by the reason of Zeus, which Chrysippus affirms to be identical with fate." In one fragment (II 975) he sets forth as a model of our relation to fate the relation of a dog to a chariot to which it is tied. The dog is fated to accompany the chariot, but it can do so in one of two ways. It can run alongside the chariot and thus "make freedom of choice help necessity" or it can refuse to move and be dragged along by the chariot; so "the same condition undoubtedly exists in the case of men. And if they be unwilling to follow, they will be wholly compelled to enter into the path laid out for them by fate." [1] Obviously the chariot-dog model is no reply to those who, like Epicurus, ask the determinist about the legitimacy of punishing the criminal. If the convicted man was fated to kill his neighbor anyway—his only option being whether or not he would do it willingly or unwillingly—then there are no grounds for punishing him. The chariot-dog model shows that free will as an efficacious causal agent is illusory.

But Chrysippus is not yet refuted. In another fragment he attempts to resolve the problem by denying that some events can occur unless they have the cooperation of the wills of men, and "we contribute much assiduous and zealous effort with respect to

---

[1] II 975. Zeno also used this. *Cf*. Cleanthes' poem (I 527), found in Epictetus' *Enchiridion* (53), and Seneca's translation (*Ep*. cvii. 10) with the added line, "ducent volentem fata, nolentem trahunt." See note on the passage in the Loeb edition of Seneca's epistles concerning the disputed authorship of the poem. *Cf*. Arnim, "Kleanthes". *Realencyclopädie*, col. 567.

these things, since it has been ordained that they occur in conjunction with our wills" (II 998). Is this attempt successful? It would seem not. To be sure, a man has the psychological experience or the consciousness of making free decisions, but this is only because his "free decision" is a component in a "condestinate fact" or a fact fated to come about in conjunction with his "decision".

Chrysippus' second distinction, as we intimated before, does not, in fact, differ from the first: it is the distinction between fate and what is in our power.[1] With respect to it the most one can say (with Oenomaus II 978) is that, if Democritus makes the soul of man a slave, Chrysippus makes it a half-slave. And one may admit that Chrysippus shows an awareness of the problem that is original. But on closer examination it turns out that his distinction does not solve the problem. In one passage (II 1000), where he makes use of his cylinder figure again, adopting an almost Aristotelian position, Chrysippus maintains that healthful, well-educated inclinations will be strong enough to remand fated forces which attack us from without and that savage and ignorant inclinations will succumb to them. But unless a man is free to participate in activities from which will emerge the corresponding character, then he is responsible neither for his character nor for the actions which are consequential to it. And Chrysippus, it seems to me, implicitly denies that a man is responsible either for the health of his body or that of his soul, when, in his book, *On Nature* (II 937), having pointed out that eternal motion is like a potion which turns and agitates the things through which it flows (undoubtedly he is thinking of the movement of pneuma through substance), he says, "And since the administration of the universe proceeds in this way, it is necessary, in keeping with this, that we be as we are at the moment, either sick, contrary to our nature, or maimed, or that we have become grammarians or musicians. ... In accordance with this doctrine we talk in a similar way about virtue and vice, and generally about the arts and the want of knowledge about them. ..." But if a man is sick or vicious as a result of fated movements in the universe, he cannot be held to be a responsible agent.

---

[1] II 977 — *aliquid in nobis*.

II 991—τὸ ἐφ' ἡμῖν καὶ τὸ καθ' εἱμαρμένη. τὸ ἐφ' ἡμῖν becomes a key term in Epictetus. His message to his contemporaries, in fact, may be fairly summed up in the expression, καταφρόνησις τὰ οὐκ ἐφ' ἡμῖν.

We conclude that Chrysippus harbored two incoherent strands of thought, both of which he prized to the extent that he would give up neither, though he was unable to reconcile them. On the one hand, there is the rigorous causal nexus from which nothing is excluded. This provides the basis for the prophecies of the diviners and a manifestation of the orderly administration of the universe. On the other hand, there is the psychological experience of freedom in thought and action—the feeling that some things are "in our power". And insofar as this feeling is veridical, it provides a basis for responsibility and moral action. To maintain both these strands of thought *together* is a logical impossibility; Chrysippus appears to have held them *successively* or *alternately*. Like oppositely-charged electric wires, when they cross one another in his thought, as in the passages we have just examined, there is a reaction, in which either the all-embracing character of fate is denied or the feeling of freedom in thought and action is, in effect, said to be illusory.[1] It is fair to add that one cannot lightheartedly condemn Chrysippus, who was one of the first [2] in the history of western philosophy to become aware of the difficulties inherent in reconciling the principle of causality and moral responsibility, for having failed to solve a problem which has exercised thinkers to the present day.[3]

---

[1] *Cf.* Spinoza's ". . . homines se liberos esse opinentur, quandoquidem suarum volitionum suique appetitus sunt conscii, et de causis, a quibus disponuntur ad appetendum et volendum, quia earum sunt ignari, nec per somnium cogitant." *Ethics*, Part I, Appendix.

[2] *Cf.* Pamela Huby, "The First Discovery of the Freewill Problem" (*Philosophy*, Vol. XLII (October, 1967), pp. 353-362). Huby makes a convincing case for the view that the Epicureans and Stoics were the first to take seriously the freewill problem. She writes, ". . . it seems to me more probable that Epicurus was the originator of the freewill controversy, and that it was only taken up with enthusiasm among the Stoics by Chrysippus, the third head of the school" (*ibid.*, p. 358). I believe that here, too, Huby is probably right. She ought, however, to have taken into account Fragments 175 and 177 of *Stoicorum Veterum Fragmenta* (Volume I) and Cleanthes' *Hymn to Zeus* before writing, "The earliest evidence we have about Stoic views is from Chrysippus . . ." (*Ibid.*, p. 359).

[3] St. Augustine, David Hume, Immanuel Kant, William James, and Gilbert Ryle, to name only a few. For an eminently clear presentation of an argument for fatalism which contains as premises some of the propositions used by Chrysippus, see Richard Taylor, *Metaphysics* (Englewood Cliffs, New Jersey: Prentice-Hall, Inc., 1963) Chap. 5. Interestingly enough Chrysippus' attempts to escape the consequences of his determinism by adopting a position roughly like that called "soft determinism" by contemporary philosophers (Taylor, *ibid.*, pp. 43-44) run into the chief difficulty

5. GOD

We have already seen[1] that Providence and Fate are, for Chrysippus, the two sides of the same coin. As Arnim has pointed out,[2] it is true of the Stoa generally that if, from the point of view of physics or natural philosophy, their view of the universe culminates in the concept of fate, it is equally true that, looked at from the point of view of "theology", in which physics terminates (II 42), their view of the universe culminates in the concept of providence. That this generalization about the Stoa is certainly applicable to Chrysippus[3] should become clear from my discussion of the subject, which will center on his proofs for the existence of God, his thoughts on the nature of God, and his opinion on providence and evil.

5a. *Proofs for the existence of God*

Three proofs by Chrysippus for the existence of God are preserved. The first of them is really a series which exhibits the first and second undemonstrated argument forms. It goes as follows:

> If there is something which man cannot produce, then he who does produce that thing is better than man.
> All celestial phenomena and those phenomena of which the order is eternal cannot be created by man.
> Therefore that by which those phenomena are created is better than man. (II 1012)
> If there is anything better than man, it is god.
> There is something better than man.
> That thing is god (or, god exists). (II 1011)
> If the gods do not exist, there is nothing in the universe better than man.
> There is something in the universe better than man.
> Therefore, the gods exist. (II 1011)

Chrysippus' second proof for the existence of God is a teleological argument (II 1022). Not that he likened the universe to a machine

---

encountered by soft determinism; that is, it tries to deny determinism with the right hand without letting the left, which is busy affirming determinism, know what it is doing.

[1] *Supra*, p. 142.

[2] ,,Kleanthes'', *Realencyclopädie*, col. 567.

[3] In application to Cleanthes it has to be qualified as Arnim himself admits (*ibid.*).

or instrument, as modern philosophers would. From "the embellishment of the world ... the variety and beauty of celestial phenomena ... the power and magnitude of sea and lands", (II 1012) men are constrained to infer that the universe was constructed to be a home for the Gods.[1] No sane man, he believed, would presume that this universe had been made for mice. The third proof (II 1019) is empirical. Gods may be known to exist, according to Chrysippus, on account of the existence of altars.

Plato had based his argument for the existence of Gods upon the priority of the self-moving principle or soul to the four elements and the regularity of the movements exhibited by the celestial bodies (*Laws* 891^b - 899^b). Aristotle, too, had reasoned that, for the existence of eternal circular motion, itself required by the imperishableness of change and time, there had to exist an eternal immaterial substance capable of causing motion.[2] True in theory, it is also shown to be the case in fact (*Meta.* 1072^a 22) by the unceasing circular motion of the heavenly vault which requires something to move it.

Chrysippus, though in his first series of proofs [3] he makes the nerve of his argument the movements of the celestial bodies, in his second argument, which accentuates the beauty and purposefulness of the universe, falls more into the kind of teleological doctrines ascribed to Socrates by Xenophon.[4] The distinctive character of this second argument may be brought out by a comparison with a relatively early Aristotelian argument. In his *On Philosophy* [5] the Stagirite had pointed out that if one came into

---

[1] The thought here (II 1012—"si tuum ac non deorum immortalium domicilium putes, nonne plane desipere videare?") is that men cannot possibly believe that the universe is their home and not *also* that of the gods. This interpretation of the report is confirmed by Chrysippus' doctrine (III 371) that all other things in the universe are born for men and the gods. *Infra*, pp. 156-157.

[2] *Meta.* 1071^b 3-1073^a 12.

[3] Cleanthes (I 528; see also *de natura deorum* ii. 5, 15, for Arnim leaves out the most interesting part of the argument) uses a similar line of reasoning, but makes it straightforwardly analogical as does his namesake in Hume's *Dialogues Concerning Natural Religion*.

[4] *Mem.* iv. 3. And this affiliation is not at all far-fetched if one recalls (D.L. vii. 3) that it was Zeno's delight in reading Xenophon's *Memorabilia* that launched his career as a philosopher.

[5] Frag. 13, the Oxford trans., Vol. 12. For the evidence that this dialogue belongs to Aristotle's "transition period" (347-335), see Jaeger, *Aristotle*, 2nd edit. (Oxford: Clarendon Press, 1948), pp. 125-166.

the universe as into a vast house or city, one would surely reason that these things had "not been framed without perfect skill but that there both was and is a framer of this universe—God". Chrysippus, too, had spoken of the variety, beauty, and power in the universe; the line of his argument, however, is not from the universe back to the existence of its producer or craftsman, but rather to the stature of the being for whose purpose such a universe exists. The purposefulness of God is such a characteristic feature of the Chrysippean and Stoic divine being, as will become more evident in the following section, that it even shifts the direction in one of the "ancient" proofs for the existence of God.

Of course, since Chrysippus identifies God with fate, the same arguments he adduces to prove the latter[1] serve to prove the existence of the former.

5b. *The nature of God*

The substance of God is the whole universe and heaven (II 1022). God is a natural force provided with divine reason (II 1025); God extends throughout the universe and is the soul and nature of all ordered existence (II 1042). God is the world itself and universal diffusion of its soul (II 1077). If Chrysippus nevertheless speaks of God and Gods interchangeably, it is because he gives a naturalistic interpretation of the Olympian gods as the following report by Cicero makes evident: "And he [Chrysippus] argues that ether is that which men call Zeus, and that Neptune is air which diffuses itself through the sea, and that earth is that which is called Demeter, and in a similar way, he treats the names of the remaining gods." [2] Only in this sense would the proofs of God's existence be at the same time proofs for the existence of the "Gods".

Origen (II 1051) implies that, for Chrysippus, God is corporeal, an assertion which is confirmed by our philosopher's identification of God with the universe. At the time of the conflagration [3] all the gods (which, as we have seen, are parts of the universe) are destroyed except Zeus (II 1049). God is fire, and since all things are destroyed into fire in the Great Year, this destruction is also expressed by

---

[1] *Supra*, pp. 146-147.
[2] II 1077. See also generally fragments II 1062-1104 for some of Chrysippus' attempts to explain the names of the gods.
[3] *Supra*, pp. 123-124.

saying that Zeus, at that time, consumes all the other gods into himself (II 1049).

In the early Platonic dialogues, up to and including the *Republic*, the words "god" and "gods" are used to describe the supra-sensuous world.[1] And even when, in the late dialogues, the gods become identified with souls they continue to be divorced from matter. Aristotle's god, too, is immaterial and not in space.[2] Without being moved it causes motion through being desired.[3] Epicurus' gods are corporeal, though, to be sure, they are of a finer texture than are other bodies.[4] In Chrysippus' philosophy everything that distinguishes god from a material being has disappeard. Even god's indestructibility at the time of the conflagration is accounted for by his being identified with the primordial fiery substance.[5] Indeed, given his materialism and his pantheism, Chrysippus could have viewed the cyclical death and rebirth of the universe as episodes in the life of god, though such a view is not attested in any of the fragments.

5c. *Providence and evil*

Like Aristotle, Chrysippus believed that nothing is done in vain by nature (II 1140); but when he says so, he means that everything except the world itself was created for an end (II 1153); and, by an end, he means human purposes.

In sharp contrast to the Epicurean School [6] Chrysippus affirmed the providential nature of the divine (II 1029), maintaining that the gods are beneficial and friendly towards men (II 1152). The gods have made men for the sake of themselves and one another; and animals, for the service of man (II 1152). Other things are born for men and the gods; man was born to contemplate and imitate the world (II 1153); men and the gods are born for the sake of fellow-

---

[1] *Cf.* G. M. A. Grube, *Plato's Thought* (Boston: Beacon Press, 1958; first published in 1935), pp. 176-177.

[2] *Physica*, 266ᵃ 10-11. For the embarrassment such a conception caused Aristotle, *cf.* Friedrich Solmsen, *Aristotle's System of the Physical World* (Ithaca, New York: Cornell University Press, 1960), pp. 193-194.

[3] *Meta.* 1072ᵃ 23-27; *de Caelo* 279ᵃ 18.

[4] *de rerum natura* v. 154; Bailey, *op. cit.*, p. 449.

[5] Plutarch says (II 1049) that, in Chrysippus' view, none of the gods except fire is indestructible. This is undoubtedly the meaning of Chrysippus' (and Zeno's) doctrine (II 1029) that god is the purest body (τὸ καθαρώτατον σῶμα).

[6] *Supra*, pp. 28-29.

ship and society (III 371). So sure was Chrysippus of this hierarchical arrangement, culminating in man and god, that he was able to detect in the pig god's plan: the pig had been given a soul for salt in order that it not putrefy, and was made more fecund than the other animals because it was such a fitting food for man.[1] This teleology is that of neither Plato nor Aristotle; or, more accurately, Chrysippus goes much further than they do. Nowhere among philosophers in antiquity does one find a more radical form of teleology in terms of human purposes.

Moreover, so great is the providence of the gods that this is the best of all possible worlds; things could not have been deployed in a more advantageous way by god; had there been a better way, things would have been arranged in accordance with it, for nothing could have occurred to hinder god (II 1150). The gods are not auxiliary causes of any disgraceful happenings (II 1125). But how can the gods be exonerated from guilt for diseases and injuries? Is their providence limited by those things which cause human suffering, or are they responsible for that suffering? These were questions which Chrysippus, the proponent of a providential god, had, of course, to confront.

He offered four different explanations for the occurrence of evil in the world. The first was an argument, the conclusion of which appears also in Plato (*Phaedo* 60C; *Theaetetus* 176A):[2] no contrary can exist without its contrary; therefore no good can exist without evil. Secondly, evil, and specifically infirmities and illnesses of the body, was not deliberately created by nature (*sive deus*); infirmities and illnesses were necessary concomitant consequences of the useful and appropriate things nature was creating (II 1170). For example, it was fitting to fashion the head with small and delicate bones, but such a structure had to be accompanied by the disadvantage that it was poorly protected and might be easily damaged.[3] Thirdly, evil in the form of famine and plague is used by god as a means of

---

[1] II 1154. See also II 1160 and 1163 for the details of the hierarchical arrangement of things in the universe.

[2] II 1169. And Chrysippus himself reminds his readers that Plato has said this ("sicuti Plato ait"). Pohlenz, in discussing the Stoa's influence on Christian thought, wrongly implies (*op. cit.*, 430; 435) that this is a distinctively Stoic notion; this is pointed out by Edelstein in his review of Pohlenz' *Die Stoa* (*op. cit.*, p. 431).

[3] This example is also found in the *Timaeus* (75AB). It is an illustration of what Plato called the necessity in the universe.

punishing the wicked so that others may be deterred from folly
(II 1175, 1176). Fourthly, local occurrences of evil are profitable
for the universe as a whole (II 1181). An earthquake which deci-
mates a city is a great evil indeed when viewed at close range; but,
when regarded as god's way of relaxing the population pressure
in an overcrowded universe, the catastrophe becomes somehow, it
is alleged, more palatable (II 1177). The harmony of the whole
requires that good deeds be balanced by wicked acts.[1] A man's role
in life may seem a degraded one in view either of the vice he
perpetrates or the suffering he bears, but that vice or suffering,
ultimately, is profitable for the universe. As Chrysippus puts it,
"Just as the writers of comedy introduce absurd epigrams which
by themselves are paltry but, taken as a whole, add a certain charm
to the poem, similarly you might censure vice by itself; but, taken
with other things, it is not unprofitable" (II 1181).

Chrysippus was neither the first nor the last to employ this kind
of theodicy. Plato had introduced it in the *Laws* [2] to round out his
argument against those who believed that gods exist, but doubted
that they cared for men. Plotinus, too, was to make use of this
notion to combat the Peripatetic view that providential effects do
not descend below the lunar sphere,[3] though he goes on (iii. 2, 8)
to inveigh against the strongly anthropomorphic teleology propounded by Chrysippus and the Stoics. Leibniz, too, defends his
teleology "mainly by opposing the perfection of the whole to the
seeming imperfection of the parts". [4]

There is a parallelism between Chrysippus' attempt to affirm

---

[1] As Plutarch says (II 1181), "Just as it is necessary for the serpent's
poison and the hyena's bile to be in some medicines, there is similarly
another fitness in things which requires the wickedness of Meletus to be
conjoined with the justice of Socrates and the dissoluteness of Cleon to go
along with the nobility and goodness of Pericles." It is not attested explicitly
that Chrysippus was the author of this analogy; in any case it certainly
mirrors his point of view.

[2] "And one of these portions of the universe is thine own, unhappy man,
which, however little, contributes to the whole; and you do not seem to be
aware that this and every other creation is for the sake of the whole, and
in order that the life of the whole may be blessed; and that you are created
for the sake of the whole, and not the whole for the sake of you." 903B,
Jowett trans.

[3] *Enneads* iii. 2, 6 and Bréhier's note on the passage in the *Budé* edition.

[4] I am indebted to an unpublished paper by Edelstein on Leibniz and
Plato for this observation (p. 5). I am aware that Ruth Lydia Saw, in her
book on Leibniz (*Leibniz*, Baltimore: Penguin Books, 1954), opposes this
interpretation of Leibniz (p. 172), but even the quotation she introduces

both that all things are determined and that some things are not, and his endeavor to maintain both that the gods, being providential, perpetrate *no* evil in the world and that they are responsible for *some* of the evil there.

While Chrysippus undoubtedly demonstrates less originality in natural philosophy than he does in logic, his contributions to the former branch of philosophy, as we have tried to make clear in this chapter, have to be assessed as more than just a shoring up of foundations laid by Zeno and Cleanthes. Though, in his attempt to give a rational account of the universe, he recognizes the same two "principles" which had seemed highly plausible to Zeno, he weds them in such an intimate fashion that they appear as two aspects of one entity—an entity which, on his view, is always coherent or "in sympathy" with itself. And apparently it was Chrysippus who worked out the most satisfactory doctrine of mixture so as to account for the presence of two bodies, substance and god, in the same place at the same time.

Similarly in psychology it was Chrysippus who emphasized the unity of the soul. Not only is every soul a fragment of the world's soul, but each soul is a bit of unified pneuma, and all psychic phenomena—including the passions or emotions—are states of this pneuma or *are* this pneuma in some degree of tension.

While giving a strong monistic thrust to Stoic physics and psychology, Chrysippus also insisted upon the distinctive character of every individual object. He appears to have been wholly committed to nominalism, and if this reading of the evidence be correct, his theory of knowledge becomes all the more comprehensible.

Chrysippus, as we have seen, was a staunch defender of Fate and Providence, which he judged to be identical. The existence of fate guarantees that divination shall be efficacious; but divination is a science of the connections of events in nature. Chrysippus, we believe, defended the doctrine of fate with so much ardor because, in his view, fate or a rigorous causal nexus is a necessary condition

---

(*ibid.*) from *de rerum originatione* in defense of her interpretation, in fact, weakens it. In the sentence, "For it is to be observed that, as in a thoroughly well-constituted commonwealth care is taken, as far as may be, for the good of individuals, so the universe will not be sufficiently perfect unless the interests of individuals are attended to, while the universal harmony is preserved" the words "as far as may be" are crucial.

for obtaining knowledge of the connections between things in nature—knowledge that can be formulated in conditional propositions interpreted in the way we have suggested in the chapter on logic. In brief, Chrysippus appears to us to have held that, without the assumption that there is a causal nexus which embraces everything that happens, there can be no knowledge of natural laws.

Such rigid adherence to a doctrine of fate seemed to many thinkers in antiquity a denial of human freedom and responsibility. Chrysippus, as we sought to show, was an equally earnest supporter of human freedom, but, on our reading of the fragments, he never reconciled these two views and could have logically sustained them only alternately. Loath to give up human freedom because of the consequences for morality and reluctant to do away with the causal chain because of the consequences for knowledge, Chrysippus has the distinction of being one of the first philosophers to grapple with an intellectual problem that was to perplex thinkers down to and in our own century.

Chrysippus, as was made plain, has an equally difficult problem on his hands when he attempts to make his view that the logos or reason operates in the world beneficently or providentially cohere with the patent evil that is present in the world.

In a world many of whose contents allegedly come into being for the sake of man; in a world every aspect of whose life is determined by an unalterable series of causes; in a world which periodically destroys itself and then renews itself again in an unending and unchanging cycle, how ought a man to live? It may seem that such a question can be permitted to arise only by a piece of illicit logic. Chrysippus' ethical theory, to which I now turn, must give an answer to this problem.

CHAPTER SIX

MORAL PHILOSOPHY

Aristotle, in the first chapters of his *Ethica Nicomachea*, formulated the problem to be dealt with in a way which became for the Hellenistic period the way of putting, from its point of view, the fundamental problem of moral philosophy: what is the final end of life or what is that which men desire for itself, all other things being desired on account of it or for its sake? [1] Aristotle's answer was that happiness is that final good to which actions and things are to be referred for their evaluation.[2] And much of his ethical treatise is devoted to a description of those virtues, moral and intellectual, activity in accordance with which is, as he believed,

---

[1] *Eth. Nic.* 1094ᵃ 18-24.

The Epicureans: Epicurus, Letter to Menoeceus, D.L. x. 128. "An unwavering understanding of these things is able to refer every desire and aversion to health of body and tranquillity of soul, since this *is the final end of the happy life*. It is for the sake of this that we do all things . . ." The Phrase I have italicized presupposes that the question, what is that thing for which we do all else, had been raised.

The Stoics: ". . . atque ita cognitione et ratione [man] collegit ut statueret in eo collocatum summum illud hominis *per se* laudandum et expetendum bonum . . .—cum igitur in eo sit id bonum quo omnia referenda sunt, honeste facta ipsumque honestum, quod *solum* in bonis ducitur . . . id solum vi sua et dignitate expetendum est..." (italicizing my own) *de finibus* iii. 21. Again such phrases as "to be praised and desired for itself" and "that good to which all things must be referred" imply that the question we have suggested above had been asked.

The Sceptics: "The Sceptics say *the end* is suspension of judgment, upon which tranquillity follows like a shadow as the followers of Timon and Aenesidemus say." (italicizing my own) D.L. ix. 107.

[2] *Eth. Nic.* 1095ᵃ 18-20. Some persons worry about translating εὐδαιμονία with "happiness". But, as Aristotle makes plain, there were a number of views about the nature of εὐδαιμονία; and this is also the case with "happiness". The ambiguity residing in both terms combined with the convention that we use the terms in somewhat similar fashion warrants the use of "happiness" for εὐδαιμονία in my opinion. One of the major preoccupations of Aristotle in the first portion of his lectures on ethics is to discover a satisfactory notion of what εὐδαιμονια is. If some English philosopher had made an attempt to state what happiness is, one may or may not wish to say that his notion of happiness is different from Aristotle's conception of εὐδαιμονία. Unless one has such analyses in mind, however, when one objects to "happiness" as a translation of εὐδαιμονία, one's objection cannot be made sufficiently strong to make us seek an alternative translation.

happiness. Moreover, perhaps it is no exaggeration to say generally of the Greek attitude towards philosophy—to speak in the words of Theophrastus—that the esteem philosophy enjoyed was thought to rest in its power to secure for men happiness—genuine happiness.[1] Certainly the various moral doctrines set forth by the major schools of philosophy claim to be in part statements of what real happiness is.

If a philosopher maintains that some one kind of thing or action is the final end of life or is that which constitutes happiness, he is obliged to say something about all the other kinds of things or actions in the world. Do they contribute to the attainment of the *summum bonum* as defined by him? Are they indifferent with respect to it or are they positive impediments in the way of its acquisition? Or do some fall into one category; some, into another? These questions were as important for Chrysippus as was that of the final end of life, and I deal with these two topics first. Thirdly, I consider his doctrine of the emotions and their therapy, the justification for treating the topic in moral philosophy being that the emotions, in Chrysippus' view, are the source in man's life of that badness and unhappiness which he is not powerless to eradicate.[2] My concluding section describes what I consider to be some conflicting tendencies in Chrysippus' moral philosophy.

1. THE FINAL GOOD

That Chrysippus, like Aristotle, believed that the final end for the sake of which all things are done by a man is happiness is expressly attested.[3] Unfortunately we have no fragment in which

---

[1] "Omnis auctoritas philosophiae, ut ait Theophrastus, consistit in beata vita comparanda; beate enim vivendi cupiditate incensi omnes sumus." *de fin.* v. 29, 86. This does not mean that Greek philosophy is "practical" rather than "theoretical" (*supra*, pp. 18ff). The desire for the highest kind of happiness might, on Aristotle's view, lead a man to become a metaphysician, a physicist, or a mathematician. *Cf.* Bréhier's "Le problème qui se pose à la morale stoicienne est, comme dans toutes les morales grecques, celui du bonheur." *Op. cit.*, p. 212. *Cf.* Ludwig Edelstein, *The Meaning of Stoicism* (Cambridge, Massachusetts: Harvard University Press, 1966), p. 1.

[2] Such an arrangement of topics does not, admittedly, conform to the arrangement of them made by "the followers of Chrysippus" (or "those around Chrysippus") and others. According to the latter arrangement (III 1), the ethical part of philosophy was subdivided into the topics of "impulse, goods and evils, the emotions, virtue, the final end, primary worth and actions, duties, exhortations to act and to refrain from acting". My ordering, in fact, captures a number of these topics, but, because of the uneven quality of the evidence, it does not do justice to all of them.

[3] (III 16). Aristotle had already observed (*EN* 1095ᵃ 17, 18) that verbally

there appears a full discussion [1] of the nature of happiness, as he conceived it. When in his writings he speaks of it, he uses Zeno's definition of happiness, "the smooth-flowing of life" (III 16, I 184).

The final end of life, on the other hand, Zeno had affirmed, was to live consistently or harmoniously (ὁμολογουμένως ζῆν).[2] Cleanthes, as if attempting to give more content to this doctrine so that it would not be misunderstood by persons outside the school, modified the formula to read "to live consistently with (or in conformity to) nature" (III 12). And Chrysippus, wishing to make this even more explicit, set forth the following formulation: the final end of life is "to live in accordance with one's experience of the things which come about by nature." [3]

In order to get at the meaning of this assertion we do well to remind ourselves of the issue that for more than a hundred years had been debated in philosophical circles, especially at Athens, of whether what is good exists by nature or by convention. In the *Republic* (359^c 3-6) Glaucon, before introducing his disquieting story about the ring of Gyges, affirms that every creature *by nature* pursues his own advantage as the good. Callicles, in the *Gorgias* (482^e 6-483^d 1), after he has chided Socrates for shifting back and forth between the point of view of nature and that of convention in his attack on Polus, states bluntly that *nature's* verdict on the distribution of the goods of the world is that more of them ought to go to the man who is stronger and, therefore, better. Hippias, in the *Protagoras*, prefaces his remarks with these words: "I think all of you present are relatives, friends, and fellow-citizens *by nature*, not by convention. For *by nature* like is related to like, but convention is a tyrant over men and forces men to do many things against nature." [4] And Aristotle, when discussing with his

most men agree that happiness is the final end of life, but that they are by no means in accord about *what* happiness is.

[1] Though we learn that virtue is sufficient for happiness (III 49), that the happiness of the good man does not differ from divine happiness (III 54), and that to live in a morally bad way is to live unhappily (III 55).

[2] (I 179). Diogenes Laertius (I 179), Cicero (I 179), and Philo (I 179) attribute to Zeno the formula "to live in conformity *with nature*"; however, from the Stobaeus fragment in (III 12) it appears that the term τῇ φύσει was added by Cleanthes. For the arguments on both sides, see Pohlenz, *op. cit.* II, 67, 68; Pearson, *op. cit.*, p. 163.

[3] (I 12). Here, where Posidonius says that Chrysippus' formula is equivalent to "to live harmoniously", he is in effect saying "Chrysippus gives a more elaborate version of Zeno's formula."

[4] *Protagoras* 337^c 6-^{d}3. The italics are mine. As has been observed by

students some problems bound up with the study of moral philosophy, observed that there is so much variety and fluctuation in opinions as to what just actions are that they are thought to exist by convention rather than by nature (*EN* 1094[b] 14-16). Whatever may be the truth in the story about Diogenes of Sinope and the command given him by the Delphic Oracle "to alter the currency", [1] Diogenes made effective use of the divine injunction in his lifelong envenomed attack on the false currency of convention. "The currency he sought to deface was that which bore in any form the superscription of νόμος." [2]

These examples suffice to show that, in the second half of the fifth and in the fourth centuries, the question as to whether values existed by convention or by nature was in the air. Moreover we may infer, it seems to me, that in this debate the term "nature", whatever else it may have meant, signified a repository of true, genuine, or real values as opposed to the counterfeit values of custom and convention. And this much of the tradition is certainly latent in Chrysippus' use of the term "nature", as is evidenced by his view that what is just exists by nature (φύσει) and not by convention (μὴ θέσει) (III 308). But the term has for him other connotations as well.

In a passage (III 4) in which Diogenes Laertius recalls the Chrysippean formulation of the final end, we learn that Chrysippus means by "nature" in this context the nature which is common to all things and the nature which is peculiarly human. The final end of man is to live in conformity with nature (ἀκολούθως φύσει) because "our natures are parts of the nature of the universe" (III 4). Indeed, Chrysippus maintained that there was no more fitting way to initiate a discussion of moral philosophy than by considering nature in general or the way in which the universe is ordered; in fact no other procedure is possible (III 68). Justice has its source in God and common nature. "And here every such thing must have its source if we are to discover anything concerning good things and bad things" (III 326). Natural philosophy aims

---

Professor Dodds (*Gorgias*, p. 264), Hippias does not infer from the distinction the radical consequences drawn from it by Callicles.

[1] D.L. vi. 20, 21. For differing critical views on Laertius' account, see Dudley, Donald R., *A History of Cynicism from Diogenes to the 6th Century A.D.* (London: Methuen & Co., Ltd., 1937), pp. 20-22.

[2] Dudley, *op. cit.*, p. 31.

primarily at helping its devotees distinguish between good things and bad things.[1]

To appreciate fully these assertions about the final end of life and about the intimate alliance between moral philosophy and natural philosophy, we ought to note the crucial shift in connotation which the term "nature" undergoes in Chrysippus' moral philosophy as compared with his natural philosophy.[2] As we have seen above,[3] a rigorous determinism pervades Chrysippus' natural philosophy. This doctrine, in one place (II 937), is cast in terms of "common nature" (ἡ κοινὴ φύσις), the expression we now find (III 4) being used in the formulation of the final end of life. The passage—particularly valuable inasmuch as Plutarch has lifted it verbatim from one of Chrysippus' books—goes as follows: "For since *common nature* extends into all things, it will be necessary that everything whatsoever which comes about in the universe and in any whatsoever of its parts happen in accordance with that (*common nature*) and its reason, one after another in an unimpeded manner; for there is nothing outside which will resist its rule nor does any part of the universe exist in such way that it will be moved or will exist unless in accordance with *common nature*." A cardinal feature of common nature, as it is characterized in this passage, is its absolute power; its rule over the existence and movements of *all* things is unobstructed; indeed it is a condition of their existence that they be subject to its sway.

Now its absolute power is the very feature common nature loses when it becomes a key ingredient in Chrysippus' moral philosophy. Life in accordance with nature is one in which we refrain from doing those things which the law common to all things is wont to forbid (III 4); the implication is clearly that it is in our power not to refrain—that is, it is supposed that we *might* perform actions contrary to the law which is common to all things. Similarly the merely imperative nature of this law is revealed in the following words from Chrysippus' book, *On the Law*: "The law of all things ... is that which enjoins men, who are by nature political animals, to do the things which must be done and that which proscribes the things which must not be done" (III 314). The non-descriptive character of common nature as conceived here is even more patent

---

[1] (III 68). *Supra*, p. 46.
[2] This has been noted by Pohlenz (*op. cit.*, I, 117) with respect to Cleanthes.
[3] *Supra*, pp. 142-144.

in the report (III 4) that Chrysippus "means by common nature and human nature the nature in accordance with which men *ought to* live (δεῖ ζῆν)"." Common nature, in natural philosophy conceived as the irresistible and unimpeded force governing the universe, becomes in Chrysippus' moral philosophy a *norm*, in conformity with which men ought to mold their lives. But what does Chrysippus mean when he says that the end of life is to live in accordance with nature, the nature common to all things and human nature? The way in which Chrysippus, in agreement with earlier philosophers, endeavors to prove that man's highest good or final end in life is rooted in nature should cast some light on the problem.

In the fourth century the philosophers, Aristippus (*D.L.* ii. 88), Eudoxos (*EN* 1172[b] 10), and Aristoxenus (Athenaeus 545[b]) had argued that pleasure is the highest good, on the ground that every animal, both the rational and irrational, aims at it; it is the final goal of life built into the structure of things by nature herself. It is no accident, then, that the Hellenistic philosophers continue to take this empirical tack in their discussions of the final good. To prove that pleasure is the final end of life Epicurus "uses the fact that living things, as soon as they are born, are well-pleased with it, but are inimical towards pain, and this naturally and apart from reason." [1] Polemo [2] appealed to the same fact of experience, but he gives it a different interpretation. That which every natural organism strives after, in his view, is its own safety and preservation. This appears also to have been Zeno's way of regarding the matter (I 198). Chrysippus sets forth the doctrine explicitly in his book (III 178), *Concerning Ends*, taking up the cudgels against the Epicurean school. He maintains that that which is first conformable to the nature of every animal is not pleasure, but rather its own constitution and its consciousness of this. By making the living being dear to itself, nature makes him in such a way that he draws near to those things which are suitable to his constitution and is repulsed by those things which might harm him. Pleasure is an incidental factor consequent to nature's having found what is suitable to the animal's constitution. Some animals continue throughout their lives to be guided by impulse or instinct; in one species, namely, man, reason supervenes on impulse. And just as it is natural for the other animals and the young of the human

---

[1] D.L. x. 137.

[2] *de finibus* iv. 6, 14; 7, 16.

species to live in accordance with instinct, it is *natural* for man after childhood, to live in accordance with reason (III 178).

To live in accordance with reason, we may infer, is to live in accordance with one's experience of the things that occur by nature. And, since to live in accordance with nature is what constitutes the virtue of the happy man (III 4), we may further infer that, for Chrysippus, a man who lives in accordance with reason lives in accordance with virtue.

But in addition Chrysippus apparently held (III 20) that for each kind of living thing there is some faculty peculiarly its own and whose perfect development and unimpaired functioning constitutes the excellence or virtue of the individuals in that species. If we may indulge in an anachronism, Chrysippus' view is best expressed by Aristotle's words, "that which is proper to each thing by nature is that which is best and most pleasant for it"; [1] on the other hand, Chrysippus' spirit, if not his very doctrine, informs Epictetus' judgment that "of those beings whose constitutions are different, their works and final ends are also different." [2] If we can trust Stobaeus (III 16), we may conclude that the morally good and beautiful for men consists in living in accordance with reason.[3] And it also becomes clear now that reason is that *with which* man ought to live in accordance with his experience of things which occur naturally.

All of this, as has been suggested, sounds quite Aristotelian; the Peripatetic too, had held that the happiness or final good of man lay in the activities of that faculty in him which is peculiarly his own.[4] Even in antiquity the similarity of Stoic doctrine to

---

[1] τὸ γὰρ οἰκεῖον ἑκάστῳ τῇ φύσει κράτιστον καὶ ἥδιστόν ἐστιν ἑκάστῳ. *EN* 1178ᵃ 5, 6. The anachronism is explicable if we remember that most ancient Greek moral theories were informed by the notion. *Cf.* Bréhier's "On sait que, dans presque toutes les morales antiques, la nature d'un être définit son bien et sa perfection, et que sa ≪vertu≫ n'est que le développement complet de la nature." *Op. cit.*, pp. 220, 221.

[2] *Discourses* i. 6, 16-17.

[3] Immediately after citing a Chrysippean doctrine, Stobaeus says (III 16) that the following expressions are equivalent in meaning: "to live in accordance with nature", "to live a morally good life", and "to live well"; and, again, "the morally beautiful and good" and "virtue and what participates in virtue".

[4] *EN* 1097ᵇ 22-1098ᵃ 17. Note how Bishop Butler later incorporates this notion, having combined it with that of an intelligent creator, at the beginning of his second sermon on human nature: "If the real nature of any creature leads him and is adapted to such and such purposes only, or more than to any other; this is a reason to believe the Author of that nature intended it for those purposes."

Aristotelian and Platonic views was a subject of invective, for it was charged that the Stoics masked this resemblance behind the guise of a new terminology.[1]

1a. *Life in accordance with reason*

In order to understand this formulation, which is equivalent to life in accordance with nature, we must recall [2] that Chrysippus viewed the soul as a unified body, all of whose functions are those of what he called the soul's ruling part or rational part. It is perhaps the most revolutionary aspect of Chrysippus' psychology that the rational faculty is regarded as the soul's only faculty; he did not think that there were any such faculties as the appetitive and spirited, which are assumed in Plato's psychology (III 259). Appetition or impulse [3] is explained by him as the reason of man commanding him to do something (III 175). Another affective state of the soul presumably would for him also be reason in some specific dispostion.[4]

The excellence or virtue of reason is knowledge or wisdom (III 256). And this wisdom is of a rather special sort; it is knowledge of what is really good and what is really evil (*ibid.*). The vice of reason is ignorance. For example, one who thinks that death or poverty or disease is an evil exhibits the vice of ignorance; for these are not *really* evils, and yet he thinks one or more of them is (*ibid.*). These statements make clear why to live in accordance with reason, or, what comes to the same thing, in accordance with knowledge of what is *really* good and evil is, by Chrysippus, judged to be that which is morally good. Men by nature have impulses towards the apparently good and away from the apparently bad. Philosophy teaches them what is really good and really bad.[5]

This notion is elaborated in another fragment. According to Diogenes Laertius (III 117), Chrysippus believed that many things commonly thought to be good, such as wealth and health, are not good, because there are circumstances in which they could conceivably be injurious;[6] while it is the property of what is good

---

[1] *de finibus* iv. *passim.*

[2] *Supra*, pp. 129-130.

[3] On the difficulties with the term "ὁρμή" in the fragments, *infra*, pp. 182-183.

[4] *Supra*, pp. 131-132.

[5] (III 256). *Cf. de anima* 433ᵃ 25-30.

[6] Kant comes to mind immediately (as does Socrates, but for the latter,

always to benefit, not to injure. It follows that wisdom, which knows how to employ health and money, by dint of its knowledge of what is really good and evil, is the only good thing there is. Or, as other fragments (II 29, 30, 157) state, what is morally good (knowledge of what is genuinely useful) is the only good thing there is. Again, it is stated that a good reputation is not worth extending one's finger for if that reputation is not accompanied by right use (III 159).

This fundamental view of Chrysippus that what is morally good is the knowledge of what is genuinely good and what is genuinely bad—a knowledge by which its possessor is enabled to use things beneficially or injuriously—and that nothing else is good except that knowledge—this basic doctrine is found in a fragment (III 165) which, though not directly referring to Chrysippus,[1] neatly expresses his view: "If to sail well is good and to sail badly is bad, then to sail is neither good nor bad. And if to live well is good, and to live badly is bad, then to live is neither good nor bad".

We may conclude, then, that to live in accordance with reason, which we previously determined was the meaning of Chrysippus' expression, "to live in accordance with one's experience of the things which occur by nature", means, in turn, to live in accordance with reason in its state of excellence, that is, in possession of the knowledge of which things are really good and which are really bad. This knowledge itself is what constitutes moral goodness; and there is nothing good other than moral goodness.

The concept of reason's virtue as the genuine knowledge of good things and bad things also explains two figures, one of them employed almost constantly when Chrysippus describes the function of reason in human life. Reason, he maintains, supervenes upon impulse like a craftsman (τεχνίτης) or like one who works according to rules (III 178). Secondly, reason is *a guide* (ἡγεμών). The rational being can be guided (κυβερνᾶσθαι) by reason in every situation (III 390). It is natural for him to follow reason and to act in

---

infra, pp. 171-172ff): ". . . but these gifts of nature may also become extremely bad and mischievous . . . It is the same with the *gifts* of *fortune*. Power, riches, honour, even health, and the general well-being and contentment with one's condition which is called *happiness*, inspire pride, and often presumption, if . . ." *Fundamental Principles of the Metaphysic of Morals*, First Section.

[1] Arnim thinks it does refer directly to Chrysippus; I rule it out as a direct reference because Chrysippus' name does not appear in it.

accordance with it as his guide (III 462). Those who are moved by reason "as though it were a guide" and who submit to its government are able to master the impulses which otherwise might overpower them (III 476).

The excellence of reason—the morally good—or the knowledge of what is really good or bad (that is, useful or harmful) is specified in definitions of the virtues, some of which have been preserved. Wisdom or prudence is knowledge of things to be chosen; courage, of things to be endured; justice is knowledge of things to be assigned or distributed; and self-control is knowledge of things with respect to which one must be steadfast (III 295). Moreover Chrysippus held that the possession of virtue not only empowers man to see or understand the things he ought to do (τὰ ποιητέα) but also enables him to do them (III 295). In this context the problem of man's power freely to make decisions regarding his action is not broached.

What is the source of the knowledge which constitutes the virtue of reason? Is this moral goodness something more than a highly-refined instrument directing man's will in such a way that he will live a long and profitable life? By "human nature" Chrysippus must have meant that complex of rudimentary tendencies in man which we may call the instinct to preserve his life, for, in order to refute Epicurus, who had considered pleasure to be the fundamental natural desire, Chrysippus, like Zeno, points to the young of the various species of animals: they seek first of all to preserve themselves; pleasure is an incidental addition. In the case of man, however, reason soon takes the place of instinct and reveals to him what is really good, i.e., advantageous, and what is really bad, i.e., harmful.

From whence does reason get such invaluable knowledge? Chrysippus maintained, we recall, that the advantage to be derived from the study of natural philosophy is the knowledge of what things are good and bad.[1] He also posited as the chief good a life in accordance with one's experience of the things which occur naturally. Nothing else is said in the extant material about our problem. Any assertion concerning the origin of moral goodness— or genuine knowledge about good things and bad things—can be but conjecture.

---

[1] *Supra*, p. 46.

Now one of the cardinal doctrines emerging from Chrysippus' natural philosophy is that every event has a cause. Might it be his meaning, when he affirms that philosophy instructs us about the goodness and badness of things, that reason generalizes from experiences of *this* benefit following on *that* action to conclusions such as "that *kind* of action issues in this *kind* of benefit"? For example, a person discovers that *this* lentil soup (one of Chrysippus' preferred dishes by the way (III 709a)) is beneficial in some way with respect to his health, and the same he discerns to be true of *that* lentil soup, and also of *that*. He then generalizes: lentil soup—any lentil soup —is *really* good or *really* advantageous. Unfortunately, as we shall see, there is a serious objection to such an hypothesis. Nevertheless, we shall allow it to stand for the moment. It will at least serve to prepare the way for another hypothesis that might do more justice to the evidence.

1b. *Historical note*

I need not emphasize how akin to Socrates' thought is Chrysippus' notion that there is only one thing that is good, and that this is the wisdom which enables a man to discern which things are injurious and which, beneficial. In the *Euthydemus* (278ᵉ - 282ᵈ) Socrates makes his young friend, Cleinias, understand that men are made happy by so-called good things (wealth, health, beauty, temperance, justice, courage) only if these things profit them; and that they are beneficial only when men use them rightly (χρῆσθαι ὀρθῶς). The upshot of the discussion is that "wisdom alone is good and ignorance alone is evil; of other things none is either good or evil." [1] The same doctrine appears also in the *Meno* (88ᵃ 1-ᵇ2): when things are rightly used, they benefit us; when wrongly used, they harm us; temperance, justice, courage, quickness of apprehension, memory, and magnanimity may be harmful unless he who possesses them has also the wisdom to direct him in their right use, "since none of the qualities of soul are in themselves either beneficial or harmful, but become beneficial or harmful when wisdom or folly is added" (88ᶜ 6-ᵈ1). In substance, then, the Chrysippean notion of the morally good is almost identical with that of Socrates. The

---

[1] *Euthydemus* 281ᵉ 3-5. These things, neither good nor bad, were labeled "indifferent" (ἀδιάφορα—(III 117)) by Chrysippus. But different degrees of value in these indifferent things were recognized by the Stoa. *Infra*, pp. 177-178.

concept of reason as a craftsman which works in accordance with rules has also its parallel in the Platonic-Socratic dictum that virtue is knowledge. But Chrysippus' view as to the origin of this knowledge is wholly different from that expressed by Plato. While in his dialogues the origin of knowledge is the transcendental Idea of the Good, which one "sees" by turning *away from* sense experience, in Chrysippus' opinion its source appears to lie in the generalizations made by reason from sensory experiences of what is advantageous and what is injurious. But, as we shall presently see, there was also a non-naturalistic tendency in Chrysippus' thought concerning the source of wisdom.

1c. *The wise man*

To live in conformity with one's experience of things which occur by nature, to live in accordance with reason, to live in accordance with virtue, to be ἀπαθές or free from emotions; all these formulae are, for Chrysippus, ways of describing the final end of life or happiness. He who lives in such a manner and thereby attains happiness is the wise man. The wise man is a ruler, knowing which things are good and which are bad (III 617). To be sure, Chrysippus did not claim that either he himself or his disciples were good, that is to say, wise (III 662, 668). In fact, he held that all men (III 668) with the exception of one or two are fools and, therefore, unhappy.[1] Yet even though few wise men exist (or have existed), Chrysippus continues to draw a picture of the wise man.

The wise man has many needs but is in want of nothing, which is to say that many things exist which he does not possess, but regards as unnecessary for happiness. Necessary for him is the one and only thing which is indispensable for happiness—knowledge of what is really good and of what is really bad (III 674). On the other hand, the wise man will not shun all activity or possessions. He will not refrain from ruling a kingdom or living with those who do so rule (III 691). He will collect fees for his lectures (III 693, 694). He will take part in government if nothing prevents his doing so (III 694); he will participate *as if* "wealth, reputation, and health were really goods" (III 698). What Chrysippus' definitive opinion on this latter subject was, though, is uncertain, for Plutarch has preserved (III 703) a passage from one of Chrysippus' books which

---

[1] (III 668). Plutarch rightly chides Chrysippus for this gloomy outlook on a world allegedly ruled by providence.

contradicts some of the statements just quoted: "I think that the wise man does not meddle in the affairs of government, is of a retiring nature, and attends to his own affairs, good men being, in a similar way, people who are concerned with their own affairs and lead a retiring life."

The ideal of the wise man, in our view, creates an internal strain in Chrysippus' philosophy. It is derived from the tradition which originated with Antisthenes, who was inspired by what he took to be Socrates' ascetic life,[1] and passed from him into Cynic philosophy and through Crates into that of Zeno.[2] But this ideal of a sage so indifferent to all the goods of the world conflicts with the view that the goods of this world, though not morally good, have a certain value insofar as they are rightly used. If it be assumed that reason's function is to generalize from particular experiences to conclusions about what is really profitable for man or conducive to the furtherance of life, and if this function, when perfectly developed, be called wisdom or knowledge, then the wise man can hardly be described as one who has no need of the goods of the world and as one to whose happiness such things as wealth and health contribute absolutely nothing; for, if nothing else, they provide the material for his inferences; they are, in part, the source of his knowledge.

The position of the wise man, then, is vulnerable even from the vantage point of Chrysippean philosophy. On one hand, he is the one of all men who has made the truest generalizations about things which are advantageous and injurious, for he alone knows what is really good and what is really bad. On the other hand, none of these things which constitute the object of the knowledge identical with his virtue contributes to his happiness. One wonders, consequently, if his wisdom after all *was* derived from a close scrutiny and reflection upon his experience with the goods of the world. It is nowhere in the extant fragments made clear what precisely is the source of the wise man's wisdom, but his *contemptus mundi* air and the fact that the ideal has been so infrequently realized lead one to dissociate him from the man who lives in accordance with his experience of natural occurrences.

---

[1] D.L. vi. 2.

[2] *Ibid.* vi. 105. One of the fragments (III 728) shows that Chrysippus also adhered to the utopianism of Zeno (I 262; *cf.* Pearson, *op. cit.*, p. 198), for he, according to it, believed that wise men ought to have their wives in common; in this way the jealousy which arises because of adultery will be avoided.

From another point of view Chrysippus' ideal does cohere with a certain *a priori* element in his conception of virtue or the knowledge of what is really good and what is really bad. It will be recalled that this knowledge is morally good, because it enables its possessor to determine which things are useful or harmful; it itself is always useful and, hence, always good. Health is not by itself *always* advantageous (it is so only if properly used) and, therefore, it is not morally or unqualifiedly good, but only something having worth.[1]

Now heretofore we have assumed that the link between Chrysippus' natural philosophy and his moral philosophy and, more specifically, the ground of his assertion that natural philosophy issues in the knowledge of good things and bad things, is the accessibility to generalized knowledge of a closed universe, in which every event has as antecedents theoretically-determinable and sufficient conditions for its occurrence. But this assumption entails a proposition that Chrysippus does not grant, namely, that natural entities like wealth, health, and life itself are good things. If reason draws generalizations concerning the goodness of various foods on the ground that they contribute to health, it errs because, though it may be true that they contribute to health, it is not true, on Chrysippus' view (III 157), that health is a *good* thing; therefore these foods do not contribute to the procurement of something good. Health, though it is not good in an unqualified way, may have value if used properly and the wise man is he who possesses the knowledge which enables him to use health and all other so-called good things fittingly.

But of what sort is *this* knowledge and how does reason come by it? Did Chrysippus mean that the knowledge of what is really good or useful is coordinate with the knowledge of what is really healthful or really economic? Given that one has a relatively clear notion as to what health is, one, with some experience, can make judgments as to whether or not this food and that activity contribute to health. But of what thing does reason have to possess a relatively clear notion in order to discern in an analogous way whether or not health, wealth, or life itself contribute to its acquisition—whether or not and when, that is, these so-called goods are *really* useful? Whatever it is of or about, is this knowledge the result of generalizations on experience by reason?

---

[1] *Infra,* pp. 177-178.

Here the evidence is ambiguous and would allow one of two answers, which it is impossible to reconcile. On one hand, it appears that this knowledge does result from reason functioning instrumentally as a generalizing faculty. This is the upshot of the propositions that the final end of life is to live in accordance with one's experiences of the things that occur by nature, that what is morally good is virtue or the excellence of reason, that this excellence is the genuine knowledge of good and bad things, and that a thing is good insofar as it is useful (III 117). On the other hand, this knowledge of what is really good and of what is really evil appears to have a source which is prior to experience. In one passage (III 314), as we have already seen, Chrysippus maintains that the law common to all things *enjoins* and *proscribes*; this law is the ruler of human and divine things (III 314) and is, therefore, we infer, reason. These imperatives issue from reason, it would seem, just by dint of its being the reason common to all things. And Chrysippus appears to be maintaining, as Kant would do later, that a man ought to do a given deed, in the last analysis, because he is a rational creature. In other words, his decision is not the outcome of prudential calculations and generalizations concerning the utility of a given act. This view of reason as "practical reason" seems also to be contained in Chrysippus' doctrine (III 295) that the virtuous man is one who "sees" the things he ought to do.

Finally, as we have already intimated, the logic of an ethics based on utility demands that the final good itself, by reference to which other things are adjudged useful, be esteemed on grounds other than its utility. And if the instrumental function of reason as a measure of the utility of a thing or an activity exhausts its ethical function relative to experience, then the ethical function of reason, as it relates to the morally good—the genuine knowledge of things good and bad—must be one, which is, in some sense, prior to experience. Thus Chrysippus' view of reason contains an antithesis and results in the paradox that to live in accordance with one's experiences of the things which occur by nature, that is, to attain the final end of life, is not a sufficient condition for the attainment of happiness, although happiness is the final end of life. Or, to state the paradox more bluntly, to attain the final end of life is not necessarily to attain the final end of life; there is required in addition the genuine knowledge of good things and bad things which constitutes reason's virtue. And, this, as we have seen, is not the product of experience, according to some of the Chrysippean evidence.

It is, then, our contention that the ideal realization of the good and of happiness in the wise man both has and has not a secure place in Chrysippus' moral philosophy. It does not fit Chrysippus' conception of reason as a generalizing instrument for determining what things and activities are useful. The wise man is too contemptuous or, at least, too indifferent towards the world's "goods". It is unthinkable that he should attend to them with a view to determining which of them is useful. He *already* knows; [1] his wisdom comes from another sphere. He is sure of what is really good because an unobfuscated reason has *told* him; he did not have to wait upon the verdict of reason's generalizations on experience. And, as we have seen, Chrysippus at times views reason in just this way and, to the extent that he does so, the wise man in his philosophy *is* an apt exemplar of the rational man, as conceived by him. But it is impossible to forget the emphasis on experience, which is so predominant in his philosophy when other questions are dealt with, and, therefore, his concept of the wise man must be judged, in part, to be an awkward excrescence on the system rather than an organic part of it.

2. HOW OTHER THINGS ARE RELATED TO THE FINAL GOOD

It is *prima facie* difficult, on the basis of the extant fragments, to make out what Chrysippus' view is with respect to other so-called goods, i.e., things other than knowledge or the morally good. The difficulty arises not from a dearth of reports but rather from the existence of seemingly contradictory reports. In one fragment (III 29) there appear two arguments which he advanced for the view that only moral goodness is good. Another fragment (III 30) informs us that Chrysippus maintained the same doctrine in his book, *On Moral Goodness*. And Plutarch quotes from Chrysippus' book, *On Justice* the following passage: "Not only justice, but also magnanimity, temperance, and all the other virtues will be destroyed, if we admit that pleasure, health, or anything else, which

---

[1] *Cf.* Edelstein, *The Meaning of Stoicism*: "And surely in the opinion of the Stoa the sage is not merely the man who lives for the sake of moral action . . . but is preeminently the man who knows and opines." (p. 16) In his chapter on the Stoic sage, Edelstein says nothing about the source of the wise man's knowledge.

is not morally good, is good" (III 157). But in other fragments we hear of Chrysippus applying the term "good" to things other than the final end, for he recognizes two goods, the final end and that which is good by reference to it (III 25). Moreover not only wisdom is a member of the class of good things; courage, continence, perseverance, and virtues similar to these are also in that class (III 24). And from Cicero we learn (III 27) that Chrysippus, inveighing against Aristo, went so far as to try to prove that if moral goodness is proven to be the only good, then care of health, diligence in private affairs, the duties of life, and finally even moral goodness itself are done away with.

2a. *Things preferred and right actions*

We suspect that Chrysippus' position is not, as these fragments might lead us to suspect, contradictory. When he states that what is morally good is the only good thing there is, he clearly means by "morally good" *unqualifiedly* good. Life, health, pleasure, beauty, strength, wealth, renown, and good birth are indifferent things (ἀδιάφορα), as are death, sickness, pain, ugliness, weakness, poverty, bad-reputation, low birth and things similar to these (III 117). But the former group are conventionally recognized as good things to possess; so, even though they might be used badly and therefore are not good in an unqualified way, they may nevertheless be distinguished by calling them "things preferred" (προηγμένα) (III 117). That is why Chrysippus did not object if men called things like life and health "good", keeping an eye on the customary use of terms (III 137). He reacted negatively to Aristo's position, because Aristo maintained that among those things which are between virtue and vice *there is no difference* whatsoever, and that they are all to be treated alike.[1] Undoubtedly Chrysippus' derisive line, preserved for us by Plutarch (III 138), is aimed at Aristo's flatly Cynical doctrine: "Those who reckon as of no value wealth, health, freedom from pain, and soundness of body, and do not care for these things are mad."

On account of this position, Chrysippus and the Stoa generally were again accused of adopting the Peripatetic view that external goods are required for happiness, and of merely changing their names from "good" things to "preferred" things.[2] The charge is

---

[1] D.L. vii. 160.

[2] *de finibus* v. 30, 90.

false, for Chrysippus, though he did call "preferred" many of the
things conventionally called "good", never waivered in the conviction that happiness consisted in one thing only, though it might
be described in several ways, namely, in a life in accordance with
virtue. This life is the happy life. It needs nothing else; not even
the "preferred" things contribute to it (III 139). Strangely enough
Cicero, when following Antiochus, the enemy of the Stoa, re-
produces Chrysippus' view much more adequately in another
place: [1] "In making the primary objects "preferred", so as to
admit a certain principle of choice among things, they [the Stoics]
seem to be following nature, but in refusing to allow them to have
anything to do with happiness, they again abandon nature." To be
sure, the imputation contained in the last words, however, is one
Chrysippus would have denied.

In sum, for Chrysippus, virtue is sufficient for happiness (III 49).
And here we must remember that by virtue he means the virtue
or excellence of reason or knowledge. Such knowledge and it alone
is good. To live in accordance with it is to live happily. Other so-
called goods, like health, wealth, and beauty, are "preferred"; they
do not merit the adjective "good" because they may be used badly.
They may be called "good" in accordance with prevailing con-
ventions, but in no way do they help to make up the happy life.

Or, to state the same thing differently, Chrysippus was obviously
trying to mediate between two traditions. On one hand, he wished
to preserve what appeared to him true in the Cynic teaching, namely,
that only what is good in an unqualified way can bear the ascription
"morally good". On the other hand, he deplored in Cynic thought
the doctrine that everything other than the morally good is, from
the point of view of value, indifferent. And the contemporary
Academic and Peripatetic schools which emphasized the value of
natural goods such as health and strength seemed to him to espouse
an eminently sensible view if one did not exaggerate it to the point
at which health, for example, becomes indentical with moral
goodness. In thus attempting to preserve what he regarded as true
in both these traditions Chrysippus certainly did not, as adversaries
of the Stoa were fond of saying, simply repeat the Peripatetic-
Academic moral theory in the guise of a new terminology. Yet,

---

[1] *de finibus* iv. 16, 43. (Rackam's trans.) In this passage we may assume
that Chrysippus is included among these "Stoics", because we know on
other more direct grounds that this was his view.

however praiseworthy his intention, one cannot deny that in carry-ing it out he undertook an impossible task. The two lines of thought which he tried to integrate do not go together; in this respect Antiochus was just in his criticism.[1] If the final end of life, happiness, is to live in accordance with nature, one of whose ends is the preservation of the species, then it cannot be the case, as Chrysippus wished to maintain, that natural goods such as health, unimpaired senses, and strength, have nothing to do with happiness. The inconsistency of Chrysippus' teaching on this topic, which we have stressed, was, in fact, recognized even by one of his successors. For in the next century Panaetius openly admitted that things like health and strength do contribute to man's complete happiness,[2] thus resolving the undesired and undesirable tension between nature and happiness in Chrysippus' moral philosophy.

2b. *The virtues*

There are only scraps of information about Chrysippus' treatment of the virtues other than knowledge, such as that it can be taught (III 223) and it can be destroyed (III 237); but if one combines it with the notion that man's final end is to live in accordance with genuine knowledge, something can be gleaned from them.

Galen reproached Chrysippus for having recognized any virtues other than knowledge, for Galen, whose thinking was rigidly geared to Platonic psychology and ethics, believed that if a philo-

---

[1] *Supra*, p. 178.

[2] Pohlenz, *op. cit.*, Vol. I, p. 199. For a more recent and more forceful statement of the problems generated by this view, see Henry Sidgwick, *The Methods of Ethics* (7th edit., New York: Dover Publications, 1966 (f.p. 1907): "The result, then, is that Virtue is knowledge of what is good and ought to be sought or chosen, and of what is bad and ought to be shunned or rejected: while at the same time there is nothing good or properly choice-worthy, nothing bad or truly formidable, except Virtue and Vice respectively. But if Virtue is thus declared to be a science that has no object except itself, the notion is inevitably emptied of all practical content. In order, therefore, to avoid this result and to reconcile their system with common sense, the Stoics explained that there were other things in human life which were in a manner preferable, though not strictly good, including in this class the primary objects of men's normal impulses. On what principle then are we to select these objects when our impulses are conflicting or ambiguous? If we can get an answer to this question, we shall at length have come to something practical. But here again the Stoic could find no other general answer except either that we were to choose what was Reasonable, or that we were to act in accordance with Nature: each of which answers obviously brings us back into the original circle at a different point." (pp. 377-378)

sopher maintained that the soul contains only one capacity, then he can talk intelligibly of one virtue only, namely, the virtue or excellence of *that* capacity (III 257, 259). Consequently, for one who maintains the rational faculty to be the only faculty of the soul, to speak about virtues other than the virtue of that faculty is to speak inconsistently. Therefore, Chrysippus, to be consistent, according to Galen, must not talk as if there existed virtues other than knowledge.

Our philosopher, however, could legitimately speak of other virtues as various manifestations of knowledge in different circumstances and actions (III 256). For, to him, courage, for example, is not the virtue of the spirited element—no such element exists in the soul; courage is knowledge of the things which one ought to confront and of the things which one ought not to confront with confidence (III 256, 285). It is in accordance with this view that Chrysippus regarded all virtues other than the four cardinal virtues, which are themselves specifications of knowledge, as being derivable from the latter: "Good counsel and quick comprehension are consequences of prudence. Moderation and decorum are consequences of temperance. Fair dealing and kindness follow upon justice. And vigor of character and unshakeable determination are consequences of courage" (III 295). This example also illustrates the Chrysippean doctrine that the virtues reciprocally entail one another (III 297, 299). He seems to have argued in the following way: since courage is a function or an expression of knowledge, we may infer that a man who possesses courage is a wise man. And if he be a wise man, he will be capable of exercising the other virtues, which are also manifestations of knowledge, acquiring their name and peculiar quality from the nature of the circumstances which bring a person's mind into play. This line of reasoning would have been applicable to any one of the virtues. The perfect man possesses all the virtues and no action is perfect which is not performed in accordance with all the virtues.[1]

Given his view of the soul as being reason itself, Chrysippus had either to deny the existence of virtues other than knowledge—and this would have been to deny obvious facts—or he had to explain those virtues as functions or specifications of the one virtue which belongs to reason, namely, knowledge. Chrysippus was consistent

---

[1] (III 299). *Cf.* Bréhier, *op. cit.*, p. 218.

in his theory of virtue and so he was in his theory of vice as a lack of knowledge. Since, however, this intellectualistic approach to the topic is more amply exemplified in Chrysippus' doctrine of the emotions and their therapy and since the emotions, in his view, are integrally related to unhappiness and badness, we shall first examine that doctrine before exploring further the problem of evil in his philosophy.

3. THE EMOTIONS

Galen says of Chrysippus' treatise on the emotions, "In short, if one were to select and add up all the things which are said by him in his book about the emotions which, while contrary to the doctrines which he lays down, bring out the plain facts and fit Plato's doctrine, the length of the book would become something immense. For the book is full of words by him, in which he expresses the notion that we are diverted from our judgments and previously discussed plans by anger or desire or pleasure or some such emotion" (III 478). The preserved fragments—and for once we have a super-abundance of them —I am afraid,[1] do not bear out Galen's verdict.

3a. *Diagnostic analysis*

The most fundamental doctrine about the emotions is that the emotions are judgments.[2] This agrees with Chrysippus' view that the soul is reason having a variety of functions, because for one who denied that the soul contains appetitive and spirited elements, it was no longer possible to describe emotions in terms of the unruly and, indeed, rebellious behavior of allegedly irrational faculties in the soul.[3] There was nothing to rebel against reason except reason itself.

Yet how can an emotion be a judgment? Is an emotion not rather the *feeling* that follows upon the judgment—the hollowness and tightness in one's viscera and the pounding of one's heart which follow upon the judgment (unarticulated perhaps) that what is before one is about to injure one?—the sense of renewed vigor and lightheartedness that supervene on the judgment that

---

[1] (III 384)-(III 487).

[2] (III 456, 459, 461, 463).

[3] For example, in Book IX of *The Republic* the appetitive and spirited elements are represented as fierce animals which have overcome the ruling and rational element, their erstwhile master.

what is in one's presence is good? Chrysippus' predecessors, Zeno and Cleanthes, certainly put the accent on this second factor—on what might be called the tonal side of the emotion rather than on the judgment which gives rise to it.[1] But Chrysippus maintained that the emotion is the judgment itself.

What sort of judgment, then, is it that, in his view, is an emotion? The most obvious characteristic of a judgment being that it is either true or false, the judgment which an emotion is alleged to be is a false judgment (III 459, 461). In addition to being false the judgment which constitutes an emotion is a recently-formed one (III 463). Yesterday's judgment by Jason that marriage with Creon's daughter would be a good thing constitutes an emotion in Jason today only if it is repeated today. Thirdly an emotion-judgment has as predicate one of the two contraries, good-bad, or perhaps "maximally good or maximally bad" (III 467, 480). Fourthly an emotion-judgment is "one which incites a forceful and excessive impulse."[2]

To show more clearly what he means by an excessive impulse, Chrysippus employs the following illustration (III 462, 476, 478): a person whose impulses are not in excess is like a man walking; his legs obey his inclination, are under his control, not moving one step unless the man feels disposed to move them one step. On the other hand, a man suffering a forceful or excessive impulse is like a man who runs; the legs of the runner do not change their pace in the obedient manner which characterizes the legs of the walker. Here Chrysippus is thinking of the experienced runner athlete. In another place he uses as a simile the unsteady motion of a child. Emotions, he says (III 459), "are perverse judgments ... certain activities which change in a moment, just as the forward motions of boys exhibit an unsteady violence and a precarious excess by reason of their weakness."

To determine just what Chrysippus intended to denote with the term "impulse" (ὁρμή) is difficult in the extreme. He, in one passage

---

[1] For Zeno, emotion is "a movement of the soul against nature", "an excessive impulse" (I 205); *cf.* especially I 209. Note how Cleanthes describes pain in I 575.

[2] (III 384). I infer that Chrysippus is one of the Stoics referred to here, for in III 459 we are told that, for Chrysippus, the governing part of the soul is said to be irrational when, through an excess of impulse which becomes strong and prevails, it is swept away towards some wrongdoing opposed to rational conviction.

(III 175), is said to have maintained that impulse is the reason of man commanding him to act. But, when he *uses* the term, [1] he suggests that impulse is something *distinct* from reason. It normally "obeys" reason; it is in harmony with other impulses by dint of reason; when it is excessive, reason exercises no control over it whatsoever. While recognizing this ambivalence in Chrysippus' conception of impulse, I, for the moment setting aside Plutarch's reading of our philosopher (III 175), make the provisional conjecture (i) that "ὁρμή" is a movement of the *body* as a whole or of a portion of it; (ii) and that, in the latter case, in which there might be a plurality of such bodily movements, the reason or λόγος can and ought to keep these well-attuned or in harmony with one another. The most important point about our conjecture is its assumption that impulses reside in the body rather than in the soul. Its significance will become apparent when we deal below [2] with one of the objections to Chrysippus' doctrine.

Before going on I should point out that one of the recent interpretations of Chrysippus' emotion-judgment is impossible. Bréhier, while admitting that, for Chrysippus, an emotion is certainly a judgment, argues [3] that the content of such a judgment does *not* relate to the goodness or badness of a thing but to the appropriateness or suitability of the emotion. But, even if Bréhier's arguments were convincing,[4] his interpretation must be rejected *a priori*,

---

[1] (III, 384, 459, 462, 463, 464, 466, 467, 476, 478, 479, 178).

[2] *Infra*, pp. 192-193.

[3] Bréhier, *Chrysippe*, pp. 249-253.

[4] Bréhier's first argument for this interpretation is that Chrysippus admits (III 475) that a passion like anger makes us act against our judgment; and this admission would be totally incompatible with his thesis, says Bréhier, if it were a question of one's judgment on the good and bad and not of the judgment which regards the anger as being appropriate. However, it ought to be noted, in the first place, that in the passage cited by Bréhier (III 475) Chrysippus does *not* affirm that a man in anger acts *against* his opinion or judgment; rather he says that such men wish to indulge their anger and be left alone for better or worse. He does not say that anger itself is a revolt *against* an opinion; it, we take him to mean, *is* an opinion. Secondly, anger is a derivative emotion; it is not one of the four basic emotions acknowledged by Chrysippus. And, though we cannot be sure that the preserved lists of definitions of the emotions belong to Chrysippus, in one of them (III 379) anger is defined in terms of desire; specifically it is "the desire for revenge upon one thought to be responsible for an injury". Chrysippus defines desire as an irrational conation (III 463); on the analogy of fear it would be the expectation of something *good* (*cf.* the definition of ἐπιθυμία given in III 391). Each of the fundamental emotions is defined in terms of a judgment about

because it is meaningless. To say that an emotion is a judgment that an emotion is appropriate is, if we substitute *definiens* for *definiendum*, to say that an emotion is a judgment that a judgment that an emotion is appropriate is appropriate; and again we have to substitue, so that we are obviously in for an infinite regress. Chrysippus, therefore, could not have meant what Bréhier interprets him to have meant if his doctrine meant anything at all. To sum up, an emotion, as Chrysippus conceived it, is a recently-formed erroneous judgment that something is good or maximally good or that something is bad or maximally bad resulting in an excessive impulse.

Let us try to get a clearer picture of Chrysippus' positive doctrine concerning the emotions or of what he wished to convey with his assertion that the emotions are judgments. A judgment for Chrysippus is a false opinion with regard to the specific character of something, namely, its goodness or badness. Medea one day in Colchis meets Jason, or as Chrysippus would put it, Medea had a presentation of a stalwart and handsome young man. The picture evokes love, the thought that to be in love with this man would be a good thing, but, between the occurrence of this thought and

---

the goodness or badness of something, and all other emotions are derivable from them.

Bréhier's second argument for his interpretation is that a Plutarchean passage (III 384), which reports that Chrysippus did not wish to place emotion "in just any judgment but in the judgment which produces a violent and exaggerated impulse", would be too insignificant if it only meant that "in order to qualify as an emotion the opinion must be accompanied by an impulse" (p. 251). Its real purpose, according to Bréhier (p. 251), would be to distinguish a judgment on the good which does not arouse an impulse from a judgment concerning appropriateness which does produce an impulse. But it is very difficult to find this "real purpose", either expressed or implied, in the text cited (III 384) by Bréhier. There is mention neither of a judgment on the good nor of one on the appropriateness of anything. The sentence reads, "not every judgment is an emotion, but only the judgment stimulating (κινετική) a forceful and exaggerated impulse"; and it appears to be full of significance to us, since it gives one of the primary differentia of that class of judgments which are emotions.

Bréhier's final proof (p. 251) is derived from "the care with which Chrysippus sets about to distinguish the judgment-passion from error". For, according to Bréhier, if it were a question of a judgment concerning the bad and good, such a distinction would be impossible. But Bréhier's assertion is hardly correct. As he himself had just pointed out (p. 251), one of the characteristics of a "judgment-passion", in addition to its being erroneous, is that it stimulates an impulse. Even if it did not have the other two features we attribute to it, then, its stimulating an impulse would be sufficient to distinguish it from a judgment which is merely erroneous.

the mind's assent to it, there is a moment of indecision. If assent
to the thought is finally given, then one may say the judgment has
been passed. While prior to this moment her thought waivered
between the rightness and wrongness of this love, now that the
mind has assented, its status may be described as "it is right to love
him and a good thing."

Immediately one grasps two features of the kind of judgment
that is an emotion. It has as its predicate "good" and is recently-
formed. Presumably a judgment may be said to be recently-formed
on each occasion the mind makes its assent, either inwardly or
outwardly.[1] Now if in addition the judgment is false, if in fact to
be in love with Jason would not be a good thing, and if this assent
or judgment incited an excessive impulse, the judgment is an
emotion.

To proceed with the discussion of the emotions, Chrysippus (and
his predecessors in the Stoa) believed, as Descartes and Spinoza
were to do, that there are certain primary or "generic" emotions
in terms of which the others can be defined.[2] Cicero even complains
that Chrysippus and other Stoics devote too much of their discourse
to defining and subdividing the emotions, and consequently spend
too little on a consideration of their therapy.[3] These generic emotions
are pain, pleasure, fear, and desire. Pain is a recently-formed
judgment that there is present something bad (III 463). Pleasure
is a recently-formed judgment that something good is present (III
463). Fear, though not mentioned in the same fragment with the
foregoing emotions, is a recently-formed judgment that something
not yet present is bad or an expectation that something not yet
present will be bad.[4] Desire is a recently-formed judgment that

---

[1] (III 481). "And he [Chrysippus] says that 'recent' (in the definition of
a 'recently-formed' judgement) is 'what is near-by in time'."

[2] (III 463). Descartes' are *l'admiration, l'amour, la haine, le desir, la joie,*
and *la tristesse.* Spinoza (*Ethica,* Bk. iii. prop. LIX, *demon.*) reduces Descartes' list to *cupiditas, laetitia,* and *tristitia. Cf.* also Hobbes, *The Leviathan,*
Pt. I, chap. vi.

[3] (III 483). For some of these definitions, see III 397, 401, 409, and 414.
There other emotions are defined in terms of pleasure, pain, desire, and fear,
the four generic emotions for the Stoics.

[4] Fear is not discussed in this fragment (III 463), but I assume that
Chrysippus regarded it, too, as one of the generic emotions, for this was a
cardinal doctrine with Zeno (*Tus. Disp.* iv. 6, 11); and if Chrysippus had
decided that fear, after all, could be explained in terms of the other basic
emotions and was, therefore, a derived emotion, Galen would have found it

something not yet present is good or an expectation that something
not yet present will be good.[1] In each of these instances the judgment
is false and gives rise to an excessive impulse.

This, it appears to me, is Chrysippus' positive doctrine about
the nature of emotion. Before we deal with Posidonius' and Galen's
criticisms of it, we shall discuss his recommendations about the
extirpation of emotions from the soul.

3b. *Therapeutic analysis*

The emotions have to be removed, because they are contrary to
nature,[2] and, as we have seen, the final good of life for Chrysippus
is to live in conformity with one's experience of the things which
occur by nature. Those things which render a man free of emotions
or make him ἀπαθής are in conformity with nature (III 144). So
important was the subject to Chrysippus that he wrote a whole
book concerning therapy of the emotions (III 457, 474).

Convinced that emotions in the soul are analogous to diseases
in the body, he was persuaded that diagnostic and therapeutic
theories concerning the emotions ought not to be inferior "in
detailed theory and in healing power" to theories which have the
diseases of the body as their subject (III 471). He believed that
the emotions depress and crush the soul and his desire to extirpate
them was, indeed, humane, as so great an analyst of human nature
as Origen was not slow to see (III 474). He deemed futile any
attempt to eradicate emotions at the time when they are inflamed
(III 474, 484). His principal recommendation for the uprooting of
emotions appears to have been that their victim be made to understand that the judgment constituting the emotion is a false one.
But he would not meddle with the *judgment* of a man troubled by
an emotion at the time that he is suffering from it, because the
overthrow of the judgments which crush the soul cannot come
about by an ill-timed effort (III 474). In other words, their extrac-
tion must be essayed when the occasion is propitious. Those in the
heat of love or anger do not wish to receive any words of counsel

---

sufficiently extraordinary to comment upon it here where he is discussing
Chrysippus' definitions of the generic emotions. Moreover (III 447) would
indicate that Chrysippus included fear in the list of the primary emotions.
See also III 424.

[1] Not fully defined in III 463, but see note 2, p. 182.

[2] (III 462). The aspect of emotion which is contrary to nature is the
excessive impulse incited by it.

(III 475). The true opportunity for therapy lies with those who are not actually suffering an inflamed emotion but who are disposed to be overwhelmed by it (III 465). Since he is always on the point of being undone, the agent must be dispossessed of the incipient emotion in his soul; and this, according to Chrysippus, can take place efficaciously only at a time when the emotion is not fired up, "for when the emotions are aroused, they repel reasonings and things which appear differently (from that which they wish) and thrust violently forward to actions contrary (to reason)" (III 390).

The best comfort for a mourner is to make him see that his belief—to mourn is a just and expected duty and therefore a good thing—is false (III 486). And, though we are not furnished with other examples, we may infer, I believe, that Chrysippus would have recommended that other emotions be driven out of the soul in an analogous way. For example, therapy for Medea would consist, I suppose, in persuading her that to fall in love with Jason would not, in fact, be good. Again, for Phaedra, it would have consisted in her becoming persuaded that to make love to Hippolytus would not be genuinely profitable.

Chrysippus' intellectualistic therapy squares with his view of the soul as being essentially rational. As we remember, to live in accordance with virtue is to live in accordance with reason; and, as we have also learned, the major function of reason, for Chrysippus, is either to induce generalizations concerning things really good or bad, useful or harmful, advantageous or disadvantageous, or to issue commands and prohibitions relating to these matters. A person suffering from an emotion has made a *false* judgment regarding the goodness or badness of some particular thing; to be retrieved from the suffering which accompanies this emotion, he requires to be shown by another or to understand by himself that he has committed a mistake. And thus it becomes understandable why Chrysippus maintained that a person who lives in accordance with nature, virtue, or perfect reason, at the same time lives free from the emotions, attains ἀπάθεια.

Included in this remedial book about the emotions must have been a section on what we would today call preventive therapy, for Chrysippus believed things unforeseen and unprepared for are more likely to alienate one from his usually sound judgments (III 417, 482). Therefore, they ought to be prepared for in advance by dealing with them in one's mind as if they were present (III 482). Chrysippus also considers the case in which one regards something as good and finds himself beginning to crave it and to judge it as the greatest good. (The example adduced is a craving for money). Reason, it is pointed out, must be applied, telling the would-be victim that, in truth, money is not a maximal good, if he is to escape the deleterious emotion of avarice: "For when money is craved and reason, as a kind of Socratic medicine, is not immediately applied to mitigate that craving, the disorder penetrates the veins and attaches itself to the viscera, and the infirmity and malady manifest themselves and, once embedded, cannot be eradicated; for this infirmity, the name is avarice" (III 424). The same Socratic medicine must be applied likewise to other incipient emotions such as the craving for honor and the passion for women, that is, pride and lust (III 424).

These appear to be the doctrines which Chrysippus set forth about the emotions. So far he has given a theory which accounts for the facts. In Galen's sentences, introduced at the beginning of this section, it was alleged that Chrysippus also made a great many assertions which are contrary to his explicit doctrine but which, according to Galen, bring out the facts and fit Plato's doctrine. In a word, Galen (following Posidonius) thought that Chrysippus' theory of the emotions was self-contradictory. That the first part of Galen's criticism is wrong ought now to be clear. I attend presently to those Chrysippean assertions which to Galen implied a Platonic theory. It will be necessary first to examine Posidonius' criticisms of Chrysippus' doctrine of the emotions.

We feel, however, not bound to refute a sniper-like attack on the doctrine launched by Origen (III 474). Chrysippus, he says in effect, says that emotions are judgments, but he has not specified the kind of emotion a true judgment is. The answer is, as we have seen, that a true judgment is not any *kind* of emotion, it is not an emotion at all. A judgment, to be an emotion, must, among other things, be false. Origen has simply blundered; having wrongly inferred that, since all emotions are judgments, all judgments are, therefore, emotions, and being inclined to agree that false judgments are emotions, he wonders how, with respect to the emotions, Chrysippus will classify *true* judgments. The problem is obviously, one of his own making. We now turn to Posidonius' objections, which are of a less artificial sort.

3c. *Posidonius' objections*

Posidonius argued (III 466) as follows against Chrysippus' view: if emotions are judgments, then any changes that take place in emotions must be evidenced in some way in the judgments which they are alleged to be. Now an obvious property of emotions is that, after a period of increased intensification, they abate. Chrysippus then ought to be able to indicate some characteristic of the judgment, in terms of which an emotion has been defined, which corresponds to or explains the well-known phenomenon of abatement in the emotions—the quiet after an outbreak of rage, the changes in intensity of a man's envy, or the cessation of pain.

Now Chrysippus was by no means unaware of this problem. He himself wrote, "One must inquire about the abatement of pain, in what way it comes about, whether some judgment is changed, or whether all of them remain the same, and (if so) through what cause *this* occurs" (III 466). He acknowledges that the cause of this phenomenon is difficult to determine, because he does not wish to say that the judgment changes. In the case of abatement of pain, the *judgment* that what is nearby is bad persists. Phaedra's love for Hippolytus was not always feverish, and yet one does not wish to say that there were corresponding fluctuations in her judgment that it would be a good thing to indulge her love. It was situations of this order, I believe, which compelled Chrysippus to maintain that the abatement of emotion was not to be explained by any change in the judgment.

For an explanation of the phenomenon he had recourse rather to what we above described [1] as the fourth characteristic of a judgment which is an emotion, namely, that such a judgment incites a forceful and excessive impulse. When the emotion is observed to abate, what in fact is occurring is not a change in the judgment, but rather a diminution in the strength of the impulse, which had been caused to become excessive by the judgment (III 466). The judgment persists but no longer incites an excessive impulse, because some other kind of disposition supervenes, which has no bearing on the judgment of what happens (III 466). Chrysippus refers to a person's weeping uncontrollably, perhaps because of the imminent departure of a friend; then one stops weeping and one's grief seems to abate somewhat because one becomes thirsty or

---

[1] *Supra*, p. 182.

hungry. Thirst and hunger do not reason about the departure of the friend, and they lay hold on the forceful impulse to weep generated by the judgment that the friend's departure is a bad thing. But the judgment that it is bad does not itself change; its loss of one of the four characteristics of a judgment-emotion—that of producing an excessive impulse—means that the judgment is no longer an emotion, or since the impulse has diminished somewhat, one might wish to say that it is no longer the strong emotion it once was. In this way emotion-abatement is explained by reference to those very factors which, in Chrysippus' view, make a judgment an emotion.

There is no evidence beyond this one brief report for this interpretation. Yet what we have serves to make the theory clear and suffices to show that, while there may be difficulties in Chrysippus' attempt to explain the phenomenon of emotion-abatement, they are not the difficulties described by Posidonius; for Posidonius says that Chrysippus' explanation *contradicts* his assumptions.[1] Nothing in Chrysippus' explanation of emotion-abatement contradicts his theory of the emotions. On the contrary, he employs, as we have seen, one of the properties of an emotion-judgment to show what is going on when the emotion abates, so that his explanation is in full accord with his theory. Posidonius' appeal to Platonic psychology for explaining emotion-abatement (III 467) is certainly legitimate, in view of his penchant for Platonic philosophy, but it is hardly to the point when criticizing Chrysippus, who rejects outright the tripartite division of the soul.

Chrysippus' endeavor to explain a slackening in emotional intensity casts an interesting sidelight on our discussion of his recommendations concerning emotional therapy. We pointed out how futile it was, from Chrysippus' point of view, to attempt to cure a person at the time he is suffering from an inflamed emotion and how important it was to begin the cure at a propitious moment.[2] And it may have seemed odd, at that point in our discussion, to speak of the cure of emotions when they are no longer at a fever heat. If Phaedra is relatively calm and is not under the sway of her passion, for what ill does she require a remedy? On what will

---

[1] (III 467). And, presumably, he means the assumptions underlying Chrysippus' theory of the emotions, and specifically the one which had it that the emotions are judgments.

[2] *Supra*, pp. 186-187.

one work if the emotion is no longer manifesting itself? Chrysippus, and here the consistency of his doctrine seems to me to be admirable indeed, replies that, though the impulse has slackened, the false judgment is still there, and this is just the time to begin trying to make the person see how mistaken his judgment is: "For this reason, one is not to despair, since though the trouble drags on in this way, the inflamed emotion does abate, and reason penetrates and, as if taking over a fortress, shows one the absurdity of the emotion" (III 467).

The two remaining objections of Posidonius to Chrysippus' theory of the emotions seem to me to result from a failure on his part to comprehend that theory. The first is that some men who think themselves to be in the midst of the greatest evils do not on that account become engulfed by emotion (III 481). But Chrysippus had not held at all that every man who judges evil to be around him was overcome by an emotion; if he had, such counter instances as these cited by Posidonius would constitute a refutation of his doctrine. Instead Chrysippus was maintaining that if, say, Dion is said to be the victim of an emotion, then we may infer that Dion has made a judgment having the four properties mentioned: (i) it asserts that something is good or bad; (ii) it was recently formed; (iii) it is false; (iv) it incites an excessive impulse. One can impair the validity of this definition by pointing to cases commonly regarded as emotions and showing that some one of these characteristics is missing. For example, Chrysippus would have been embarrassed by a case in which the agent, on one hand, is commonly regarded as suffering some emotion and, on the other, is known to have made no false judgments. But one embarks on a fruitless enterprise if, like Posidonius, one hopes to weaken Chrysippus' position by showing that where some one of these properties is present there emotion is not.

Posidonius' remaining objection turns on a detail. He wants to know why not mere belief, but only recently-formed belief that something bad is present, generates pain (III 481). Unfortunately no fragment tells what Chrysippus would have replied to such an objection, but he could have said that a recently-formed belief is something like an actual assertion made within oneself. A man may believe mistakenly that his wife's behaviour harms him. But for a long time this belief may have lain in the back of his mind like so many beliefs or opinions men have. But when he asserts and

admits this belief to himself, it becomes a "recently-formed" judgment, and it is an emotion if it is false and incites a forceful impulse.
Or Chrysippus may have taken the tack that only beliefs which
are strictly new, in conjunction with their being at the same time
false and containing "good" or "bad" as a predicate, are capable
of inciting an excessive impulse. In any event it appears that
Posidonius' objection is not insuperable.

3d. Galen's objections

We now turn to those Chrysippean tenets which appeared to Galen
to imply a view about the emotions eminently Platonic, true, and
contrary to Chrysippus' false theory about the emotions. It might
be noted here that Galen's criticisms are themselves probably influenced, if indeed not furnished, by Posidonius.[1] We discussed
above the criticisms of Chrysippus' doctrine explicitly attributable
to Posidonius.

To Galen, Chrysippus' expositions of his theories about the
emotions and the therapy for them seemed often to commit Chrysippus to a Platonic psychology inasmuch as he talked in a way that
suggested there were in the soul irrational elements. To say an emotion is a judgment which incites a forceful and excessive impulse
implies that there is one thing in man which judges and another
which feels (III 384). The impulses of a man living in accordance
with reason are obedient as are the legs of him who walks. This
presupposes, in Galen's opinion, that there is one thing in us which
commands and another which obeys or is recalcitrant and, therefore, sounds much like the Platonic doctrine, according to which
the soul has as its regent part reason whose proper function it is to
reign over the appetites which tend to get out of hand.

Galen, then, assumes that Chrysippus' mind was divided between
his own monistic intellectualistic psychology and the Platonic view
of the soul (III 461). Though he explicitly maintains the monistic
position in his books on the emotions, in his first book about the
soul, he is alleged (III 461) not to have denied the tripartite division
of the soul, nay, to have explained the properties of each of the three
faculties, and even to have assigned to each a position in the body.
If this is so, Chrysippus was of two minds indeed. But Galen does
not cite any specific passages for this particular charge. What he

---

[1] Reinhardt, "Poseidonios", *Realencyclopädie*, cols. 734-736.

says reads as if he had taken an exposition of Platonic psychology, given as a point of departure of the view of Chrysippus. And Chrysippus, as we have tried to make evident above,[1] would not have found unmanageable the two-things-in-us view implied in expositions of his own doctrine. Since all of a man's soul is reason, in Chrysippus' view, anything in him which either obeys the soul or rebels against it must belong to the body.[2] One who speaks of a faculty in man which persuades and another which is persuaded is not thereby necessarily committed to the view that the *soul* has two or three faculties. Galen assumed mistakenly that the first view does entail the second, and on this false assumption he grounded his criticism of Chrysippus.

Galen's next move is to attack Chrysippus' conception of emotion as an irrational movement of the soul and an excessive impulse (III 462). He says that Chrysippus "defined" emotion in this way. If he did, there is no denying that he tried to embrace contradictory notions. But most of the reports Galen records represent emotions, in Chrysippus' view, as being judgments which *issue in* excessive impulses (III 462). By "irrational" Chrysippus, according to Galen (III 462), meant alien to reason and without judgment, and he pounces with obvious satisfaction on the phrase "without judgment". Here, he seems to say, we have a philosopher who tells us out of one side of his mouth that emotions are judgments and out of the other that emotions are without judgment (III 462). One cannot help suspecting that Galen, because of his Platonic bias, is reading Chrysippus in an unsympathetic manner. Chrysippus' view, as we have seen, is that an emotion is a judgment which *unleashes* an excessive impulse. The movements which it triggers are irrational in the sense that they are so intense and excessive that reason is powerless to regain control over them. But to say that *they* are irrational, i.e., without judgment, is not in contradiction to saying that *the emotions* which incite them are judgments. These are, *malgré* Galen, two different things. There may be something wrong with Chrysippus' doctrine as such, but it does not involve the contradiction Galen professes to have found in it.

Again, Chrysippus believed that the emotions were infirmities of

---

[1] *Supra*, pp. 182-183.

[2] We admit that if Plutarch has read Chrysippus correctly—that is, if the impulse is itself reason (III 175), then Galen's objection has some point. *Supra*, pp. 182-183 and *infra*, p. 198.

the soul just as diseases are impairments of the body. Galen observes that, in expounding this analogy, Chrysippus frequently betrayed a tacit conviction that the soul consists of several parts or divisions. Disease in the body is a certain disorder of the hot, cold, wet, and dry elements in it; ugliness of the body is a certain disorder of its limbs (III 471). Now if one wishes to liken an infirmity of the soul to a disease of the body or the ugliness of the soul to the ugliness of the body, one is obliged, Galen feels, to assume that the soul has elements and parts (III 471a, 472), for, as Chrysippus put it, "the parts of the soul are those through which the reason and its disposition exist in it. And the beautiful or ugly soul exists in accordance with the ruling part which is in this or that condition by reason of its own divisions" (471a). There is no way, I believe, to absolve Chrysippus from this blunder. If the soul consists of reason alone, one may speak of its functions, but not of its parts, though there is a possibility that one may be employing the term "parts" in a curious way, i.e., to refer to the reason's functions. Perhaps Chrysippus' use of the disease/body, emotion/soul analogy wooed him into modes of speech which were discordant with his monistic psychology.[1]

Galen's last criticism concerns Chrysippus' view that an emotion is a judgment, which, if we consider merely its truth value, is false. But the question is—why does the mind assent to a false judgment? Anger impedes our seeing things which are plain to see (III 390); and emotion generally repels reasoning and thrusts violently towards actions contrary to reason (III 390). And what caused those emotions to be aroused in the first place? Or, in other words, how did the false judgments which constitute those emotions ever come about? (III 473) One who has excluded the appetitive and spirited faculty from the soul, making the whole soul to consist of its rational governing element (III 462), cannot fall back on unruly and rebellious forces *within* the soul as an explanation of false judgment. Apparently Chrysippus was aware of this problem; at any rate Galen reports that, for Chrysippus, the soul has a sinewy structure whose relaxed and flabby condition makes us "shun things rightly known" (III 473). This must be interpreted to mean, I should have thought, that an assent to false judgments is the result of reason obfuscated by the flabby nature of the soul. Other-

---

[1] Edelstein pointed out to me that this is the one doctrine of Chrysippus which Posidonius finds acceptable.

wise one hardly does justice to the very words of Chrysippus, which are as follows: "as the tensions, flabby conditions, and taut states in the body are said to be in the sinews, because, it is said, we are capable or incapable with respect to works that are achieved through them, so the tension in the soul is spoken of, because vigor and flabbiness are found there too" (III 473). Chrysippus, we must remember, is logically entitled to speak, with respect to the soul, of a tension and flabbiness, properties one usually associates only with corporeal entities, because the soul, from his point of view, is a body.[1] The kind of false judgment that is an emotion may occur, then, because of excessive impulses, themselves caused by other false judgments or by the flabby condition of the corporeal soul.

Of course, in one sense, Chrysippus, rather than solving the problem, in fact, pushes it further back. For, if lack of vigor and flabbiness in the soul explain why men initially make false judgments, one wishes then to know why a man's soul ever finds itself in this condition. Chrysippus maintained that men assent to false presentations because they are "bad and weak" (III 177). But why are they bad and weak? Our philosopher had a distinctly optimistic view of human nature, as is evidenced in his reply to this question (II 229a). Men, if they are well-educated, will become wise, and this accords with Chrysippus' doctrine that virtue is knowledge. If they become bad, this is attributable to their association with bad men. Presumably Chrysippus would also maintain that the souls of men become flabby and enervated when they associate with men whose souls are already in that condition. Chrysippus, insofar as we know, never encountered any proponents of the doctrine of original sin, but had he done so there can be little doubt but that there would have been a head-on clash. And this is at no time more dramatically confirmed than within the century after Chrysippus' death when his disciples were vehemently taken to task by Posidonius for their failure to understand that one portion of every man's soul is "infested by a bad and godless demon" (III 460). For, as Posidonius argued, if men are made bad through their association with bad men, who "persuaded the first men" to become bad?[2]

The material is too sparse to appreciate fully the criticism that was made. It is obvious that much of the material comes from

---

[1] *Supra*, p. 129.
[2] Galen, *de Sequela Potentiarum*, 819.

writers unsympathetic with Chrysippus' views. Nevertheless, one may maintain that some of it is petty and verbal. Some of it could have been refuted by Chrysippus, granted his basic principles. That there are difficulties in his view, as in any intellectualist ethics, I am far from denying. But they seem not to lie where Galen, or rather Posidonius, so often finds them.

4. CONFLICTING TENDENCIES

If my attempted reconstruction of Chrysippus' moral philosophy has succeeded in any way in restoring at least the main contours of the original edifice, then that philosophy was an endeavor to affirm the value of such "natural" goods as health, strength, and unimpaired senses, while insisting that the possession of them is not to be equated with the morally good life. Chrysippus wished to steer a course between, on one hand, the Cynic tradition, which adjudged all things other than wisdom to be indifferent, that is, of no value; and, on the other hand, the naturalistic theories of the Academy and the Peripatos, which tended to equate the moral life with life in possession of the primarily natural goods. But, unless Chrysippus in his books more successfully maneuvered between this Scylla and Charybdis than the preserved fragments indicate, it would seem that his position was seriously encumbered by his holding conflicting views, which he neither could reconcile nor was willing to jettison.

In the first place, his formulation of the final end—to live in accordance with one's experience of the things that occur by nature (be it common nature or human nature)—contains one term which he uses both descriptively and normatively. In natural philosophy "common nature" means the law or rule in accordance with which all events in the universe *do* occur; in moral philosophy it is the law in accordance with which certain acts of men *ought to* occur. And, though in his moral philosophy, Chrysippus assumes throughout that man is a responsible and, therefore, a free agent, the upshot of his natural philosophy is, as we have seen, that the universe is a closed system in which there is no free or uncaused motion. The radical shift in the significance of the term, "common nature", as one passes from its use in natural philosophy to its use in moral philosophy, has as its counterpart Chrysippus' assumption, on one hand, of a rigorous determinism in a universe embracing man, and his silent supposition, on the other, when he deals with moral phenomena, that man can make decisions freely.

The second set of conflicting tendencies in Chrysippus' moral philosophy stems from his ambivalent view concerning reason, or more precisely, the source of reason's knowledge. In his logic and natural philosophy this knowledge is derived from sensory experience and generalizations made thereon; his moral philosophy asserts that one learns in natural philosophy which things are genuinely good and which are genuinely bad, and postulates that the good is identical with the profitable or beneficial, thus presupposing a world structure amenable to knowledge, which is acquired through generalizations mounted on experience, and reason, which is an instrument competent to make such generalizations. But this conception of reason is contravened by the view that reason enjoins those things which a man ought to do and proscribes those things from which he ought to refrain. One might be tempted to argue that Chrysippus in his moral philosophy is enlarging the conception of reason to include a practical function and that reason, conceived as practical, is not inconsistent with his other view of reason as a generalizing instrument. But when trying to resolve the difficulty in this way, one is confronted by two obstacles which seem to me insuperable.

In the first place, if reason can be sure enough of its generalized knowledge to issue on its basis incontestable injunctions, it must, at the very least, have attended to experience in a most assiduous manner, not allowing anything to escape its attention; yet the wise man, who is the paradigm of the man whose knowledge is perfect, as Chrysippus describes him, pays little attention to the so-called natural goods and can get along without them—those very things which are the basis for inference concerning what is useful and what is harmful. So confident is the wise man about his knowledge and yet so detached from the goods of the world that it is difficult not to feel that in the last analysis his knowledge is prior to experience; it is, as it were, encased in reason itself as an innate possession.[1]

In the second place, that this knowledge is *a priori* is suggested by Chrysippus' view that the virtue of reason is genuine knowledge of good things and bad things or of things really useful and really

---

[1] *Supra*, p. 64 where we discuss the possibility that πρόληψις in the Chrysippean fragments signifies innate ideas.

harmful. For, though by means of generalization, one may infer, for example, that a specified amount of sleep is useful in the procurement of health, and even that good health is conducive to a long life, it is difficult to imagine from which sensory experiences one can infer that a long life is *ipso facto* a good life. These two considerations, it appears, heavily weigh against the assumption that Chrysippus could have consistently conceived reason as an instrument to generalize on experience and, as such, a source of dicta about those things in the world which are genuinely good or genuinely bad.

Thirdly, Antiochus' criticism cannot easily be done away with. Chrysippus believed that to live in conformity with nature is the final end of life. He also believed that even if one does not possess such natural goods as health and unimpaired senses, one can nevertheless be happy. There is no evidence that Chrysippus ever reconciled these two views.

Finally, it is difficult to understand how Chrysippus conceived the relation between reason and impulse. On one hand, he says impulse is reason itself commanding man to do something; that is, impulse is part and parcel of the soul. On the other hand, he maintains that this impulse, on occasion, is something over which reason has no control though, on other occasions, it is "obedient" to reason. Impulse seems to be both reason *and* something distinct from reason. Each of these concepts of impulse is maintained by Chrysippus in the fragments, and to the extent to which he maintained the first, Galen was justified in saying that at times Chrysippus spoke like a Platonist.

I have stated the contradictions as plainly and as forcefully as I could. In their extenuation I shall plead only what I before mentioned in passing. The brilliant essay to synthesize what was true in Cynic thought with what was true in Peripatetic and Academic naturalism is hardly more encumbered by difficulties than any other solution that tries to do justice to the complexity of moral phenomena, and it seems in many respects superior to the onesidedness of the philosophies through and beyond which Chrysippus sought to work.

CHAPTER SEVEN

CONCLUSION

In the chapters that precede I have sought to reconstruct the philosophy of Chrysippus, one of the most eminent of the leaders of the Stoa. I have endeavored to restore the original features of his thought on the basis of those remnants of it to be found in the books of other writers. The study has been limited, as was indicated at the outset, to those passages which are in an obvious way pertinent to Chrysippus. Each of the passages introduced as evidence contains his name; some of them contain an author's summary and assessment of a Chrysippean doctrine; some—and these are obviously the most valuable—contain a quotation from one of his books. I admitted no fragment inferred to be Chrysippean on any hypothesis beyond the one that if a fragment contains Chrysippus' name, it is Chrysippean (i.e., it can be used as evidence for assertions about the man and his thought). For example, I excluded fragments which do not bear Chrysippus' name but which may be thought to be Chrysippean, on the ground that the author of the treatise in which they are found had probably read Chrysippus' books. On the basis of such evidence I have, after a presentation of background material dealing with Chrysippus' life and reputation in antiquity and with philosophy in his century, attempted to restate Chrysippus' doctrines in each of the three major branches of philosophy. What were the dominant themes in his philosophy? Do they interlock with one another so as to form a coherent system of thought? These are the questions to which I attend in this summary of the results set forth in the chapters on Chrysippus' logic, his natural philosophy, and his moral philosophy.

In his theory of knowledge Chrysippus insists that the senses constitute man's immediate cognitive relation to the world. The senses are "messengers", which bear reports about the nature of the external world. The soul, of which the senses are functions, remembers these messages; it compares them with other accounts that have been classified and, as it were, stored away. In this manner it determines whether or not the report being made at a given moment is veridical. The soul also "foresees" what will happen inasmuch as it can, by virtue of its experience, declare that a given object has a particular property, one which at the time, is, in fact, not perceived by any of the senses; or it can predict, again on the basis of its experience, that if a particular event occurs, another event which can be characterized will occur.

The soul contains no innate ideas. Every mental phenomenon related to cognition—presentation, notion, common notion, and anticipation, to use Chrysippean terminology—can be explained in terms of the natural functions of the soul. Chrysippus, then, was an empiricist in epistemology. Of the classical British empiricists, Chrysippus has more affinities with Berkeley and Hume, because of their rejection of abstract ideas, than with Locke.

If one examines the Zenonian and Cleanthian fragments relating to logic, one will note, on the one hand, that in their brief, almost epigrammatic, sentences, there appear expressions—"presentation", "assent", "impression", and "memory"—which Chrysippus employs in his epistemology, and, on the other, that there is nothing which would indicate that either of Chrysippus' predecessors was concerned with formal logic, i.e., with the study of arguments, their components, and the norms of valid argumentation. This testimony relating to the earlier heads of the Stoic school lends weight to the conclusion that Chrysippus developed and made more articulate the epistemology he learned in the school, and that he, by dealing in such a thorough way with propositions and arguments, made a distinctive contribution to Stoic philosophy.

The manner in which Chrysippus relates epistemology to formal logic may be discerned in his conception of dialectic as the discipline whose purpose it is to discover truths and the organization of them. Atomic propositions are true when the states of affairs they denote, in fact, exist. But events do not occur haphazardly in the world as it is conceived by Chrysippus. Every happening has natural grounds or causes and these are, in principle, discoverable. Some events are sufficiently like others so that if a man determines the cause of one of them, he may conclude that the causes of the remainder of them are similar to it. That is, as Chrysippus maintains, one may generalize and affirm that if events of a particular sort occur, then other events of a specified sort will occur. Such generalizations may be expressed in conditional propositions which are true only if it is empirically impossible for the antecedents in them to be true while the consequents are false. These kinds of generalizations, then, are true only when they denote connections between things or events in nature. In this portion of his logic Chrysippus evinces his constantly-held conviction that the nature of the world can and ought to be known.

His formulation of argument schemata for arguments containing compound propositions — today called the *modus ponens*, the *modus tollens*, and the disjunctive syllogism—constituted a brilliant supplement to Aristotle's logic of classes. And, though it is by no means clear that Chrysippus was the first to formulate a logic of propositions, he was certainly the first Stoic to understand the import of this kind of logic. His conception of the truth condition of a conditional proposition, described in the preceding paragraph leaves no room for doubt that he views the new logic, not as an intellectual toy, but as an instrument for deepening man's knowledge of nature.

Now that the relation between two of the principal branches of Chrysippus' logic has been sketched, I shall summarize the chief notions in his natural philosophy, after which I shall show how the leading conceptions in his logic are related to those of his natural philosophy.

The fundamental feature of Chrysippus' natural philosophy is its monism. Taking over from the school tradition the two "principles" which underlay Zeno's rational account of the universe, he knitted them together in such fashion that they become two aspects of one primordial substance whose eternal duration is characterized by a cyclical pattern. The minimum qualification of this substance as a fiery mass and its maximum qualification as a universe are the polar points in each cycle of its existence. All the events which take place and all the individuals which come to be are the manifestations in given regions of space of the divine reason, logos, or pneuma, penetrating and fructifying substance. This is why there is a "sympathy" between all the parts of the universe; as constituents of the same substance there is among them an ineluctable kinship.

Chrysippus welds to this monistic way of looking at things a nominalism, which perhaps stems from his recognition of the unbounded richness of the primordial substance, of the copiously-varied progeny which will issue from the always integrated substance and divine reason. Every thing, and every event, constitutes an individuating property of the primordial substance. Though there are obvious similarities among things in the universe, there are no identical twins; no man, leaf, or fish is exactly like any other man, leaf, or fish.

A third prominent feature of Chrysippus' natural philosophy is its determinism or its providentialism, for the phenomena described by these terms are really one and the same. The first accents the inevitable character of the course of events, in theory predictable in the degree that one can unveil the causal chain which binds these happenings together. The second emphasizes the goodness of what takes place. The first signifies that there is an efficient cause or set of efficient causes in terms of which the emergence of any given individual or event may be explained. The second is Chrysippus' final answer to the query, Why does the primordial substance successively become a universe and then revert to its original state? His determinism is an expression of his view that nothing could happen in a way different from that in which it does happen. His providentialism exhibits his conviction that nothing which happens could have occurred in a better way—or to use language that was to become fashionable in another era—that this is the best of all possible worlds.

A fourth distinctive doctrine in Chrysippus' natural philosophy is his psychological monism. Abandoning the Platonic tripartite soul, he affirms the soul to be reason alone; it has diverse functions and it can be "disposed" in various ways or can be in one state or another, but throughout it is one corporeal entity. It does not have parts or divisions among which there might erupt internecine warfare. Accompanying this view of the soul's unity is a doctrine which relates Chrysippus' psychology to his metaphysical monism, and this is the tenet that every soul is a fragment of the soul or reason of the universe.

Though our philosopher held that there are three distinct departments of philosophy—logic, natural philosophy, and ethics—he did not believe that the notions in any branch were without reference to those in another. And before I proceed to a summary of the leading ideas in his moral philosophy I shall briefly discuss how his logic and natural philosophy elucidate one another.

Chrysippus' doctrine that the soul is a unity, reason capable of being in one condition or another, relates to his empiricist epistemology and specifically to the conception of a presentation as being an alteration of the soul. The soul in the presence of an external object assumes a certain state which, as we have seen, plays a role in the cognition of that object. Chrysippus' nominalism, his teaching that everything is, in the strict sense of the word, an individual, in company with the view that there is nothing in the reason which was not first present to the senses or to the memory, is the metaphysical basis of his doctrine that common notions are not innate ideas or abstract ideas, but rather are families of remembered similar presentations. Finally, his determinism or his doctrine that every event has causal antecedents which, when unveiled, explain their occurrence, is reflected in his logical doctrine of implication. The truth of a conditional proposition signifies that it is empirically impossible for its antecedent to be true when its consequent is false, and this suggests, if there are any true conditional propositions, that in nature one kind of event is always the cause of another kind of event. And, in his natural philosophy, Chrysippus implies this to be the case with his doctrine that, though no event is exactly like another, there are similarities among occurrences such that one can classify them into families and thus speak intelligibly of "kinds" of events.

Chrysippus' moral philosophy is built around his conceptions of the final end of life, virtue, and the passions. His formula for the final end of life is "to live in accordance with one's experience of the things which occur by nature". I first pointed out that the term "common nature", signifying in natural philosophy the inviolable laws in accordance with which all things exist, undergoes a shift in meaning when employed in Chrysippus' moral philosophy; for here it signifies the law in obedience to which men ought to act. Secondly, it was shown that the final end of life could, for Chrysippus, equally well be described as "to live in accordance with reason", and this was to be understood as "reason functioning in accordance with excellence or virtue". The excellence of reason is the knowledge of what is really good and what is really bad. Such knowledge is the one thing that is "morally" or unqualifiedly good. In an attempt to open up further Chrysippus' conception of the final end of life I sought to discover what in his mind was regarded as the source of the knowledge that constitutes the excellence of reason. On one hand, the strong empirical current running through his philosophy supports the hypothesis that the source of this knowledge are the senses and the generalizations made by reason from their reports concerning the advantageousness or the harmfulness of the various kinds of things experienced. On the other hand, this hypothesis is weakened by the circumstance that, in Chrysippus' philosophy, nothing can be called unqualifiedly good except the morally good itself; consequently, the conception of reason as an instrument which makes generalizations about the goodness of things breaks down. For an object or activity which is deemed useful can, in addition, be adjudged good only if the purpose which it serves is good. And, on Chrysippus' view, nothing is good except the morally good or genuine knowledge of good things and bad things. Anything, then, which does not contribute to the acquisition of this knowledge, no matter how useful it may be in other respects, cannot be adjudged good. A counter-hypothesis of an *a priori* source of this knowledge is supported by Chrysippus' ideal of the wise man—the exemplary case of the man who lives in accordance with reason—who seems to have no need of the goods of the world and whose knowledge, so indubitable and forthright, does not issue, it seems, from long and arduous reflection upon experience. Such an hypothesis also finds some confirmation in the assertion that reason commands and proscribes regarding the things one ought to undertake and those from which one ought to refrain. The evidence for an empirical source of this knowledge outweighs that which points to an *a priori* source for it, but the presence of the latter makes problematic the interpretation of this part of Chrysippus' moral philosophy.

With respect to the relation of other things to the final good, Chrysippus seeks to steer between the Cynic view, which was that nothing is good besides virtue, and the Peripatetic doctrine, which emphasized the value of natural goods. The undertaking fails, because Chrysippus insists that natural goods such as health, though "preferred", do not contribute to happiness. And this proved to be a difficult position indeed for a philosopher who maintained both that the final end of life was happiness and that the final end of life was to live in accordance with nature.

Insofar as the knowledge which constitutes reason's excellence has its source in the senses and reason's generalizations made upon sensory reports, it is evident how Chrysippus' theory of-knowledge squares with his moral philosophy. And his conception of the cardinal virtues as various specifications of knowledge coheres with the conception of the soul as essentially reason, a conception he sets forth in his natural philosophy.

A further connection between his doctrine of the soul as a unified body, namely, reason, and his moral philosophy emerges in his doctrine of the emotions and his recommendation regarding the therapy for them. An emotion is a recently-formed false judgment which has as its predicate "good" or "bad" and which incites an excessive impulse. And such a judgment may be viewed as a perverted state or condition of reason. The extirpation of emotions comes about when their victims comprehend that the judgments which constitute them are mistaken ones; and this comprehension can be most efficaciously induced at a time when the impulse set off by the judgment is not at fever-heat pitch.

In Chrysippus' natural philosophy we found a forcefully-articulated doctrine of determinism, and I there raised the question, how Chrysippus, aware as he was of the consequences of such a doctrine for morality, could legitimately go on to discuss the problems commonly raised in moral philosophy. The answer is, as we are led to suspect even in his discussions of fate, that he, in effect, concedes that men are responsible for some of their behavior. In none of the extant fragments of his moral philosophy does Chrysippus broach the subject of determinism versus freedom. For example, in his discussions of therapy for the emotions, he never waivers in his conviction, tacit though it be, that man himself is responsible for the emotions whose harmful effects he suffers.

Chrysippus' philosophy, taken as a whole, must have been, if not thoroughly well-knit, comprehensive and attractive. Even the little that is preserved in the fragments still shows why his reflections aroused the interests of so many generations of men. His system attempts to lay the philosophical foundations for an empirical view of knowledge. It makes of each man and of every other entity in the universe a distinct individual, and yet places all things in sympathetic relations with one another by conceiving them as the parts of one substance. It explains the evolution of the universe from a primordial substance and its periodic resolution into that substance in terms of the beneficent ends of a wholly immanent divine force. Like Greek philosophy generally, it posits happiness as the final end of life; but it refuses to identify happiness with either the "gifts of nature" or the "gifts of fortune" and conceives it rather as the possession of the man who is morally good. And, though eternal life is denied to man, an opportunity to "re-play" the same role in another of the cycles of the universe is a certainty. Chrysippus' way of seeing the world, as I have reconstructed it, though not without its difficulties, can boast several philosophically noteworthy features; and, in its original form, it must have constituted an overwhelmingly impressive system of thought.

Early in this investigation [1] there were set forth descriptions that have been given by modern scholars of Chrysippus' position within the Stoa. What can be said of them in the light of the results of the present investigation of Chrysippus' philosophy?

Now as for the description concerning our philosopher's position in the Stoa—his relation to Zeno and Cleanthes—this study would point to the conclusion that, while Chrysippus accepted some of the doctrines as such of his predecessors and developed others of them, he, in several ways, demonstrated a bold and striking originality. The results of my study constitute, I trust, a refutation of Pearson's view that Zeno and Cleanthes alone are responsible for the true essence of Stoicism. Chrysippus' conception of a presentation as an alteration of the soul is new and gives to Stoic materialism a greater degree of plausibility. The development of a logic of propositions in the context of dialectic, conceived as the search for truth by means of argument, is a wholly novel idea and a rich contribution by Chrysippus to Stoic thought. The embryonic elements of a metaphysical monism may be found in Zeno and Cleanthes, but it was Chrysippus who gave the most forthright and highly-developed statement of this doctrine, and psychological monism in the Stoa is almost entirely the product of his own reflections. His formulation of the doctrine of mixture was the one most highly esteemed among the Stoics. Determinism and providentialism are to be found in Chrysippus' predecessors, but it was he who systematized and defended these doctrines against the mounting attacks of the opposing schools. Chrysippus clearly enunciates a doctrine of sympathy among the parts of the universe; consequently, the Stoa did not have to wait for Posidonius to formulate such a view. In ethics, and particularly in his conception of the emotions, Chrysippus introduces a radical intellectualism of which there are few traces in the doctrines of Zeno and Cleanthes. Though he employed two of the elements in what was to become a Stoic "doctrine of categories", he himself had no systematic teaching about the categories either of being or of terms.

---

[1] *Supra*, pp. 14-17.

Secondly, in regard to the description—Chrysippus argued more acutely than Zeno and Cleanthes and was responsible for the importance logic assumed in the Stoa—our enquiry has both confirmed it and, more importantly, specified the sense in which it is true. Thirdly, with respect to the view that Chrysippus systematizes and strengthens Stoic doctrine, my picture of Chrysippus' philosophy tends, with some qualifications, to confirm it. My reservations about Chrysippus having strengthened the Stoa turn on the conflicting tendencies I noted in his thought and the opposition some of them created in antiquity towards the Stoa. This is the case in regard to his unsuccessful attempt to reconcile his doctrine of determinism with his assumption that men are responsible for some of their conduct, and the unresolved difficulties caused by his doctrine of "conformity to nature" as being the final end of life together with his denial that natural goods like health and unimpaired senses contribute to happiness.

Turning to the final description of Chrysippus' position in the Stoa—his philosophy remained for centuries the standard of orthodoxy—a judicious evaluation of it would require a comparison of the results of my research with the philosophies of Stoics who lived during the four hundred years following Chrysippus' demise, and such an investigation is beyond the scope of the present work. However—and this study could perhaps conclude on no more fitting note—we can indicate, by means of examples, how this attempted reconstruction of Chrysippus' philosophy could contribute to a truly scientific assessment of any hypothesis concerning Chrysippus' influence on Stoics who lived after him; for, by referring to it, one can trace that influence with a higher degree of precision or with greater specificity.

I have already indicated with what esteem Chrysippus was regarded by later Stoics, such as Seneca and Epictetus, and one can undoubtedly affirm that these philosophers in a general way were influenced by Chrysippus. The present restoration of Chrysippus' thought, however, enables one to discuss the question of influence in a more specific way. Seneca, in a passage, to which reference has once been made,[1] says that every body has "its own color and its own shape and size" and that each single leaf is "stamped with its own property". It is highly probable, though of course not

---

[1] Note 1, p. 106.

demonstrable, that Seneca's thought in this passage is a reflection of Chrysippus' radical nominalism. In Epictetus' philosophy the distinction between things in our power (τὰ ἐφ'ἡμῖν) and things not in our power (τὰ οὐκ ἐφ' ἡμῖν) occupies a pivotal position;[1] Marcus Aurelius, too, made much of this distinction.[2] Now, while I do not wish to deny that Zeno is the author of this distinction (I 177), it ought to be born in mind that Chrysippus made use of a similar distinction in order to reconcile free will with fate;[3] and, though it was concluded that the reconciliation was not satisfactorily effected by this device, it can hardly be doubted that Chrysippus made much use of it in his defense of Stoic doctrine. And, if one wishes to be specific when one speaks of Chrysippus' influence on Epictetus and Marcus Aurelius, one can with some degree of confidence cite the distinction to which we have alluded. In the *Meditations* of Marcus Aurelius one may find a strong monistic note accompanied by an emphasis on the sympathy of the parts of the universe for one another. There is but one substance or universe and all other things are parts of it.[4] All things are "mutually-intertwined" and thus "have a liking for one another" by reason of "the sympathy that breathes through them".[5] Again he who remembers Chrysippus' formulation of both these doctrines and the esteem in which the Roman emperor held Chrysippus,[6] can make, it seems to me, some rather concrete observations about the influence of our philosopher on Aurelius.

In this way, then, the picture of Chrysippus' philosophy that has been presented ought to be of use in tracing with more precision, at least, the similarities—and, in some cases, the affiliations—of doctrines in post-Chrysippean Stoics with those of Chrysippus. In addition, it can be of use in helping one to decide, when presented with a doctrine ascribed to "the Stoics", whether or not Chrysippus is a member of that group. For example, Diogenes Laertius, in his account of "Stoic" doctrine, says in one passage (vii. 138), "The individuating quality (ἰδίως ποιός) of the substance of all things is the world." "Is Chrysippus one of "the Stoics" who adhered to this doctrine?" an investigator might ask himself. If the reader

---

[1] The *Discources* as reported by Arrian, Book i, Chapter 1.

[2] *Meditations* vi. 41; viii. 7.

[3] *Supra*, p. 151.

[4] *Meditations* iii. 9; *cf.* iv. 29; viii. 34; xi. 8.

[5] *Ibid.*, vi. 38.

[6] *Supra*, p. 13.

refers to the account given of Chrysippus' nominalism [1] and remembers Chrysippus' use of the expression, ἰδίως ποιός, as a
terminus technicus in the explication of this doctrine, he can only
conclude that Chrysippus is certainly one of the anonymous Stoics
to whom the view set forth in the Laertius' passage is ascribed. And,
in this case, there is some evidence for going one step further. For,
since the expression, ἰδίως ποιός, appears in none of the preserved
fragments of Stoic philosophers who came before Chrysippus, it is
likely that our philosopher is the author of the doctrine set forth by
Laertius and attributed to the Stoa generally. This procedure
exemplifies, I believe, the way in which this reconstruction of
Chrysippus' philosophy can be useful in working with fragments
about the Stoa in general with a view to specifying the adherents,
if not the authors, of the doctrines set forth in those fragments.

This study of Chrysippus' philosophy ought, then, not only to
help one to determine the extent of Chrysippus' influence on subsequent Stoic philosophers, but ought also to contribute to a history
of the Stoa, in which, more than before, lines of influence can be
more finely drawn and sources of doctrines, identified with more
exactitude.

---

[1] *Supra*, pp. 103-106.

BIBLIOGRAPHY

I. ANCIENT SOURCES

Aristotle. *Analytica Posteriora*. Trans. by G. R. G. Mure. London: Oxford Univ. Press, 1928.
——. *Analytica Priora*. Trans. by A. J. Jenkinson. London: Oxford Univ. Press, 1928.
——. *Categoriae* and *De Interpretatione*. Trans. by E. M. Edghill. London: Oxford Univ. Press, 1928.
——. *De Anima*. Trans. by J. A. Smith. Oxford: The Clarendon Press, 1931.
——. *De Caelo*. Trans. by J. L. Stocks. Oxford: The Clarendon Press, 1930.
——. *De Generatione Animalium*. Trans. by Arthur Platt. Oxford: The Clarendon Press, 1912.
——. *De Generatione et Corruptione*. Trans. by H. H. Joachim. Oxford: The Clarendon Press, 1930.
——. *De Mundo*. Trans. by E. S. Forster. Oxford: The Clarendon Press, 1923.
——. *Ethica Nicomachea*. Trans. by W. D. Ross. London: Oxford Univ. Press, 1915.
——. *Metaphysica*. 2nd edit. Trans. by W. D. Ross. Oxford: The Clarendon Press, 1928.
——. *Meteorologica*. Trans. by E. W. Webster. Oxford: The Clarendon Press, 1931.
——. *Physica*. Trans. by R. P. Hardie and R. K. Gaye. Oxford: The Clarendon Press, 1930.
——. *Physics*. Rev. text with introduction and commentary by W. D. Ross. Oxford: The Clarendon Press, 1936.
——. *Prior and Posterior Analytics*. A revised text with introduction and commentary by W. D. Ross. Oxford: The Clarendon Press, 1949.
——. *Select Fragments*. Trans. by W. D. Ross. Oxford: The Clarendon Press, 1952.
——. *Topica* and *De Sophisticis Elenchis*. Trans. by W. A. Pickard-Cambridge. London: Oxford Univ. Press, 1928.
Athenaeus. *The Deipnosophists*. Trans. by Charles B. Gulick (Loeb Classical Library, Vol. V), Cambridge, Massachusetts: Harvard Univ. Press, 1955.
Aurelius, M. Antoninus. *The Communings with Himself of Marcus Aurelius Antoninus, Emperor of Rome*, Together with His Speeches and Sayings. A rev. text. Trans. by C. R. Haines (Loeb Classical Library), Cambridge, Massachusetts: Harvard Univ. Press, 1953.
Chrysippe. "De la partie hégémonique de l'âme"—fragments du traité *De l'ame* traduit du grec par Georges Blin et Monette Keim, *Mesures* (15 avril 1939), pp. 163-174.
Cicero. *Academica*. Trans. by H. Rackham (Loeb Classical Library), Cambridge, Massachusetts: Harvard Univ. Press, 1951.
——. *De Fato*. Trans. by H. Rackham (Loeb Classical Library), Cambridge, Massachusetts: Harvard Univ. Press, 1948.
——. *De Finibus Bonorum et Malorum*. Trans. by H. Rackham (Loeb Classical Library), Cambridge, Massachusetts: Harvard Univ. Press, 1951.

——. *De Natura Deorum.* Trans. by H. Rackham (Loeb Classical Library), Cambridge, Massachusetts: Harvard Univ. Press, 1951.
——. *De Oratore.* 2 vols. Trans. by E. W. Sutton and H. Rackham (Loeb Classical Library), Cambridge, Massachusetts: Harvard Univ. Press, 1959.
Diogenes Laertius. *Lives of Eminent Philosophers.* 2 vols. Trans. by R. D. Hicks (Loeb Classical Library), Cambridge, Massachusetts: Harvard Univ. Press, 1950.
Epictetus. *The Discourses as Reported by Arrian, The Manual and Fragments.* 2 vols. Trans. by W. A. Oldfather (Loeb Classical Library), Cambridge, Massachusetts: Harvard Univ. Press, 1956.
Galen. *De Placitis Hippocratis et Platonis.* ed. I. Mueller. Leipzig: Teubner, 1874.
——. *De Sequela Potentiarum.* From *Scripta Minora* ed. I. Marquardt, I. Mueller, and G. Helmreich, Vol. 1, Leipzig: Teubner, 1884.
——. *On the Natural Faculties.* Trans. by John Brock (Loeb Classical Library), Cambridge, Massachusetts: Harvard Univ. Press, 1952.
Lucrezio. *Il Poema della Natura,* testo Latino e versione poetica di Pietro Parrella. 2 vols. Bologna: Niccola Zanichelli, 1953.
Lucretius. *The Nature of the Universe.* Trans. by Ronald Latham. Baltimore, Maryland: Penguin Books, 1951.
Musonius, C. Rufus. *Reliquiae.* ed. O. Hense. Leipzig: Teubner, 1905.
Panaetius. *Fragmenta.* ed. Modestus Van Straaten, Leiden: E. J. Brill, 1952.
Plato. *Euthydemus.* Trans. by B. Jowett. New York: Random House, 1937 (first published, 1892).
——. *Gorgias.* A revised text with intro. and commentary by E. R. Dodds, Oxford: The Clarendon Press, 1959.
——. *Laws.* Trans. by B. Jowett. New York: Random House, 1937 (first published, 1892).
——. *Laws.* 2 vols. Trans. by R. G. Bury (Loeb Classical Library), Cambridge, Massachusetts: Harvard Univ. Press, 1952.
——. *Meno.* Trans. by B. Jowett. New York: Random House, 1937 (first published, 1892).
——. *Phaedo.* Trans. by R. S. Bluck. New York: The Liberal Arts Press, 1955.
——. *Protagoras.* Trans. by B. Jowett and extensively rev. by Martin Ostwald. New York: The Liberal Arts Press, 1956.
——. *The Republic.* 2 vols. Trans. by Paul Shorey (Loeb Classical Library), Cambridge, Massachusetts: Harvard Univ. Press, 1953.
——. *Sophist.* Trans. by B. Jowett, New York: Random House, 1937 (first published, 1892).
——. *Theaetetus.* Trans. by Francis M. Cornford. New York: The Liberal Arts Press, 1959.
——. *Timaeus.* Trans. by R. G. Bury (Loeb Classical Library), Cambridge, Massachusetts: Harvard Univ. Press, 1961.
Plotin. *Ennéades.* III, Texte établi et traduit par Émile Bréhier. Paris, 1956.
Plutarch. *Adversus Colotem,* from *Plutarchi Moralia,* Vol. VI. Fasc. 2. Recensvit et emendavit Max Pohlenz. Leipzig: B. G. Teubner, 1959.
——. *De Communibus Notitiis.* from *Plutarchi Moralia,* Vol. VI. Fasc. 2. Recensvit et emendavit Max Pohlenz. Leipzig: B. G. Teubner, 1959.
——. *De Stoicorum Repugnantiis.* from *Plutarchi Moralia,* Vol. VI. Fasc. 2. Recensvit et emendavit Max Pohlenz. Leipzig: B. G. Teubner, 1959.
Seneca. *Epistulae Morales.* 3 vols. Trans. by Richard M. Gummere (Loeb

Classical Library), Cambridge, Massachusetts: Harvard Univ. Press, 1953.
——. *Moral Essays*. 3 vols. Trans. by John W. Basore (Loeb Classical Library), Cambridge, Massachusetts: Harvard Univ. Press, 1958.
Sextus Empiricus. *Outlines of Pyrrhonism. Against the Logicians* (Books vii and viii of *Adversus Mathematicos*). *Against the Physicists* (Books ix and x of *Adversus Mathematicos*). *Against the Ethicists* (Book xi of *Adversus Mathematicos*). *Against the Professors* (Books i-vi of *Adversus Mathematicos*). 4 vols. Trans. by R. G. Bury (Loeb Classical Library), Cambridge, Massachusetts: Harvard Univ. Press, 1949 (Vol. I), 1953 (Vol. II), 1955 (Vol. III), 1957 (Vol. IV).
Simplicius. *In Aristotelis Categorias Commentarium*. ed. Kalbfleisch. Berlin: George Reimer, 1907.
St. Augustine. *Confessions*. 2 vols. Trans. by William Watts (Loeb Classical Library), Cambridge, Massachusetts: Harvard Univ. Press, 1950.
Theophrastus. *Metaphysics*. Trans. with commentary and intro. by W. D. Ross and F. H. Fobes. Oxford: The Clarendon Press, 1929.
——. *De Igne*. from *Opera Quae Supersunt Omnia*. 3rd vol. *Fragmenta*. Friderick Wimmer. Leipzig: Teubner, 1862.
Xenophon. *Memorabilia*. Trans. by E. C. Marchant (Loeb Classical Library). Cambridge, Massachusetts: Harvard Univ. Press, 1959.

II. MODERN SOURCES

Arnim, Hans von. "Chrysippos", *Realencyclopädie der Classischen Altertumswissenschaft*, Stuttgart: J. B. Metzlersche, 1899. Cols. 2502-2509.
——. "Diogenianus", *Realencyclopädie der Classischen Altertumswissenschaft*. Stuttgart: J. B. Metzlersche, 1903. Cols. 777-778.
—— "Kleanthes", *Realencyclopädie der Classischen Altertumswissenschaft*. Stuttgart: J. B. Metzlersche, 1921. Cols. 558-574.
——. *Stoicorum Veterum Fragmenta*. 4 vols. Leipzig: B. G. Teubner, Vol. I, 1905; Vol. II, 1903; Vol. III, 1903; Vol. IV (Index), 1914.
Arnold, E. Vernon. *Roman Stoicism*. New York: The Humanities Press, 1958 (first published, 1911).
Ayer, A. J. "Negation", *Journal of Philosophy*, Vol. XLIX (Dec. 18, 1952), pp. 797-815.
Baguet, F. N. G. *De Chrysippo*. Annales Accademiae Lovaniensis, 1822.
Bailey, Cyril. *The Greek Atomists and Epicurus*. Oxford: Clarendon Press, 1928.
Barth, Paul. *Die Stoa*. Stuttgart: Fr. Frommann, 1903.
Bevan, Edwyn. *Stoics and Sceptics*. Cambridge: W. Heffer and Sons, Ltd., 1959 (original edition, 1913).
Bochénski, Innocentius M. *A History of Formal Logic*. South Bend, Indiana: University of Notre Dame Press, 1961.
Bréhier, Émile. *Chrysippe*. Paris: Felix Alcan, 1910 (edition of 1951 entitled *Chrysippe et L'Ancien Stoicisme*).
——, *La Théorie des Incorporels dans L'Ancien Stoïcisme*. Deuxième Édition. Paris: Librairie Philosophique J. Vrin, 1928 (first edition, 1908).
——, *Les Stoïciens*. Textes traduits par Émile Bréhier édités sous la direction de Pierre-Maxime Schuhl. Paris: Éditions Gallimard, 1962.
Brink, K. O. "Peripatos", *Realencyclopädie der Classischen Altertumswissenschaft*. Stuttgart: Alfred Druckenmuller, 1940. Cols. 899-949.
Brochard, Victor, "Sur la Logique des Stoiciens", *Archiv für Geschichte der Philosophie*, Vol. V (1892), pp. 449-468.

Burnet, John. *Early Greek Philosophy*. 4th edit. London: Adam and Charles Black, 1930.

Butler, Joseph. "Sermon II. Upon Human Nature", from *Fifteen Sermons Preached at the Rolls Chapel*. London: G. Bell and Sons, Ltd., 1958.

Callahan, John F. *Four Views of Time in Ancient Philosophy*. Cambridge, Massachusetts: Harvard Univ. Press, 1948.

Cherniss, Harold. *Aristotle's Criticism of Presocratic Philosophy*. Baltimore: The Johns Hopkins Press, 1935.

Clagett, Marshall. *Greek Science in Antiquity*. 2nd edit. New York: Collier Books, 1963.

Copi, Irving M. *Introduction to Logic*. 2nd edit. New York: The MacMillan Co., 1961.

Cornford, F. M. *Before and After Socrates*. Cambridge: University Press, 1960 (first printed, 1932).

——. Plato's *Cosmology*. The *Timaeus* of Plato translated with a running commentary. New York: The Liberal Arts Press, 1957.

DeLacy, Phillip. "The Stoic Categories as Methodological Principles", *Proceedings of the American Philological Association*, LXXVI (1945), pp. 246-263.

——. "Stoic Views of Poetry", *American Journal of Philology*, Vol. LXIX (July, 1948), pp. 241-271.

Descartes. *Les Passions de L'Ame*. from *Oeuvres et Lettres*. Textes présentés par André Bridoux. Paris: Librairie Gallimard, 1952.

——, *Rules for the Direction of the Mind*. Chicago: Encyclopaedia Britannica, Inc., 1952.

DeWitt, Norman Wentworth. *Epicurus and His Philosophy*. Minneapolis, Minnesota: University of Minnesota Press, 1954.

Diels, Hermann. *Die Fragmente der Vorsokratiker*. 5th edit. Herausgegeben von Walther Kranz. Berlin: Weidmannsche Buchhandlung, 1934.

——. *Doxographi Graeci*. Editio iterata. Berlin: Walter de Gruyter, 1929.

Dobson, J. F. "Erasistratus", *Proceedings of the Royal Society of Medicine*. Vol. XX (April, 1927), pp. 825-832.

Dudley, Donald R. *A History of Cynicism* from Diogenes to the 6th Century A.D. London: Methuen & Co., 1937.

Duhem, Pierre. *Le Système du Monde. Histoire des doctrines cosmologiques de Platon à Copernic*. Paris: Librairie Scientifique A. Hermann et Fils, 1913.

Edelstein, Ludwig, "Max Pohlenz. Die Stoa, Geschichte einer geistigen Bewegung. Göttingen, Vandenhoeck und Ruprecht, I (1948), pp. 490; II (1949), pp. 230" *American Journal of Philology*, Vol. LXXII (October, 1951), pp. 426-432.

——. "Motives and Incentives of Science in Antiquity", paper read at the International Conference on the History of Science, Oxford, July, 1961, printed in A. C. Crombie (Ed.), *Scientific Change* (London 1963), pp. 15-41.

——. *The Meaning of Stoicism*. Cambridge, Massachusetts: Harvard University Press, 1966.

——. "Recent Trends in the Interpretations of Ancient Science", *Journal of the History of Ideas*, Vol. XIII, (October, 1952), pp. 573-604.

——. "Review of Fritz Wehrli's *Die Schule des Aristoteles*, Texte und Kommentar. Heft IV: Demetrios von Phaleron. Heft V: Straton von Lampsakos. Heft VI: Lykon und Ariston von Keos. Heft VII: Herakleides Pontikos", *American Journal of Philology*. Vol. LXXVI (October, 1955), pp. 414-422.

——, "Review of M. Pohlenz. *Hippokrates und die Begründung der wissen-schaftlichen Medizin*. Berlin: de Gruyter, 1938" *American Journal of Philology*. Vol. LXI (April, 1940), pp. 221-229.

——. "The Development of Greek Anatomy", paper read in a seminar course in the history of anatomy. For a detailed argumentation, see "Die Geschichte der Sektion in der Antike", *Quellen und Studien zur Geschichte der Naturwissenschaften und der Medizin*, III (Berlin, 1932), pp. 100-156.

——. *The Fragments of Posidonius* with a commentary (unpublished).

——. "The Genuine Works of Hippokrates", *Bulletin of the History of Medicine*, Vol. VII (1939), pp. 236-248.

——. "The Philosophical System of Posidonius", *American Journal of Philology*. Vol. LVII, 1936, pp. 286-325.

——. "The Professional Ethics of the Greek Physician", *Bulletin of the History of Medicine*, Vol. XXX (1956), pp. 391-419.

Farrington, Benjamin. *Greek Science*. Baltimore: Penguin Books, 1953 (Pt. 1, 1944; pt. 2, 1949).

——. *The Faith of Epicurus*. London: Weidenfeld and Nicolson, 1967.

Faust, August. *Der Möglichkeitsgedanke*. Erster Teil, Heidelberg: Carl Winters Universitätsbuchhandlung, 1931.

Festa, Nicola. I. *Frammenti degli Stoici antichi*. Vol. II. Bari: Gius. Laterza & Figli, 1935.

Frank, Erich. *Philosophical Understanding and Religious Truth*. New York: Oxford Univ. Press, 1945.

Gomperz, Theodor. *Greek Thinkers*. Trans. by Laurie Magnus. London: John Murray, 1901.

Grote, George. *Plato and the Other Companions of Socrates*. Vol. III. London: John Murray, 1865.

Grube, G. M. A. *Plato's Thought*. Boston: Beacon Press, 1958 (first published, 1935).

Hare, R. M. *The Language of Morals*. Oxford: The Clarendon Press, 1952.

Hicks, R. D. *Stoic and Epicurean*. New York: Charles Scribner's Sons, 1910.

Hobbes, *Leviathan*. reprinted from the edition of 1651. Oxford: The Clarendon Press, 1909.

Huby, Pamela. "The First Discovery of the Freewill Problem", *Philosophy*, Vol. XLII (October, 1967), pp. 353-362.

Hume, David. *A Treatise of Human Nature*. Reprinted from the original edition in three volumes. ed. Selby-Biggs. Oxford: The Clarendon Press, 1888.

——. *Dialogues Concerning Natural Religion*. New York: Hafner Publishing Co., 1948.

Hurst, Martha. "Implication in the Fourth Century B.C.", *Mind*, Vol. XLIV (October, 1935), pp. 484-495.

Jaeger, Werner. *Aristotle*. Fundamentals of the History of His Development. 2nd edit. Trans. by Richard Robinson. Oxford: The Clarendon Press, 1948.

——. "Das Pneuma in Lykeion", *Hermes*, Vol. XLVIII (1913), pp. 29-74.

——. *Diokles von Karystos*. *Die griechische Medizin und die Schule des Aristoteles*. Berlin: W. de Gruyter & Co., 1938.

Jammer, Max. *Concepts of Space*. The History of the Theories of Space in Physics. New York: Harper & Brothers, 1960 (f.p. 1954).

Kant, Immanuel. *Foundations of the Metaphysics of Morals*. Trans. with an introduction by Lewis White Beck. New York: The Liberal Arts Press, 1959.

Kirk, G. E. and Raven, J. E. *The Presocratic Philosophers*. Cambridge: The University Press, 1957.

Kuhn, Thomas. *The Structure of Scientific Revolutions*. Chicago: The University of Chicago Press, 1962.

Lewis, Clarence I. and Langford, Cooper H. *Symbolic Logic*. 2nd edit. New York: Dover Publications, 1959.

Lovejoy, Arthur O. *The Great Chain of Being*. New York: Harper Torchbooks, 1960 (first published, 1936).

Lukasiewicz, Jan. *Aristotle's Syllogistic*. Oxford: The Clarendon Press, 1951.

Luria, S. "Die Infinitesimaltheorie der antiken Atomisten", *Quellen und Studien zur Geschichte der Mathematik, Astronomie und Physik*. Berlin: Julius Springer, 1932, pp. 106-185.

Mates, Benson. *Stoic Logic*. Berkeley: Univ. of Calif. Press, 1961. (originally published, 1953).

——. *Elementary Logic*. New York: Oxford Univ. Press, 1965.

Mette, H. J. "Review of *Die Stoa* by Max Pohlenz", Gnomon (Band 23/1951), pp. 27-39.

Patrick, Mary Mills. *The Greek Sceptics*. New York: Columbia University Press, 1929.

Pearson, A. C. *The Fragments of Zeno and Cleanthes*. London: C. J. Clay and Sons, 1891.

Petersen, Christian. *Philosophiae Chrysippi fundamenta*. Altona and Hamburg, 1827.

Pohlenz, Max. *Die Stoa*. Geschichte einer geistigen Bewegung. 2nd edit. Gottingen: Vandenhoeck & Ruprecht, 1959.

——. "Review of *Stoicorum Veterum Fragmenta*. Vol. II", *Berliner Philologische Wochenschrift*, XXIII (August 1, 1903), pp. 962-971.

——. "Zenon und Chrysipp", *Nachrichten von der Gesellschaft der Wissenschaften zu Göttingen*. Philologisch-historische Klasse. Neue Folge. Fachgruppe I. 1936-38 (lecture given on April 8, 1938). Göttingen: Vandenhoeck & Ruprecht, 1938, pp. 173-210.

——. "Plutarchs Schriften gegen die Stoiker", *Hermes*, Vol. 74 (1939), pp. 1-33.

Praechter, Karl. *Die Philosophie des Altertums*. 12th edit. Berlin: E. S. Mittler & Sohn, 1926.

Reesor, Margaret E. "The Stoic Concept of Quality", *American Journal of Philology*, Vol. LXXV (January, 1954), pp. 40-58.

Reiche, Harald A. T. *Empedocles' Mixture, Eudoxan Astronomy and Aristotle's Connate Pneuma*. Amsterdam: Adolf M. Hakkert, 1959.

Reinhardt, K. "Poseidonios", *Realencyclopädie der Classischen Altertumswissenschaft*. Stuttgart: J. B. Metzlersche, 1953. Cols. 558-826.

Reith, Otto. *Grundbegriffe der Stoischen Ethik*. Eine Traditionsgeschichtliche Untersuchung. Berlin: Weidmannsche Buchhandlung, 1933.

Robinson, Richard. *Plato's Earlier Dialectic*. 2nd edit. Oxford: The Clarendon Press, 1953.

Ross, W. D. *Aristotle*. 5th edit. New York: Barnes & Noble, Inc., 1949.

Russell, Bertrand. *The Problems of Philosophy*. New York: Oxford Univ. Press, 1959 (first published, 1912).

Ryle, Gilbert. *The Concept of Mind*. New York: Barnes & Noble, Inc., 1949.

Sambursky, Samuel. *Physics of the Stoics*. London: Routledge and Kegan Paul, 1959.

——. *The Physical World of the Greeks*. Trans. by Merton Dagut. London: Routledge and Kegan Paul, 1956.

Sarton, George. *Ancient Science and Modern Civilization*. New York: Harper & Brothers, 1959 (f.p. 1954).

Saw, Ruth Lydia. *Leibniz*. Baltimore, Maryland: Penguin Books, 1954.

Schmekel, A. *Die positive Philosophie in ihrer geschichtlichen Entwicklung*. Berlin: Weidmannsche Verlagsbuchhandlung, 1938.

Sidgwick, Henry. *The Methods of Ethics*, 7th edit. New York: Dover Publications, 1966 (f.p. 1907).

Solmsen, Friedrich. *Aristotle's System of the Physical World*. Ithaca, New York: Cornell Univ. Press, 1960.

——. *Cleanthes or Posidonius? The Basis of Stoic Physics*. Amsterdam: North Holland Publishing Co., 1961.

——. "Greek Philosophy and the Discovery of the Nerves", *Museum Helveticum*, Vol. 18, Fasc. 3 (1961), pp. 150-167; Vol. 18, Fasc. 4 (1961), pp. 169-197.

Spinoza. *Éthique*. 2 vols. Trad. par Charles Appuhn. Paris: Garnier Frères, n.d.

Steckerl, Fritz. *The Fragments of Praxagoras of Cos and His School*. Leiden: E. J. Brill, 1958.

Stein, Ludwig. *Die Erkenntnistheorie der Stoa*, Berlin: S. Calvary & Co., 1888.

Tarn, Sir William. *Hellenistic Civilisation*. 3rd ed. revised by the author and G. T. Griffith. London: Edward Arnold & Co., 1952.

Taylor, Richard. *Metaphysics*. Englewood Cliffs, N. J.: Prentice-Hall, Inc., 1963.

Toulmin, Stephen. *Reason in Ethics*. Cambridge: The University Press, 1960.

Überweg, Friedrich. *Grundriss der Geschichte des Altertums*. 10th edit. rev. Berlin: Ernst Siegrief Mittler und Sohn, 1909.

Verbeke, G. *L'Évolution de la Doctrine du Pneuma* du Stoicisme à S. Augustin. Paris: Desclée de Brouwer, 1945.

Voelke, André-Jean. *Les rapports avec Autrui dans la philosophie grecque d'Aristote à Panétius*. Paris: Librairie Philosophique J. Vrin, 1961.

Wehrli, Fritz. *Die Schule des Aristoteles, Texte und Kommentar*. Heft V: Straton von Lampsakos. Basel: Benno Schwabe & Co., 1950.

Windelband, W. *A History of Philosophy*, 2nd edit. rev. Trans. by James H. Tufts. New York: The Macmillan Co., 1901.

Zeller, Eduard. *Die Philosophie der Griechen in ihrer geschichtlichen Entwicklung*. 5. Auflage. Dritter Teil. Erste Abteilung. Darmstadt: Wissenschaftliche Buchgesellschaft, 1963.

GENERAL INDEX

Academic sceptics 9, 35, 44, 58
Academy 9, 21 n. 5, 24, 25-26, 27,
  59, 196
Ackrill, J. L. 139 n. 5
active principle (or power) 32, 59,
  93, 96, 97, 102, 122
Alexander the Great 20
Alexander of Aphrodisias 13, 61,
  100, 112, 131 n. 2, 144 n. 1
alteration 54, 202, 206
Ammonius 45 n. 4
Anaxagoras 94 n. 1, 117, 128 n. 1
Anaximenes 126, 126 n. 6
Anscombe, G. E. M. 139 n. 5
anticipation 62-64, 200
Antiochus 45 n. 4, 178, 179, 198
Antipater 12, 13 n. 7
Antisthenes 13, 108, 173
apprehension 49 n. 1, 53, 58
Arcesilaus 9, 26, 49
Archedemus 12
argument forms (or schemata) 82-
  87, 88, 153, 201
Aristeides 13
Aristippus 166
Aristo 177
Aristotle 10, 16, 20, 21, 22, 23, 24,
  34, 38 n. 3, 40, 41, 42, 43, 45, 45
  n. 4, 48, 48 n. 1, 49, 50, 60, 66, 67,
  68, 82, 83 n. 3, 85, 87, 92, 93, 93
  n. 1, 94, 95, 95 n. 2, 96, 96 n. 2, 98,
  100, 108, 109, 110, 111, 113, 114,
  114 n. 1, 116, 119, 120, 120 n. 3,
  122, 122 n. 1, 123, 124, 127, 135
  n. 2, 138, 139, 140, 142, 146, 147,
  154, 156, 157, 161, 162, 162 n. 1,
  163, 167, 201
Aristoxenus 166
Arius Didymus 113, 114, 119, 120
  n. 1
v. Arnim, H. 1, 1 n. 2, 2, 10, 13 n.5,
  14, 16, 16 n. 6, 17, 34 nn. 4 and
  5, 35 nn. 3 and 5, 45 n. 1, 49 n. 5,
  64 nn. 2 and 3, 101 n. 2, 116, 119
  n. 1, 121 n. 1, 128 n. 1, 131, 133
  nn. 4 and 5, 142 n. 2, 150, 153, 153
  n. 3, 154 n. 3, 169 n. 1

Arnold, E. V. 9 n. 3, 12 n. 1, 14, 22
  n. 3
assent 49 n. 1, 57, 58, 59, 62, 65,
  89, 130, 149, 185, 194, 195
Augustine 115 n. 2, 116, 152 n. 3
Aurelius, M. 10, 13, 17, 208
Ayer, A. J. 47 n. 3

Baguet, F. N. G. 16
Bailey, C. 27 n. 1, 62 n. 3, 110 nn. 3,
  5 and 8, 111 nn. 1 and 2, 122 n. 1,
  140 n. 7, 141 nn. 3, 5 and 7, 156 n.4
Barth, P. 19 n. 2
Basore, J. W. 11 n. 7
Berkeley, G. 63 n. 1, 200
Bevan, E. 18 n. 3, 19 n. 4, 20 n. 1
Blin, G. 133 n. 4
Bochénski, I. M. 83 n. 1
Bréhier, É. 1 n. 2, 2 n. 2, 3-4, 14,
  15, 16 n. 6, 17, 37 n. 3, 45 n. 1, 64
  n. 3, 67, 67 n. 1, 109 n. 2, 128 n. 2,
  133 n. 1, 143 n. 1, 158 n. 3, 162
  n. 1, 167 n. 1, 183
Brink, K. O. 25 n. 6
Brochard, V. 49 n. 1, 75, 75 n. 6, 81
Burnet, J. 92 n. 3, 127 n. 3
Bury, R. G. 42 n. 3
Butler, J. 167 n. 4

canonic 45 n. 4
Carneades 9, 17, 49
categories 15, 93, 103-107, 118, 206
causation 29, 41, 76, 90, 148
cause 29, 30, 30 n. 5, 57 n. 2, 94,
  95, 96, 107, 108, 138, 139, 141, 142,
  143, 144 n. 1, 146, 147, 148, 149,
  150, 160, 171, 200, 202, 203
Chalcidius 51, 56, 58, 59, 65, 96,
  96 nn. 1 and 3, 98
Cherniss, H. 67 n. 3, 92 n. 2
Cicero 5, 8, 28 n. 1, 29, 30 n. 5, 45
  n. 4, 62 n. 3, 74, 75, 76, 77, 78, 79,
  81, 87, 127 n. 2, 140 n. 5, 140 n. 7,
  141 n. 1, 143, 146, 147, 155, 163
  n. 2, 177, 178, 185
Clagett, N. 37 n. 3, 38, 40 n. 4
class 82, 83, 201